Everything

Roy A. Minet

Everything

Second Edition.   May 24, 2026.

Copyright © 2026 Roy A. Minet

Written and published by Roy A. Minet

0. Preface

We Homo sapiens are the first and, for the moment, still the only species that has the capacity for rational thought. Clearly, rational thinking has helped us tremendously in many ways, but equally clearly, we have flopped badly in other crucial areas. We have been hanging around for nearly 300,000 years so far. It is high time for us to "pull up our socks" and use our brains to clean up our act for whatever time we have remaining.

The purpose of this book is to explore and present fundamental principles and truths that are universal and apply to and throughout substantially everything. Having stated such an expansive purpose, the mission does need to be somewhat further qualified.

Physicists have undertaken to understand and explain everything about the entire universe, including what actually constitutes the entire universe. Excellent and fairly sustained progress is being made, but we are sure that we do not yet comprehend it all. We do know quite a lot and have benefited greatly from utilizing that knowledge to dramatically improve human life.

This book primarily deals with the universe of all thinking, reasoning individuals, including their interactions, their institutions, and their societies. All of that universe exists inside the physicists' entire universe and is therefore completely subject to all the laws that physicists have discovered. The most important things that have happened over the past million years or so are examined and projected into the future.

Most often, books and courses focus on some specific area of study. However, virtually everything interacts with everything else, and certain fundamental principles underlie everything as well. The purpose here is to pull back with a wide-angle lens, focus on the big picture, and understand how the whole mess functions under the governance of the laws and principles. A topic of particular interest is how rational thought might best be utilized to maximize the happiness of our species.

The most serious and fundamental problem of civilization is that there are far too few people who think rationally. By clearly defining what rational thinking is and providing examples, perhaps a few more rational thinkers can be brought online.

This material should be accessible to virtually anybody who has an interest. If you have understood this preface, you probably are good to go. However, and as always, the price for gaining understanding is the effort that is required to *think*.

This book was written because greater understanding fosters peace, progress, prosperity, and, above all, liberty.

Table of Contents

1. The Beginning

In the beginning, God created the heavens and the earth. Now the earth was formless and empty, darkness was over the surface of the deep, and the Spirit of God was hovering over the waters.

And God said, "Let there be light," and there was light. God saw that the light was good, and he separated the light from the darkness. God called the light "day," and the darkness he called "night." And there was evening, and there was morning — the first day.

And God said, "Let there be a vault between the waters to separate water from water." So God made the vault and separated the water under the vault from the water above it. And it was so. God called the vault "sky." And there was evening, and there was morning — the second day.

And God said, "Let the water under the sky be gathered to one place, and let dry ground appear." And it was so. God called the dry ground "land," and the gathered waters he called "seas." And God saw that it was good.

Then God said, "Let the land produce vegetation: seed-bearing plants and trees on the land that bear fruit with seed in it, according to their various kinds." And it was so. The land produced vegetation: plants bearing seed according to their kinds and trees bearing fruit with seed in it according to their kinds. And God saw that it was good. And there was evening, and there was morning — the third day.

And God said, "Let there be lights in the vault of the sky to separate the day from the night, and let them serve as signs to mark sacred times, and days and years, and let them be lights in the vault of the sky to give light on the earth." And it was so. God made two great lights—the greater light to govern the day and the lesser light to govern the night.

Wait a minute. WAIT A MINUTE! Stop the music, kill the lighting, and shut down the fog machine. Is that really correct? Is that actually how the earth was created? If it is, how do we know that it is? The above account was translated from ancient Hebrew text. How did the ancient Hebrews know it is correct, and why should we believe them?

Each individual must decide what they will consider to be true and correct. There is the obvious possibility that two individuals may decide that different and incompatible things are true and correct. At most, one of them can be right, although both definitely could be wrong. Clearly, there are cases where such a difference is of no consequence, but equally clearly, there are many other cases where such a difference can be of crucial importance.

Human history is replete with instances where strongly held but conflicting views have caused problems small and large. Most human individuals tend to feel threatened if or when their core belief systems are seriously challenged. Everything from fist fights to duels to large armed conflicts has been the result.

Those who maintain a worldview that differs wildly from that held by most people are labeled mentally ill (or worse). It could well be argued that holding any worldview that significantly contradicts reality is at least a symptom of mental illness. There have been some self-resolving problems where a sizable group held the same crazy worldview that ultimately led to all of them committing suicide.

However, there are plenty of examples of those branded mentally ill later proving to be sane after all. Consider poor Galileo Galilei, who was excommunicated and sentenced to house arrest merely for pointing out that the earth revolves around the sun rather than the reverse.

It would seem incredibly useful and important to have some way to peacefully determine with reasonable certainty which view is the correct one, if any. That is an issue that needs to be well addressed early on.

2. Rational Thinking — From Consciousness to Wisdom

If asked to define *rational thinking*, many would equate it to *logical thinking*. That is a correct but incomplete definition. Rational thinking definitely is logical thinking, but logical thinking is not necessarily rational thinking.

Logical Thinking

The formalization of logical thinking began in ancient Greece circa 350 BCE. Aristotle is regarded as the father of logic. The first formal deductive reasoning took the form of the "syllogism." Here is the most famous example:

All men are mortal;   (major premise)

Socrates is a man;   (minor premise)

Therefore, Socrates is mortal.   (conclusion)

The premises are always given as true. The conclusion, then, is necessarily true. If the major premise were, "All men have three eyes," then the syllogism would prove that Socrates has three eyes. The logic would be correct, although the conclusion would clearly be wrong when compared to reality.

Of course, a logical argument can be much more complex than a simple syllogism. However, there are always a number of premises given to be true and some number of logic steps ending in a conclusion. The conclusion must be correct (based upon the premises) if there have been no mistakes in the logic steps.

<u>**Logical Thinking**</u>
<u>**(or Deductive Reasoning)**</u>

<u>Premises</u>

Logic Step 1

Logic Step 2

... (additional logic steps)

<u>Conclusion(s)</u>

Englishman George Boole, known as the father of modern logic, developed symbolic logic circa 1850. Boolean logic replaces language with symbols. It provided an excellent tool for designing digital circuits when the computer age arrived.

Although the statements are terser and more concise, the same principles underlie symbolic logic, and it is sometimes utilized in areas other than mathematics and computer science.

Rational Thinking

The basis for rational thinking is the demonstrable fact that there is a single shared reality that is the same for everyone. With some careful and methodical work, we can discover and understand many of the properties and basic principles that make up and govern our reality. Building upon solid basic principles with sound logical thinking, we can deduce useful higher-level conclusions that increase and deepen our understanding of the nature of reality and how things work. The dramatic and beneficial success that humans have had in this cooperative endeavor is an extremely strong endorsement of it.

Rational thinking can be regarded as logical thinking, but certain restrictions need to be placed on the premises. *There must be a high degree of confidence that all premises can be verified as valid representations of reality.* If all premises are grounded in reality and the logic is correct, then the conclusions must also be an aspect of reality. The correct logic of the syllogism above did not establish that Socrates had three eyes because one of its premises ("All men have three eyes") was not grounded in reality.

It is important that all properties, principles, and conclusions be validated against reality with documented (published) tests or experiments and logic. Then others anywhere and at any time can repeat such a test or experiment to prove to themselves that results really are consistent with the reality we all share.

If you claim something is an aspect of reality, you must be able to tell others how they can independently demonstrate or verify for themselves that it actually is real. You could refer them to results published by others, or you would need to supply them with a detailed description of a logical proof, a test, or an experiment that they could perform and (presumably) obtain the same result.

What we have defined as rational thinking pretty much corresponds to what is commonly known as the *scientific method.* However, rational thinking does not just apply to "science." It is universal and applies to everything everywhere. There is no boundary walling off "science" from "nonscience," within which rational thought applies and outside of which it does not. More correctly, there is nothing that is outside of science.

Save for a sprinkling of serendipitous discoveries, it is safe to say that substantially all of the progress our species has made must be attributed to rational thinking.

Resolving Disagreements

All too often, people are so strongly polarized on key issues that attempts to discuss them escalate quickly to acrimony. Even good friends and families learn to avoid certain topics so they can keep their gatherings cordial. This is uncomfortable at a minimum, and it definitely impedes progress toward resolving such issues.

The intense polarization in our society has reached unhealthy and perhaps unprecedented levels. What might be done to defuse this serious problem?

When two individuals or groups disagree about something, there are only three things they can do.

1. They can "agree to disagree" and walk away. This may occur after a little or a lot of unproductive argument. Of course, the issue has not been resolved and will return to haunt them. The vast majority of disagreements follow this path of inaction and continue to fester.

2. The stronger side could use force to impose its view on the weaker side. The weaker side may still harbor its "incorrect" (now repressed) view, so a longer-lasting resolution may require the "elimination" of the weaker side. History is replete with examples ranging from two-person duels to persecution, religious crusades, and wars.

3. Both sides could agree to settle their issue(s) by employing rational thought. This is the *only* path guaranteed to actually resolve an issue — that is, both

sides end up in agreement — and to resolve it peacefully without the use of any force!

If two parties disagree about some aspect of reality, they can't both be right. Of course, they might both be wrong, but at most, one of them can be right.

The beautiful thing is that any such disputes can usually be cleared up peacefully and conclusively. Cooperatively, both parties can go back to known and agreed-to basic principles (all grounded in reality) and review each logic step (being careful to correct any mistakes) until a conclusion is reached. Having agreed upon the premises and with each logic step, both must then agree with the conclusion. No claim is asserted that this will always be easy, just that it is possible.

Additionally, a test might be devised to prove which conclusion is consistent with reality. Such a test or logic process can be duplicated by any rational person anywhere to verify the result. Should verification fail, we know we must look for the mistake(s) in the (current or original) test design or logic. If no explanation is found there, the veracity of the premises must be checked! For complex cases, this could indeed be a long, arduous process, but it would certainly be worth the effort to resolve issues of great significance.

Even for extremely complex issues where the verification process would be impractically lengthy and mistake-prone, the understanding by all parties that it is possible can maintain cooperation and collegiality.

Probably needless to say, differences in personal preference (you want to paint the room blue, but your partner likes green) cannot be settled this way. We deal only with disputes over our shared reality (e.g., imposing a minimum wage law will or will not increase unemployment).

An assertion about reality that has not been proven is called a conjecture or a hypothesis. A conjecture might be thought of as "spitballing" or throwing out ideas, while a hypothesis is usually regarded as a more serious theory that has some reasonable probability of being substantiated.

A word of caution is in order: once in a great while, a "proven" hypothesis turns out to not be correct after all. One notable example would be the laws governing the motion of objects as worked out by Sir Isaac Newton circa 1687. "Newtonian mechanics" or "classical mechanics" served the world extremely well and was fundamental to great technological progress for hundreds of years. Newton's laws and equations were validated and verified many times over.

Nevertheless, along came Albert Einstein in 1905 to point out that Newton's description isn't quite right. There were errors so small that they escaped notice within the limited range of conditions under which Newton's laws were validated. However, under other conditions, the errors would be so large as to be impossible to ignore. For example, the modern GPS satellite system cannot depend upon classical mechanics and must take these relativistic "errors" into account to function properly. The simpler Newtonian mechanics is still fine and widely used wherever its errors are known to be small enough that they can be safely ignored.

The point here is that a rational person must always be open not only to new theories and new test results but also to the revalidation of prior results, perhaps under different conditions or to greater precision.

Characteristics of Rational Thinkers

People who adopt rational thinking as their standard and appreciate its importance tend to share certain characteristics:

- goal-directed behavior that seeks to understand as much of reality as possible with the highest possible degree of certainty;

- willing to reevaluate, refine, and update this understanding as an ongoing process;

- willing (even eager) to revise understanding based upon new information or correction; of logic mistakes

- willing to invest the often hard work of *thinking* to gain or cement understanding.

A rational discussion with a nonrational "thinker" is very difficult, often impossible, and extremely unlikely to be productive! It is an exercise in futility and frustration for a rational thinker to attempt to debate anyone who has no understanding of or respect for the tenets of rational thought.

Typically, nonrationals seek "safety in numbers," surrounding themselves with or possibly citing others who hold the same opinion rather than directly addressing the position's veracity. By itself, the fact that others hold the same position proves nothing, but it could possibly warrant checking something out more carefully if doubt has been raised.

When pressed to support their positions, a favorite tactic of last resort might be called argument by intimidation. This strategy involves adopting a haughty, holier-than-thou demeanor intended to imply that you are a stupid lowlife (and probably much worse) for questioning their infallibility. If that still fails to cow you into accepting their position (or at least shutting you down), they will usually disengage with a sniff as though it's not worth their valuable time to continue.

A Trap for Which to Be Prepared

The universe does not provide any guarantee that every problem has a great solution. Some problems simply have no solution at all. Quite often, complex issues are optimization problems in which desirable things must be maximized while undesirable things are simultaneously minimized. It is sometimes possible to determine with certainty precisely where the optimum lies, but often, that is either not easy or not possible.

The point here is that someone arguing against a solution that is an optimization will always be able to point to some specific thing that, in isolation, is not desirable. Of course, if that particular thing was not comprehended as part of the optimization, it could be a valid argument against the optimization. However, if that thing was indeed considered in the optimization process, it is not a valid argument against the optimization solution.

Unfortunately, citing a specific undesirable aspect of an optimization solution can be very persuasive to those who have not expended the time and effort to understand the entire complex problem. Thus, the defender of an optimization solution is always at a disadvantage. Like a Boy Scout, be prepared.

Why Rational Thinkers Are a Minority

The two main reasons for the paucity of rational thinkers are ignorance and laziness. Being surrounded by many other careless thinkers certainly doesn't help.

Most people just don't know much about rational thought. Schools virtually never specifically teach and don't consistently emphasize these foundationally important concepts. It's rare to find a teacher capable of teaching them. The scientific method may be taught in science courses, but the implication usually is that it can be safely forgotten elsewhere.

Of those who may vaguely recognize that rational thought is important, many will have nothing to do with it. "That's just scientific stuff, and science is not my thing" is frequently their excuse.

Yet another factor is faith-based institutions that teach and encourage the opposite of rational thinking. Merriam-Webster defines faith as a "firm belief in something for which there is no proof." However, this counterproductive influence appears to be in a long, gradual decline.

Others may allow their emotions to overrule the rational thought process, either generally or just in certain subject areas.

Of the remaining group, who do understand the concept and its importance, apparently few are willing to put forth the required effort. Digging a ditch by hand is hard physical work. Rational thinking is usually equally difficult mental work. You must focus hard on a thorny problem for a sustained time and commit to carefully reasoning it all the way through. In our age of flashing screens and short attention spans, vanishingly few are able and willing to tackle the hard work of rational thought.

So, sadly, there are precious few consistently rational thinkers.

Overwhelmingly, people have little appreciation for basic principles. They adopt issue positions fairly indiscriminately because they feel or sound right, they're what their friends think, their church or political party told them so, or even just because they heard it fifty times in a catchy sound bite. Or they are willing to believe things as a matter of faith, which by its very definition is not rational.

If peace on Earth is ever to be achieved, less irrationality and more rationality will be necessary. Until we have more rational thinkers, or at least more people who appreciate, respect, and value the process, we'll continue to have lots of strong polarization, irrational shouting, acrimony, and unresolved issues.

Consciousness, Self-Awareness, Intelligence, and Wisdom

The nature of *consciousness* has been debated for years. What actually is it? Consciousness probably occurs spontaneously when an entity attains a level of complexity that can support rational thinking. It is simply the process of observing reality and its characteristics, plus trying to understand the principles that govern how reality works.

Self-awareness is a half-step higher than consciousness. It occurs when a conscious entity observes, deduces, and comprehends that it is a specific part of reality and is able to clearly identify the part of reality that is itself and distinguish it from the part of reality that is not itself.

True intelligence can be considered a measure of an entity's rational thinking capability. A balanced combination of the *depth, breadth, accuracy*, and *speed* of rational thought is what is important. Most intelligence tests tend to measure logical thinking, leaving open the possibility of high-IQ people who are not tethered to reality.

Wisdom can develop from lots of rational thinking, experience, and observations. It's the ability to quickly and correctly predict the consequences or outcome of an action based upon similar circumstances recalled from either previously thinking them through or from previous observations. This ability probably depends upon discovering underlying patterns and storing them as a handy "reference library" of shortcuts.

Rational thinking underlies all of this. In view of its importance and value, children should be encouraged and guided to think rationally from an early age. The subject should be formally covered in an early grade and reinforced throughout the education system. The rub is that this requires teachers who are rational thinkers, or at least ones who understand and respect rational thinking.

The Real Beginning

The *real* beginning for Homo sapiens on Earth was the advent of rational thinking. This could occur only after suitable and sufficiently complex structures had evolved to enable it. We should all work on advancing rational thinking and try hard not to screw it up.

3. Debunking Illusions of "Spirituality"

There are many things we can't explain — at least, we haven't explained them yet — but we are working on them. If you are disturbed by your inability to understand something, why ever would it make sense to concoct an "explanation" based on something even harder to explain (e.g., a deity) and then, apparently, not be disturbed by your inability to explain that?

Dreaming up wild conjectures that have no basis in reality just because you can't understand something is not helpful; that is, unless you are seriously proposing a hypothesis to be tested by an experiment intended to either prove or disprove said hypothesis. Proving it would require demonstrating that your hypothesis is actually grounded in the reality that we all share. You would need to provide some documented reproducible test or demonstration that could be carried out by anyone else, which would also convince them that your hypothesis is indeed true and correct.

MKS

We keep chipping away at all the stuff in our bin of unexplained things, and when we do find a new explanation for something, it has always been (thus far) describable in terms of just a very few base physical units: length, mass, and time. The international standard units are the *meter* for length, the *kilogram* for mass, and the *second* for time. This system of units is almost always abbreviated as MKS.

Higher-level (derived) units are defined in terms of MKS. The *velocity* or *speed* of an object is the number of meters it moves in one second relative to something else, that is, meters per second or m/s.

The unit of force is the *newton*, which is the amount of constant force that it takes to accelerate a mass of 1 kilogram to a velocity of 1 m/s in 1 second, which is an acceleration of 1 meter per second per second (1 m/s^2). Therefore, the MKS "signature" for the newton is kg m/s^2.

The unit of energy is the *joule*, which is defined as the energy needed to move something 1 meter while exerting a constant force on it of 1 newton; this is newton meters or just n m. In terms of the base units, the joule is kg m^2/s^2.

The unit of *power*, or the rate at which energy is being expended, is the *watt,* which is 1 joule per second (kg m^2/s^3).

The point is that everything is built upon and ties back to MKS, but we assign names to higher-level (derived) units that are easier to use than their MKS unit signatures, which are longer and harder to recognize quickly.

There are other systems of units, most notably CGS, which uses the centimeter as the unit of length, the gram as the unit of mass, and the second as the unit of time. Some of the higher level derived units for CGS are more logically defined, but of course, they all still tie back to the base units of length, mass, and time. CGS actually is a more convenient system of unit definitions for physicists, but MKS is highlighted since it has been adopted as the international standard.

Obviously, use of the scientific method has been highly successful, to put it mildly. We began by building our understanding of the things immediately around us that we interacted with all the time. Then, we later expanded our knowledge in all directions from our local, directly experienceable reality.

Astronomers have built more and more powerful instruments to observe and measure things at greater and greater distances. The diameter of the observable universe is approximately 10^{27} meters. A guesstimate of the total mass in the observable universe is about 10^{53} kilograms. The age of our universe is about 13.8 billion years or 4.3×10^{17} seconds. Our earth formed roughly 4.5 billion years ago (about 1.4×10^{17} seconds).

The ancient Greeks postulated that all matter was composed of atoms too small for them to see. Today, we are all over atoms, which are only about 10^{-10} meter in size. We even understand that atoms are comprised of even smaller components, some of which are in turn built from even smaller things called quarks, which are less than 10^{-18} meter in size! Some quarks have an electric charge of approximately 10^{-19} coulomb.

Thus, our understanding spans an astoundingly large range. By example, in distance, from 10^{-18} to 10^{27} meters, which is a factor of 10^{45} or

1,000,000,000,000,000,000,000,000,000,000,000,000,000,000,000.

As we venture away from our "neighborhood" toward the extremes, the number of unanswered questions increases. For one example, we don't know if anything of interest happens at scales smaller than 10^{-19} meter; although it very well might, and we suspect that it could possibly turn out to be quite important and may help resolve some things that we do not yet understand.

Some specific areas have been identified where we know our understanding is incomplete. Physicists have been struggling for most of the past hundred years to construct a so-called "theory of everything" that would bridge some of these gaps. We are actively working on those and other questions.

Looking at the big picture, progress over the past few centuries has been outstanding. There is no apparent reason to expect that to change. We have every confidence that doing the hard work of rational thinking will continue to expand and deepen our understanding of reality, even if it should turn out to require some refinement or extension of the current framework.

Nevertheless, and in spite of the record of success, there are many cases in which people insist that there are things that cannot *ever* be explained by our scientific framework and approach. Instead, they must be attributed to some other spiritual world (or worlds). Well, by definition, our universe, our reality, is all-inclusive, so such claims have to mean that there is something yet undiscovered and apparently not explainable within MKS or any future enhancement of it.

By far, most such spirituality claims are made by people who do not adhere to the tenets of rational thought and may not even understand what rational thinking is. However, there are plenty of examples from those who do claim to be rational thinkers, and even from scientists who are presumed to respect and adhere to the scientific method. However, no one is able to describe any test or experiment that could be carried out by anyone anywhere which would reproduce or otherwise verify or explain these spiritual phenomena.

Can all these people who insist that various spiritual things are a part of our shared reality be safely ignored? There usually is no way to prove that they are incorrect. To adapt a Bertrand Russell argument, suppose someone claims that there is a small black marble orbiting the planet Neptune. They insist that this is true and challenge you to prove that it is not. That's ridiculous. It is the burden of anyone making a claim or assertion to prove its validity. That you have no handy way to disprove the assertion is not a proof that it is correct.

Unfortunately, it is just not going to be possible to resolve these sometimes strongly held beliefs to everyone's satisfaction. What might be helpful, though, is to explain some of the understandable things that likely give rise to spiritual illusions and irrational thinking for many people.

Indoctrination and Brainwashing

There is an extremely wide variety of groups and organizations whose business is to actively encourage the suspension of rational thought in order to get people to believe in some spiritual realm that they have defined. Since they can in no way prove or demonstrate its validity, they urge its acceptance as a matter of faith. Merriam-Webster: faith: firm belief in something for which there is no proof.

A common tactic is to threaten people with some horrible fate if they fail to fully adopt the tenets of the faith and adhere to some set of prescribed rules: "You will eternally burn in hell if you don't buy into our pitch."

Usually, there is regular reinforcement, often accompanied by rituals. Participation in rituals tends to strengthen the mental acceptance that you have bought into and are submitting to the cult and are indeed a member of it. In many cases, this amounts to mild indoctrination, but in some cases, the sustained intensity is high enough to qualify as brainwashing. Many people have great difficulty escaping the spell, especially when their parents are coconspirators and indoctrination begins during childhood. Breaking free takes a sufficiently strong and independent person who is willing to expend the considerable effort required to think things through carefully in spite of very powerful peer pressure.

It must be acknowledged that some such organizations are helpful to people who are unable to rationally derive and adhere to a "good moral code" on their own. They seem to need the framework and guidance provided by spiritual constructs as direction in their lives.

However, this sort of indoctrination surely does far more harm than good. It prevents some from ever becoming rational thinkers and delays many others from getting onto a path of rationality. Some compartmentalize the irrational (faith) and the rational (scientific stuff). It can surely cause considerable mental angst to those making the transition to complete rationality.

Throughout recorded history, faith-based organizations attempting to force others to buy their particular brand of dog food appear to have been the largest single cause of violence and bloodshed. Most unfortunately and incredibly, this still seems to be true today. Assorted ruthless tyrants — like Joe Stalin — surely have provided significant competition.

Fear of Death

Substantially everyone understands that, with the technology available right now and in the immediate future, there is a finite limit to how long human life can be extended. Some are comfortable with this, but others are not. They are unable to accept that their life will end — period. This is a powerful motivation for them to buy into any spiritual fantasy that promises life after death, reincarnation, or whatever. The most effective hook that faith-based organizations have to capture and hold members may be the fear of death.

Guilt

There are all kinds of people in the world, ranging from serial killers to "saints." Certainly, a majority are raised to have some reasonable understanding of, and commitment to, honesty and fair play. Equally certain, a very large percentage of that majority will occasionally violate that commitment and experience feelings of guilt as a result of doing so.

Some purveyors of spiritual powers offer followers a path to absolution from that guilt. Such paths frequently involve the performance of a ritual and/or an open discussion of the transgression with some appropriate functionary of the faith. Most significantly, the path to absolution for some major faiths is private and much easier than properly rectifying the transgression with the harmed party. The morality and advisability of providing such an "escape hatch" for wrongdoers seems shaky at best. However — and nevertheless — this probably is the second most effective hook used to capture and retain adherents.

Peer Pressure

Some humans are loners, but most of us enjoy being accepted as part of a group. Frequently, group acceptance is enhanced by, and occasionally requires, subscribing to the important parts of a group's philosophy. When a group endorses some form of spirituality, it can become a strong motivation to buy into it.

Seemingly Impossible Occurrences

There are two subcategories to the "impossible occurrences" category. The first is that of cataclysmic, potentially life-altering events. Examples are, say, surviving a serious automobile accident or a building collapse.

Often, the survivors of a calamity point to one particular small detail that "saved them"— it could easily have been otherwise, and they would have perished. There are countless variations on this theme. The survivors are deeply affected emotionally and frequently attribute their survival to some spiritual intervention; they tend to broadcast that notion widely. Sorry, this is just part of the normal operation of the universe under MKS. Remember, there are plenty of completely analogous cases where people did not survive, but they are no longer around to say, "Gee, if such-and-such a little detail had been different, I would have survived, but I got screwed." So, we only ever get to hear one side of such "spiritual occurrences."

There is a well-known phenomenon called *confirmation bias*. Those holding a certain view tend to notice and cite instances that support or confirm the view that they favor while tending to ignore or overlook occurrences that undermine their view. Advocates of spiritual things frequently fall victim to this subconscious bias.

The second subcategory revolves around the underappreciation of the awesome power of natural selection (evolution). Occasionally, even otherwise rational thinkers and scientists who should know better will succumb to this one.

They observe the incredible intricacy, beauty, complexity (insert here whatever additional adjectives may be desired) of the world around us and refuse to accept that it could have happened "accidentally." That is just too unlikely or *improbable*. Clearly, such an amazing thing had to have been designed and created by some superior intelligence; this is the argument for so-called intelligent design.

How could any logical person make such a statement? It just attempts to explain one hard-to-explain thing with another even harder-to-explain (and unexplained) thing. That's zero help for gaining a true and correct understanding of reality. If anything, it is a step backward.

In fact, the complex (etc., etc.) world around us exists *because it is probable* under the principles and laws of the universe. It is easy to underestimate what the process of natural selection or evolution can do, especially regarding various life-forms. Complex things do not often evolve quickly. However, when there are billions and billions of trials occurring over millions of years, the results can be and are astounding.

The many, many less successful "trials" (random mutations) perish or die out, but the occasional important improvement survives, persists, and multiplies. When this basically simple process proceeds with millions of trials happening at the same time and with millions of repetitions (generations) over time, exquisite designs emerge.

Natural selection can be programmatically utilized on a computer to find reasonable solutions to certain types of intractable problems. It is shocking how much progress can be made toward a good solution in just twenty or thirty "generations," which can happen in a flash on a computer.

A great example of the tremendous power of evolution is the eye. Charles Darwin himself, in his *On the Origin of Species*, admitted that the eye is so complex and sophisticated that its evolution seems "absurd to the highest degree," but he nevertheless argued that it was indeed a product of the evolutionary process.

Biologists have by now traced the eye from its beginning as a few light-sensitive cells on the skin of marine animals through many, many, many steps to its manifestation as a lens capable of focusing an image on a retina connected to an optic nerve. The first eyes appeared about 541 million years ago, and their journey from light-sensitive cells to eyeball happened over a mere half-million years.

The natural selection process is still and always active, determining what will evolve in the future. Never underestimate what the simple and basic mechanism of natural selection can accomplish.

It's All in Your Head!

The endpoint of any explanation is always to be found here — in your head. A human brain is about two kilograms of mass and is made up of approximately 86 billion neurons. Each neuron is complexly connected to a substantial number of other neurons, and they exchange electrochemically encoded information. This forms a network that is almost incomprehensibly large and complex. In addition, the way synaptic connections convey information from one neuron to others is "conditioned" or modified by experiences and even by thoughts. The damned thing is astonishingly (and thankfully) complicated and adaptable — another excellent product of the natural selection process.

A typical human body is roughly 100 kg of mass. It takes about 100 watts (W) of power to run a body. Most of this power comes from the oxidation of glucose. The brain requires about a fifth of this power, or 20 W, to operate. Thus, the brain requires ten times the power per kilogram (10 W/kg) to operate it than does the rest of the body (which requires only 0.92 W/kg). The brain's complexity and relatively large power consumption are indicative of its importance to human survival. Every thought, every understanding a person has of the real world, is controlled by the brain. Every thought is a neural pattern in the brain. Your brain is you.

It's not surprising that a brain is capable of a wide and wild array of thoughts, both rational and irrational, including those that "explain" complex, hard-to-understand things by attributing them to some notion of "spirituality." Everyone is aware that dreams may or may not correspond to reality. Even when awake, brains can sometimes produce thoughts and images that seem vividly real but have no basis in reality. Often, this happens under the influence of drugs or extreme physical or emotional stress. There is absolutely nothing going on here that is outside of MKS.

To maximize its probability of survival, it is important for each brain to reliably identify and utilize the thoughts that actually are grounded in reality; that is, they need to think rationally. Harboring illusions and delusions is harmless as long as it is just for entertainment value and you can tell the difference. However, basing important life decisions on such things definitely could be dangerous.

4. Rational Self-Interest

This chapter attempts to describe with some rigor how human individuals make decisions. Decision-making clearly is quite important. We make untold numbers of decisions every day. One might reasonably characterize life as just serial decision-making.

Some decisions have major and long-lasting impacts on life. Other decisions may not be of great consequence, yet they too must be timely made. This may seem like a somewhat odd topic, but in view of the central importance of decision-making in everyone's life, it would seem worth the effort to better understand it in some depth.

> **<u>Axiom</u>: Human individuals *always* make decisions in such a way as to optimize their own rational self-interest.**

The entire science of economics is based on the fact that every person can be counted upon to always make choices based strictly upon their rational self-interest. Because of this, the basic laws of microeconomics do not fail and can be relied upon.

To understand how the brain makes decisions, it will be helpful to have a more useful definition of *rational self-interest*. So, to restate the above axiom: An individual will *always* make the choice that they believe will maximize their total future happiness.

Doubtless, someone will immediately jump up and say, "But what about altruism? There are plenty of examples of people sacrificing their own happiness for the benefit of others." Nope. Sorry, but that just never happens. The romantic notion of altruism is a fallacy. People *always* act selfishly to maximize their own happiness. Not to do so would manifest a fairly serious brain malfunction.

Yes, there certainly are examples of people appearing to act altruistically. However, they would not do so if that act didn't make them happy in some way meaningful to them. In blatant cases, a charitable donation might get the donor's name on a building, on a supporters' plaque, or listed in an event program. Only a slight step removed from that is a donation to a cause that would "benefit all mankind," including, of course, the donor. Sometimes, it's just admiration and acknowledgment from peers that does the trick. There are even cases where an act of kindness is done anonymously, but still, it is done because it results in increased happiness for the doer.

The first person to gain an understanding of economics was Scottish scholar Adam Smith. Here is what Adam had to say about altruism back in 1776: "How selfish soever man may be supposed, there are evidently some principles in his nature which interest him in the fortune of others and render their happiness necessary to him though he derives nothing from it except the pleasure of seeing it."

There should be no reason to be embarrassed about always making decisions that maximize your own expected future happiness. It's just how natural selection evolved our brains to function in order to maximize the probability of each individual's survival. It's the nature of the beast. You could cite it as evidence of good mental health. However, most people do tend to be somewhat embarrassed in these situations. To the extent that their potential embarrassment affects the estimate of their expected future happiness, it can affect their decisions.

Perhaps this tweaks decision making to maximize the probability of survival for the Homo sapiens species. Natural selection has resulted in astoundingly nuanced complexity.

Suppose you are faced with a basic decision between two options, A and B. Your brain will estimate your expected total future happiness that would result if option A were chosen, and separately estimate your expected total future happiness that would result if option B were chosen. That's the hard part. Then, the choice is simply the option that is expected to result in the greatest total future happiness. A and B might be two courses of action that you must choose between, or the decision might just be whether to do something (A) or not do it (B). Of course, there are multioption decisions as well (A, B, C, D…).

"Maximizing expected total future happiness" provides a somewhat more specific and actionable definition of rational self-interest. In our *Declaration of Independence*, Thomas Jefferson aptly called this "the pursuit of happiness" and stated that it is a "right." However, there is more work to do to understand and formalize how brains might go about trying to achieve this goal.

A person's happiness no doubt depends upon many factors that are unique to each individual. They will inevitably change over time. It is clear that brains have the ability to evaluate all these complex considerations by means of some internal calculation, since that is what determines each individual's happiness at each moment in time.

However, to make decisions based on "expected total future happiness," brains must also be able to project happiness calculations into the future for hypothetical situations. That is, they must be able to project into the future what will happen to all the salient factors that affect their happiness and also calculate the future happiness that will result from the projected factors. This must be done separately for each hypothetical situation.

To formalize this, we can say that the brain is able to form a "happiness function" of some sort by which it is able to estimate instantaneous happiness at a future time for each hypothetical situation it is evaluating. The happiness functions for options A and B could be written, $h_A(t)$ and $h_B(t)$. Note that $t = 0$ is always the present time, and positive values of t are future times. All happiness functions have as their result instantaneous happiness values in some units that the brain understands and are comparable with each other. We will lightheartedly call the unit of instantaneous happiness the *hap*. There is no way we can hope to know exactly how the brain accomplishes this or how such happiness functions work internally. As we have seen, brains are almost inconceivably complex. Some illustrative examples should help clarify how the overall decision-making process operates.

Suppose you are twenty-three years old and your TV set has just died. You plan to give yourself a brand-new TV set for your upcoming twenty-fourth birthday. Your investigation of TVs has boiled the choices down to a final two, and they happen to have the same price. Below is a chart showing the two happiness functions for TV set A and TV set B.

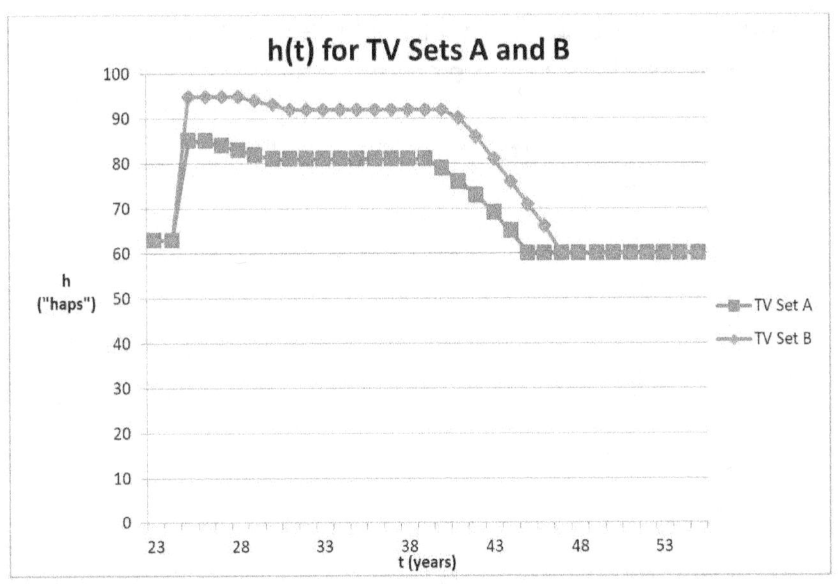

In this example, the decision is as easy as it gets. TV set B has a better picture and sound than TV set A. It also has more neat features. Your brain estimates that TV set B will bump your happiness up to about 93 haps while TV set A only manages 81 haps. The expected lifetime for both sets is about 18 years, so the happy party can be expected to come to an end with you, once again, having to buy a new TV in your early forties. Since the estimated hap levels for TV B are always equal to or noticeably greater than those for TV A, it's a no brainer that you will buy TV B.

However, were the characteristics of the two TV sets somewhat different, the decision would be a lot more difficult. Suppose now that TV B is still just as wonderful and still would give you 93 haps, but it uses a new screen technology that has a more limited service life — say, about 12 years. TV A still gives you 81 haps, but it has been specially engineered for long life — say about 24 years. Now, your brain estimates the two happiness functions as shown on the chart below.

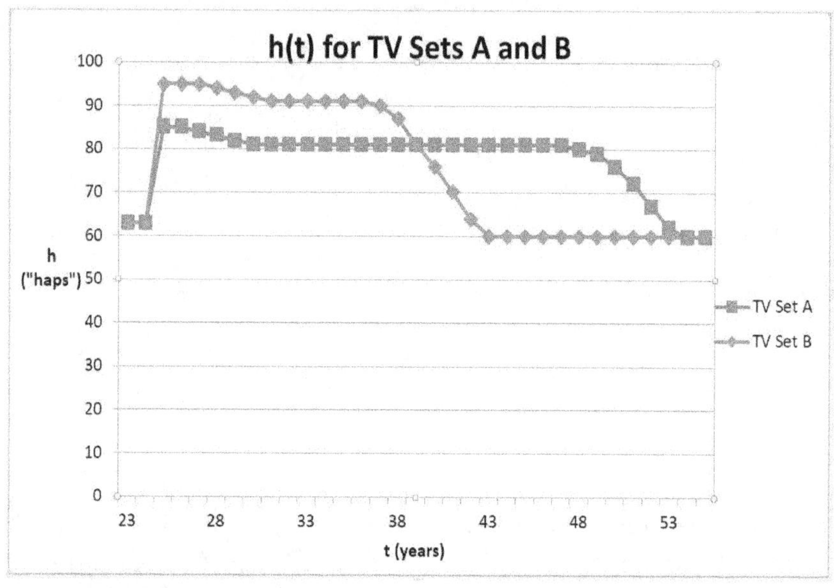

The decision now is not obvious at all. How would your brain go about making it?

As previously stated, decisions are based on expected total future happiness. Total happiness depends not only upon instantaneous happiness but also on the length of time you are able to enjoy that happiness. Suppose you experience great happiness, say 200 haps, but it lasts for only a half-second. That's not much total happiness — only 100 hap-seconds (0.5 × 200). However, suppose you are able to experience a happiness level of 80 haps and sustain that for 20 years. That's a whole lot more total happiness — 1,600 hap-years (20 × 80), which is more than 500 million times the total happiness of a mere 100 hap-seconds!

It turns out that the total happiness for the $h(t)$ functions shown in the two charts above is equal to the area below each of the functions. To illustrate, in the chart below, the total happiness for TV set B is the shaded area.

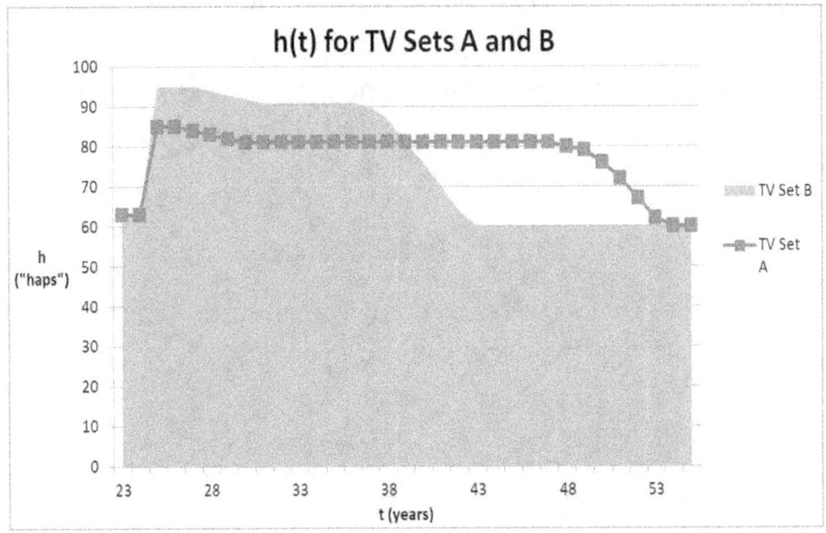

The total happiness for TV B (the shaded area) is calculated as 2,484 hap-years. Calculating the total happiness for TV A (the area under the plotted line) gives 2,559 hap-years. The longer life of TV A has "tipped the scales" in its favor. The correct decision this time is to buy TV A.

Jumping back to the first chart and calculating the total happiness for each TV, we have 2,314 hap-years for TV A and 2,560 hap-years for TV B. This confirms that the no brainer decision to purchase TV B was indeed correct.

The branch of mathematics that deals with (among other things) the areas under various functions is called *integral calculus*. Human brains are capable of doing calculus (or its equivalent), and so much more. They are truly awesome.

As a third example, let's reuse the last example, except for one small change. Instead of your TV failing when you were twenty-three and buying a new one for your twenty-fourth birthday, your TV dies when you are fifty-five, and you are going to buy yourself a new TV for your fifty-sixth birthday. The chart updated for this change is shown below.

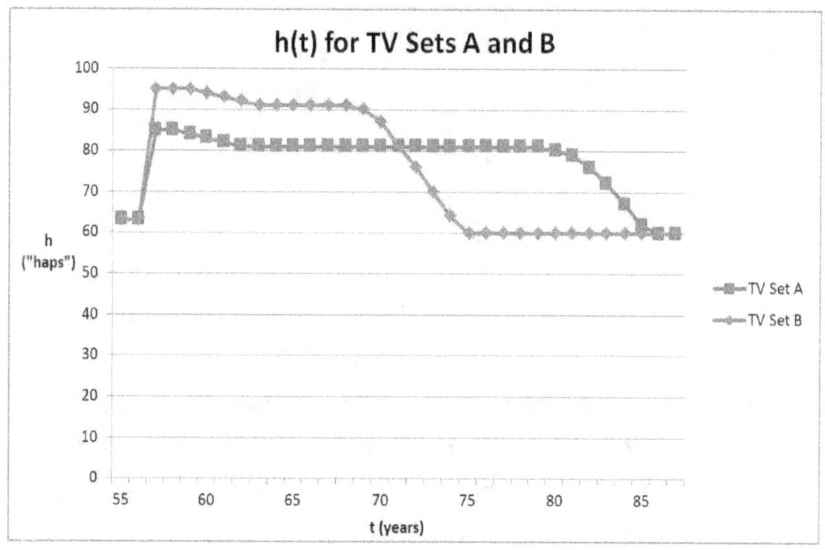

Of course, the chart is virtually identical. However, one can't help but notice that the extra-long life of TV A extends through your seventies and into your eighties. By then, there is an increasing likelihood of death or life in an assisted care facility where you will no longer be the one selecting the TV. For these and possibly other reasons, you may not be able to enjoy some part of the happiness provided by TV A. This is a very important consideration that has not yet been comprehended by the decision-making mechanism. The expected future happiness, $h(t)$, needs to be "discounted" for the possibility that you may not be able to enjoy it for one reason or another — most notably death.

Therefore, the brain separately estimates the probability that it will be able to experience the happiness estimated by $h(t)$. This will be a separate function, $p(t)$. In the best possible case, $p(t)$ will just be the probability of being alive at each time — that is, the normal life expectancy. However, the brain may know of other considerations that could cause $p(t)$ to be less than normal life expectancy. Probabilities must always be between 0 and 1, inclusive. Every $p(t)$ will have its highest value of 1 at $t = 0$, since the person must be alive to be making a decision. It will decrease to 0 at some future time, and it can never increase.

If your probability of being alive is 76% (or 0.76) at some future time, there is no possibility (with the current capabilities of medical technology) that you will later come back to life. Therefore, the probability at an even later time must be something less than 76%.

The chart below shows some examples for $p(t)$.

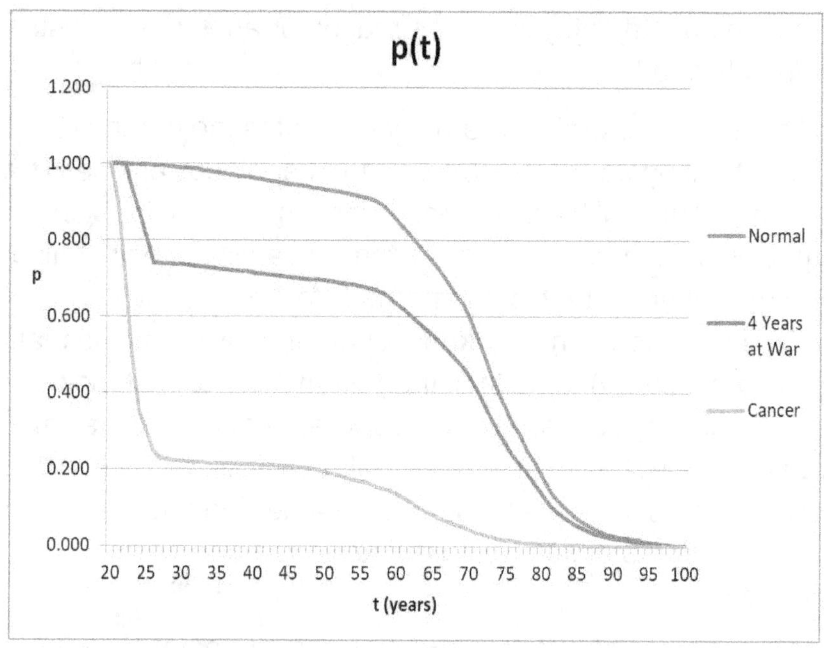

The upper curve is the normal life expectancy that a twenty-year-old would be facing.

The middle plot might be for a twenty-year-old man who has signed up with the Army. Following basic training, he anticipates being shipped off to fight in a hot war for four years and estimates a 75% probability of surviving. If he survives, he would expect a more or less normal life expectancy thereafter.

The lowest curve is the $p(t)$ estimated for a twenty-year-old who has just been diagnosed with cancer and is entering a four-year treatment program. There is a 25% probability he will beat the cancer, but even if he does, his life expectancy would then be ten years shorter than normal.

It should be obvious how important the brain's estimate of $p(t)$ can be to making good decisions. The following two charts revisit the TV set decision when $p(t)$ is taken into consideration. Instead of showing $h(t)$, these two charts show $h(t)p(t)$. The $p(t)$ is for normal life expectancy — the top curve from the above chart.

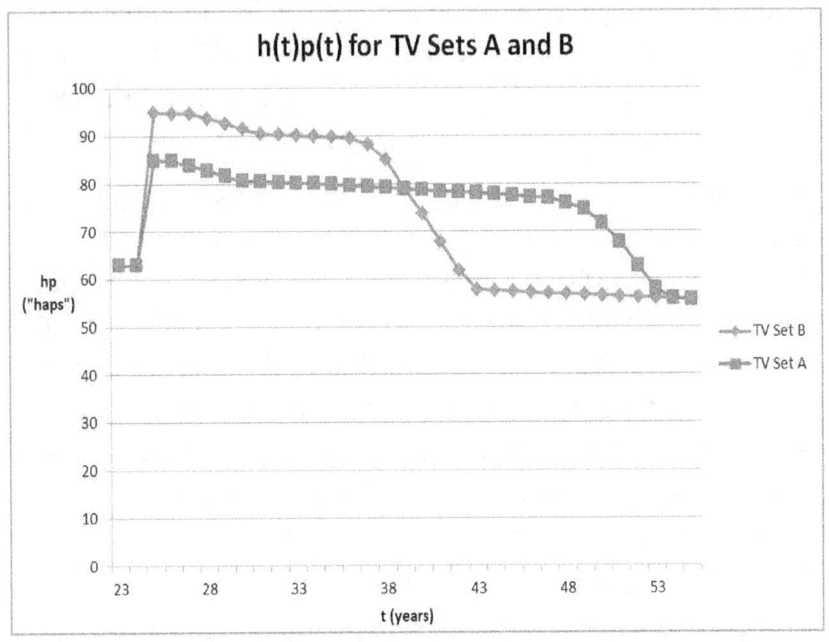

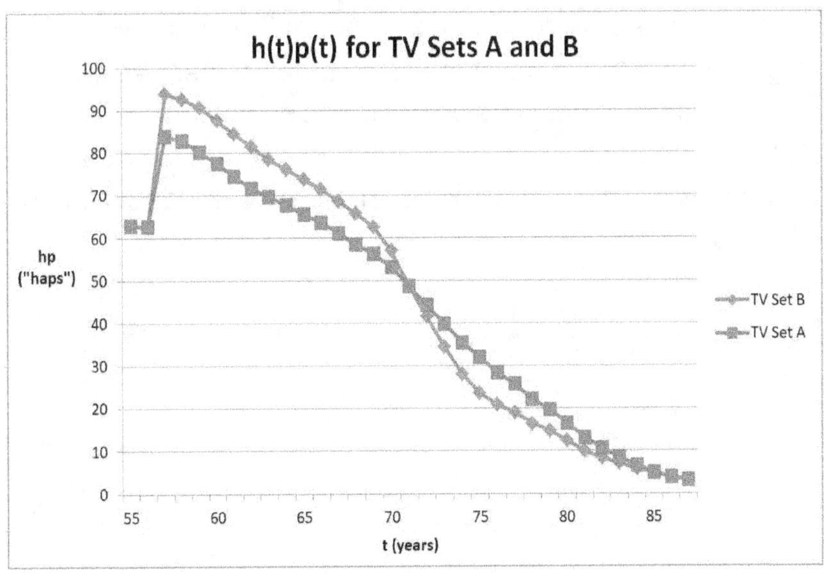

When you are making this purchase decision at age twenty-three, the effect of $p(t)$ is rather mild. In the corresponding earlier chart with just $h(t)$, the expected total happiness was 2,559 hap-years for TV A and 2,484 hap-years for TV B, so the decision was to buy TV A. Applying $p(t)$ reduces both slightly to 2,487, and 2,421, respectively. So, the correct decision still is to purchase TV A.

However, if you are making the same decision at age fifty-five, the change wrought by $p(t)$ is far more significant. Using only $h(t)$, the expected total future happiness was (again) 2,559 for TV A and 2,484 for TV B. Using $h(t)p(t)$ reduces total happiness to 1,456 for TV A and 1,513 for TV B. This reverses the decision. At the more advanced age, your total expected future happiness is greater if you enjoy the better performance of TV B while you can because of the probability that you may not be around to enjoy the longer life that TV A can offer.

Suppose now that you are walking alone down a dark, deserted street. A robber jumps out of the shadows, points a gun at you and demands that you hand over everything of value in your possession. The decision you face is whether to meekly comply or instead attempt to wrestle the gun away from your assailant. The next chart depicts this decision.

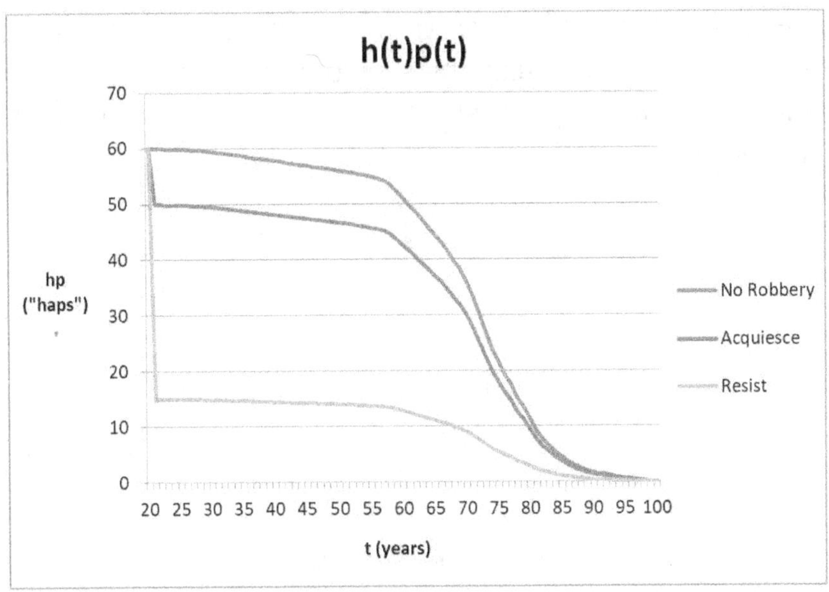

The top curve is there just for reference and represents your normal baseline happiness as it would have been if the robbery had not occurred. Your decision is between the middle and bottom curves. If you just hand over all your stuff, your $h(t)$ drops some because of your loss of wealth, but your life is not threatened and goes forward normally following the robbery. If you grab for the gun or otherwise fend off the robber, your $p(t)$ takes a major hit because you estimate the probability of your survival at about 25%. If you do survive, you keep your valuables, and your life proceeds normally from there. The decision is not close: You hand over your stuff. Of course, your brain's $h(t)p(t)$ could vary widely from those shown depending on the exact circumstances — especially your estimate of the relative size and strength of the robber and you.

It is worth specifically noting that human brains are perfectly capable of making decisions that sacrifice (reduce) near-term happiness with the expectation that increased happiness later will more than make up for it. A simple and obvious example would be the decision to invest $1,000 in a thirty-six-month certificate of deposit that yields 4% interest.

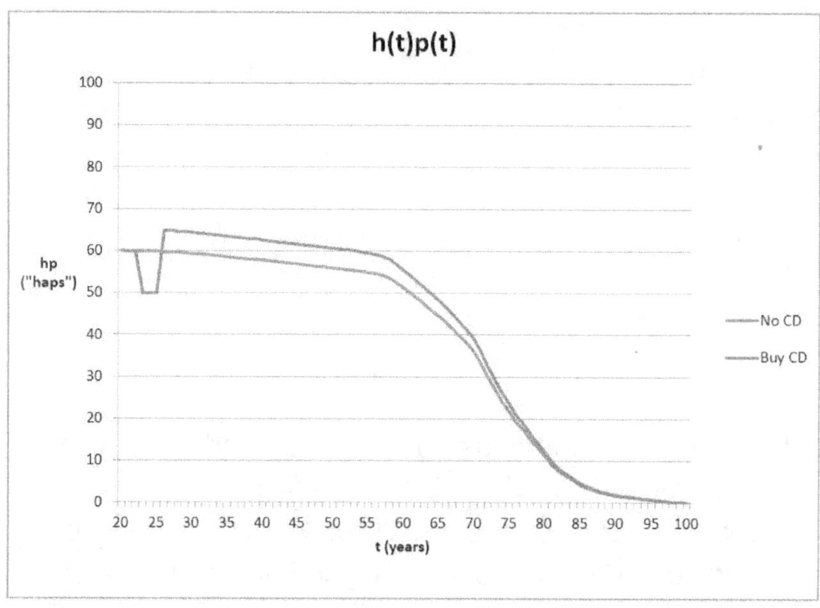

As depicted above, being without $1,000 for 36 months will reduce happiness for that period, but the return of approximately $1,170 at the end of that period boosts happiness some going forward. If you have the $1,000 lying around and do not need it for three years, the decision will be to buy the CD. If you need the $1,000 soon for something important, the larger reduction in happiness for the 36-month period will likely tip the balance against buying the CD.

As mentioned earlier in this chapter, the branch of mathematics that comprehends the calculation of areas under curves is the purview of integral calculus. Thus, it is possible to succinctly state the calculation of expected total future happiness, H, as in the equation below (where t_0 is the present time).

$$H = \int_{t_0}^{\infty} h(t)\, p(t)\, dt$$

As has been illustrated, in most cases, this is an extremely complex calculation. It is very likely that brains simplify decision-making as much as they can by isolating just the parameters and factors pertinent to the decision at hand. That is, they do not project forward the entirety of everything that bears upon their future happiness. Rather, the alternatives being considered actually are variations from some baseline $h(t)p(t)$ that is expected to be the same for all alternatives being considered.

Some people are amazingly adept at estimating their integrals quickly. Others take longer or are rather poor estimators. Still others make shortsighted decisions as though there is no tomorrow — their estimate of $p(t)$ declines unrealistically rapidly. As is clearly observable in the real world, some people make good decisions fairly consistently, while others make mostly awful ones. Of course, substantially everyone gets it wrong once in a while.

Can a person's instantaneous happiness be negative? Yes, of course, it can; there certainly are unhappy people. Can someone's integral be negative? Yes. There are even extremely unfortunate cases where someone is unable to think of any hypothetical circumstance or any decision they could make that would get expected instantaneous happiness, $h(t)$, back up into positive territory far enough, soon enough, and long enough to achieve a positive integral. The only way such an unfortunate person can maximize the happiness integral under such circumstances is to force the probability of being alive, $p(t)$, to be zero. This is when people decide to commit suicide (presumably after double checking their calculations). Remember, people always, *always* make the choice that they believe will maximize total future happiness.

No-brainer decisions can be made reasonably quickly, but other more complex and sometimes quite important ones can take a significant amount of time using the rational decision process. You may ponder tough problems for days or even longer. Some decisions must be made more quickly than the rational process can accommodate. Occasionally, life-or-death decisions have to be made almost instantly. How does that work?

Before launching the integral estimations, brains likely devote some consideration to the importance of the decision and to comparing its complexity to the time available to make it. Balancing these considerations may require some compromises in the process to shorten the time required to make the decision so that some deadline can be met. Such compromises might well be expected to adversely affect accuracy — that is, increase the likelihood of mistakes (bad decisions).

Organisms lacking the brainpower for rational thought must make decisions too, and sometimes quickly. Evolution endows them with a "library" of "hard-wired" responses to a fairly wide range of basic situations. These are called *instincts*, and they can be "looked up" and executed quickly. Such instincts may be further conditioned, refined, or extended by experience during the life of the organism. Thus, improved instincts might be passed along to future generations. Organisms primarily dependent upon instincts have an extremely limited ability to optimize choices that require accepting a near-term negative that is more than offset by long-term positives.

Of course, evolution has endowed Homo sapiens with an instinct library as well. Certain situations (predominantly those involving or implying imminent danger) will trigger fast instinctive reactions (e.g., flight). If rational processes catch up soon enough, they may modify or overrule the instinctive response.

5. Rights and Morality

Impassioned orators of every ilk, especially those in the highest places, sling around the noun *right* as if it were something extremely important about which they have a deep understanding. In 99% of such cases, the users of this word probably haven't given its meaning much serious thought. In 99.9% of the cases (and this percentage could be even a little bit higher), the statements made are incorrect in some sense, and the speakers do not actually have an in-depth understanding of this word at all.

Some say that every person has a right to life. Some think people have a right to liberty. Others claim the right to own and control property. The US *Declaration of Independence* insists that we all have certain inalienable rights, and that among these are life, liberty, and the pursuit of happiness.

Still others insist that people have a right to health care, to a decent standard of living, and on and on. What do they mean, or think they mean, when they make these statements? How many things are really rights, if any? Is there some list of guaranteed rights written down somewhere? If they do exist, from where do rights come?

In view of the visceral reactions people frequently have to statements containing the word *right*, not to mention the major decisions affecting everyone's lives that are justified by using the term, it is past time for a calm and logical examination to bring some clarity to this concept.

The most common understanding of the noun *right* in the above context is that it is a liberty of action or a benefit to which every individual is entitled and that cannot be taken away. Widespread agreement about what rights people have might be expected.

Of course, problems abound because people do not all agree about rights, and careless uses of the term are rampant.

Most religious people say rights are conferred upon humans by God or some other deity. Statists of every flavor (socialists, communists, Marxists, fascists, monarchists) insist that rights are granted to people by the state. Non- (or less-) religious people tend to claim that rights come from "nature," which belief might itself be considered a religion of a sort.

In an effort to shed more light on the subject in a manner with which rational people can agree, let us try a thought experiment. Imagine that there is only one person in the world — a very simple version of the "state of nature" as explored by Thomas Hobbes, John Locke, and others. What rights would this lonely person have? One might think that he would have any and all possible rights. At least, with no other people, there could be no problem with anyone disagreeing that he has any particular right, so we would only have to worry about the part of the definition that says the right cannot be taken away.

How about one of the most basic: the right to life? The right to a natural life should be OK because there is no one else around to commit murder. Of course, there could be large, carnivorous animals that would rather have a tasty dinner than respect the individual's right to life, so even this basic right is not inalienable under all circumstances. It would require the individual to have sufficient strength or intelligence to either overpower or outsmart such animals and protect himself in order to defend the right to life.

How about private property ownership? No problem. There's no one around to take his stuff.

Liberty? Certainly! Anything he can do he may do.

How about rights to health care and a decent standard of living? Sure! However, these would obviously and necessarily be *limited to whatever he could provide for himself.*

Suppose that we now add a few more people to this world. As long as they are very widely separated and never come into contact, all the above remains true. However, when the population density reaches the point at which there is contact and potential interference, problems quickly multiply.

Eventually, someone will disagree that another person should have some particular right or just arbitrarily decide to take the right away. The probability of rights abrogation approaches certainty as the population density grows large. Whether or not someone can hang onto (what they think are) their rights depends on their strength relative to the strength of whatever person or group decides to deny those rights.

Suppose now that our hero is able to assemble a large group of like-minded individuals who reach a consensus as to what rights they should have. They form a posse of burly people to secure these rights. The posse promises to come to the aid of any person whose rights are threatened. This might work as long as the posse behaves well, is responsive, and commands sufficient muscle to defend the rights against any person or other posse. In our modern world, the posse is often called a government.

Several conclusions may be drawn from the thought experiment:

- Whether or not a person is entitled to some particular right based upon an abstract argument or a theory, the right has zero practical value to the person unless it can be defended and secured by sufficient force.

- The only thing certain is that the so-called law of the jungle (survival of the fittest under the physical laws of the universe) always applies, with no exceptions. It is the ultimate hubris to think that the vast MKS universe somehow guarantees some special set of rights just for our species.

- There is just no such thing as an inalienable right or even one about which every person agrees.

- Conversely, almost anything can be made into a right as long as a sufficient force structure exists to secure it. This explains why the rights topic can seem pretty fuzzy; there is no automatic bright line dividing rights and not-rights.

- Since rights just do not exist in the romantic way people traditionally think of them, they do not come from anywhere as a tidy, preordained list.

The fact is that *the entire concept of rights is purely a construct of the human intellect* and is still a work in progress.

Since rights are a human idea, their purpose and definition must be entirely up to humans. For thousands of years, various people in power have been defining rights in accordance with their ideas, prejudices, and purposes. They largely controlled the rights that those not in power could enjoy.

A long line of scholars (John Locke, John Rawls, Robert Nozick, Friedrich Hayek, Murray Rothbard, and recently, Hans Hermann Hoppe, to name just a few) have arduously worked to convince everyone that a basic set of rights is provided as a part of nature. These have been dubbed *natural rights*. The idea that natural rights exist actually has been quite influential and beneficial. The interested reader may wish to explore some of the clever arguments these scholars have deployed.

However, the reader is also referred to a very interesting paper by Georgetown University Professor John Hasnas[1] in which he convincingly argues that those who advocate for the existence of natural rights have not at all proved their case. We will look at this interesting paper in more depth for a different purpose in the next chapter.

But more directly, if rights actually are an aspect of our shared reality, rational people should be able to construct a logical argument, based upon premises all can agree are solidly grounded in reality, that proves the existence of one or more such rights. Furthermore, it should be possible to devise a test that could be reproduced by anyone anywhere which demonstrates the existence of one or more of these rights as an integral feature of our universe. But if as stated above, rights are merely a human idea, this will never be possible. Take that bet.

---

[1] John Hasnas, *Toward a Theory of Empirical Natural Rights* (Social Philosophy and Policy Foundation, 2005), p. 124.

Those claiming the existence of natural rights sometimes argue that their chosen set of rights exists because it is required by morality; that is, their certain set of rights would result in the most "moral society." But once again, morality is just another human idea rather like rights. What is moral or not moral is purely a matter of personal opinion. Even all humans agreeing about what is or is not moral would not mean that a code of morality was provided for us as a part of our universe. If someone offers to bet you that an objective test can and will be devised to demonstrate that "natural morality" is part of our reality, take that bet too.

None of this is intended to argue that rights have no value. Rights certainly do have great and demonstrated value to us human individuals. However, we waste time and effort attempting to coax a list of rights out of nature when none exists. Human individuals came up with the concept of rights, and human individuals must face up to the responsibility of implementing that idea by

1. Providing the rationale for rights,

2. Defining what rights individuals should have, and

3. Devising some way to secure rights so that substantially all individuals can benefit from and enjoy these rights substantially all the time.

It is unfortunate that the very considerable amount of perfectly good brainpower wasted on attempts to concoct some justification for natural rights as an integral part of nature was not expended instead on the above three steps. Number 3 is especially a problem for which an effective and safe solution is critically important.

If anyone refuses to concede that natural rights don't exist, simply point out to them that, if they do exist, it is irrelevant because they don't seem to be having any effect. As a practical matter, we human individuals quite apparently are still on the hook to carry out the above three tasks.

The only reasonable approach that could be successful is to define rights in a way that all rational people can agree is best. Sorry, but for reasons previously discussed, irrational people are unable to participate in this process. However, one of the first things the rational people will probably conclude fairly quickly is that all individuals should have the same rights. It can be hoped that the definition forged by the rational people will likely also be best (or very close to it) for any irrational people. Hey, it's the messy real world we must deal with, and the real world is not necessarily perfect for our species; it's a mistake to expect or pretend that it is.

6. Defining and Securing Rights

Starting Point

Definition: A right is a liberty of action or a benefit to which an individual is entitled, that cannot be taken away (i.e., the individual is normally able to enjoy the right substantially all the time).

The concept that individuals should have rights at all is purely a human idea — a product of the human intellect. There is, therefore, no a priori list of rights that can be consulted or followed. If there are to be rights, it is completely up to humans to decide what rights should be, for whom they are to be guaranteed or secured, and how the rights are to be secured. If we want rights, we need to step up to the plate on this undertaking.

It is useful to think of rights as belonging to one of two categories. *Negative rights* do not normally require the expenditure of effort or resources by others; that is, the individual can enjoy the right simply by being left alone, free of force or coercion from others. *Positive rights*, on the other hand, do (or may) require the expenditure of effort or resources by others to provide or fulfill the right.

Liberty is the cleanest example of a negative right; one need only be left alone to enjoy the right to liberty. "Good" health care or a "reasonable" standard of living, on the other hand, are positive rights. Ignoring, for the moment, how to define *good* and *reasonable* in this context, it seems virtually certain that the efforts, skills, and resources of others would be required to guarantee such rights.

We have had a fair amount of experience with rights in recent centuries. In 1690, John Locke identified what he designated as the three fundamental "natural rights" of life, liberty, and property. Locke's thinking was truly revolutionary. He got a lot of things right — that is, correct. His ideas, especially about governments, were (at least predominantly) libertarian and uplifting.

Those who have lived only under extremely oppressive regimes may not appreciate what rights are, but most other human individuals value rights highly, and for very good reasons. Whenever and wherever basic individual rights are reasonably well secured, violence tends to decrease and prosperity tends to grow. People are much happier living with more wealth and less aggression.

Pure and simple, that is the sole rationale for defining and securing the best possible set of rights: to increase (maximize to the extent possible) the happiness of human individuals. There is no reason or need to dream up fictions such as natural law or morality to justify this. What *is* natural is that human individuals always make decisions based upon their rational self-interest, so it is entirely natural that they would decide to define and secure rights for the purpose of increasing their happiness.

Having dispatched the fantasies of rights conferred by a deity and rights provided automagically by nature, it is time to examine some ways in which rights can be defined more rationally by humans.

Approaches to Defining Rights

Since Locke kicked off the revolution in thinking, humans have come up with many ways to define rights. It will be worth examining several of them.

> **Equal Liberties**: Individuals have the right to do anything they like with the proviso that they not do anything that infringes upon any other individual's equal liberties.

This definition from John Rawls is one that everyone has probably heard many times. Few would disagree with it. It is succinct and sounds great … until you start asking questions about the billions of possible specific situations and possible conflicts. The soaring, but very general, statement does nothing to assist with drawing all those detailed lines in the gray areas. It also provides zero help regarding how such rights would be secured and how to deal with the inevitable transgressions.

> **The Non-Aggression Principle (NAP)**: Nobody* may deal fraudulently with anybody* else, and nobody* may *initiate* the use of force (or the credible threat of force) against anybody* else for any reason except for that minimum amount of force necessary to enforce this non-aggression principle.

The words *nobody* and *anybody* are starred because they refer to *any* societal entity. Individuals are the "atoms" of society. Therefore, the smallest societal entity is a single individual. Larger societal entities (organizations, businesses, corporations, governments, etc.) are built from and comprised of one or multiple individuals. A societal entity is normally considered to include the entity's justly owned property.

The NAP is at the heart of libertarian philosophy. It is a good and powerful principle that renders it easy to analyze even complex issues and consistently arrive at the correct conclusions. The NAP is just a more rigorous and formal statement of the old saying, "live and let live." It aims to minimize the use of force on those who are peaceful and honest. Note that the use of force on peaceful, honest people can never be completely eliminated, only minimized.

A very simple way to think of the NAP is that it is essentially the same as the instructions you might give to children the first time they are turned loose to play on a playground with other children: "Don't hit any of the other kids, don't take their stuff, and don't cheat playing games; but if another kid hits you first, you certainly may hit back to defend yourself."

Some statements of the NAP sloppily omit the explicit exception to use whatever minimum force may be necessary to enforce the NAP. This can lead to erroneous conclusions and unwarranted criticisms of the NAP. In any realistic world populated by many human individuals, there *will* be violations of the NAP; so it is folly to ignore the inevitable need for its enforcement.

Somewhat complementary to the equal liberties approach, the NAP does not say what rights should be, but instead proscribes aggressive behaviors. Rights, then, can be defined as anything that does not violate the NAP. It provides a more useful definition of rights than does the equal liberties approach; however, many gray areas remain. One example is the proper line between self-defense and aggression. Another would be the many possible situations in which one societal entity might knowingly place others involuntarily at undue risk.

Of course, just like the equal liberties approach, the NAP provides little help with how rights are to be secured (other than sanctioning the use of a minimum amount of force for that purpose).

Note that the objective of minimizing the use of force on people who are peaceful and honest is the equivalent of maximizing their liberty or freedom.

> **<u>Self-Ownership</u>: Private property ownership is a natural right. The very first thing that an individual owns is oneself. It follows that you then have the right to do anything you wish with yourself so long as no other individual is harmed. Each individual then also automatically owns the fruits of their own labor.**

This way of defining rights comes from Locke and is favored by quite a few libertarians. Extending from this as a basis to define all rights runs into several problems and limitations that have been pointed out by multiple scholars. An obvious one that should spring immediately to mind is the problem of the zygote. Does a human developing in a mother's womb own itself? For that matter, does or should a young and immature child own itself?

As with several of the other approaches, self-ownership does little to draw lines in gray areas and affords no help with how rights would be secured.

> **<u>Rational Rights</u>: The sole rationale for defining and securing rights is to increase (maximize to the extent possible) the happiness of human individuals. Rational Rights is the set of rights, *and the mechanism that secures them*, that maximizes the total happiness of all individuals.**

Since the rationale for defining and securing rights is to increase the happiness of individuals, then a wholly rational approach would seem to be to pursue that objective directly. In the Rational Self-Interest chapter, we learned that individuals always, always make every decision to maximize their expected total future happiness. A mathematical expression was derived for an individual's expected total future happiness and is reproduced below:

$$H = \int_{t_0}^{\infty} h(t)\, p(t)\, dt$$

This integral calculates the expected total future happiness of a single individual under some set of circumstances. The sum of all individuals' happiness can then be written as follows:

$$H_T = \sum_{i=1}^{n} H_i$$

H_T is the total of all individuals' happiness, H_i is the happiness of each single individual, and n is the number of individuals.

Well, there we have it. Pragmatically, one would not expect many objections to defining something aimed directly and purely at helping people be happy since this is exactly in accord with everyone's built-in primary motivation. Note also the comprehensive nature of this approach. All we need to do is figure out what set of rights *and* what mechanism to secure them will maximize H_T and we're finished. However, having adopted a definition based upon a calculation that we can never hope to compute, that challenge is daunting.

Perhaps surprisingly, some of the broad features for a set of rights can actually be deduced rather easily from the nature of the mathematical expressions. It is not very difficult to conclude that the three primary negative rights to life, liberty, and property need to be secured.

Interestingly, the right to commit suicide also turns out to be important. Obviously, cases in which one individual gains happiness but does so in some way that decreases the happiness of many others need to be prevented whenever the total decrease in happiness exceeds the increase.

We will not further explore here the voluminous and tedious details of how rights may be deduced from this definition (or whether it is even possible to derive a complete set) but will instead offer these observations: The definition is based directly (and exclusively) upon the stated rationale for defining and securing rights: increasing individuals' happiness. The definition is comprehensive: the mechanism that secures rights must be considered as an integral package along with the rights it secures, and the best lines in all the fuzzy or gray areas must be clearly drawn as well.

> **<u>Empirical Natural Rights</u>: The rights people actually decide to secure when left to do so on their own.**

This is the approach suggested by John Hasnas in his essay *Toward a Theory of Empirical Natural Rights*. The "Petri dish" chosen by Hasnas is Norman England following the collapse of Roman rule in the fifth century. The disappearance of all central authority left the English people in something akin to a Lockean "state of nature." Problems had to be resolved solely through interactions among themselves.

Over the ensuing few hundred years, *common law* was hammered out as a practical and effective means for dispute resolution and violence avoidance. The laws form a detailed definition of rights to be secured, and those turn out to bear a striking similarity to the three negative Lockean natural rights to life, liberty, and property; no positive rights evolved. This is an extremely terse summary of the core idea, and one really should read the entire essay for its many interesting insights.

Empirical natural rights differ markedly from theoretical rights in several significant ways. Instead of being derived in a "clean room" as an end in themselves, empirical rights developed in the rough and tumble real world *in parallel with, and actually defined by, the very mechanisms that secure them.* The process was rather Darwinian, with "good" laws surviving and propagating widely while "bad" laws were discarded or mutated.

Theoretical rights tend to be thought of as cleanly (simplistically) defined philosophical entities, while empirical rights tend to be a bit messy. As stated by Hasnas, "The empirical natural right to property can only be described in extremely inelegant terms as the right to a great amount of use and control of an object most of the time, with exclusive use and control at some time, and no use or control at others."[2] A large part of the evolution of common law was concerned with drawing the lines between rights and not-rights in the best places in the many gray areas.

Interestingly, there is no hard end to the evolutionary process for empirical natural rights. Presumably, they are still evolving. Such an evolutionary process would gradually adapt in response to changing conditions. Might

---

[2] John Hasnas, *Toward a Theory of Empirical Natural Rights* (Social Philosophy and Policy Foundation, 2005), 135.

some positive rights emerge, possibly as a result of increased prosperity? Perhaps some already have.

<u>A Document</u>: Rights and the mechanism that will guarantee them are both defined in a document.

Instead of depending almost exclusively on a pithy principle or an elegant rule, one could define a set of rights using a document. A document allows rather complete flexibility, which, among other things, certainly includes the possibility of citing or incorporating pithy principles and elegant rules. There are by now several precedents.

The most memorable early attempt was probably the Magna Carta of the thirteenth century. The most significant and groundbreaking attempt was the US Constitution, which was crafted in 1787.

While writing the US Constitution, the Founding Fathers were focused primarily on defining a central government to replace the inadequate and failing one established by the Articles of Confederation. They greatly feared such a concentration of power and worked hard to design it in such a way that it would not escape citizens' ability to maintain control over it. This quotation, widely attributed to George Washington, clearly conveys the Fathers' concerns regarding the fundamental nature of government, its inclination to accumulate power, and the difficulty of keeping it under citizens' control: "Government is not reason; it is not eloquent; it is force. Like fire, it is a dangerous servant and a fearful master."

Defining individual rights was not the primary focus of the Constitution. However, ten amendments (known as the Bill of Rights) were hastily added to beef up its enumeration of rights and restrictions on government.

Conveniently, the use of a document enables both the definition of rights and the specification of the machinery needed to secure them.

Additional Considerations

There is a strong tendency to think of a right as a simple thing. However, as mentioned above in connection with the empirical right to property ownership, this is not necessarily or even usually the case. There almost always are gray or fuzzy areas around the edges of rights. As examples, here are some of them; the reader may be able to think of others.

Self-defense versus aggression. Obviously, the use of force must be condoned for self-defense. If confronted by an unarmed adversary of equal or lesser size, one might very well wait until the thug throws the first punch to respond with force. If the adversary is armed with deadly force, you obviously can't wait until you're dead to respond, so you must preemptively pull your trigger first — as soon as you're "sure" there is a bona fide threat. Thus, human advancement of technology (in this case, firearms) changes the game considerably.

Even higher-tech stuff now makes the problem of defining a proper preemptive action far more complex and difficult. Does a country wait for the first mushroom cloud or the first pandemic from the intentional release of a deadly virus, or does it take out the threat before this can happen? How much before, under what conditions, and so on? There is nothing at variance with the principle; it's just very tough to draw a bright, clear line between aggression and self-defense. It's difficult to define some simple rules to follow that adequately cover all the possible situations, not to mention the situations that will become possible in the future.

Clearly, to optimize this trade-off, there must also be some reasonable burden to avoid doing anything that would reasonably be interpreted by another party as a serious and immediate threat.

Placing others involuntarily at undue risk. These are the many cases where we ask the question of whether force should be used to restrict someone's liberty for the preemptive protection of others.

Should someone be allowed to do research on a dangerous virus in their home laboratory? Or should laws force certain minimum safety measures upon the laboratory? Should there be laws forcing certain types of buildings to have automatic sprinkler systems or fire exits? Should a penalty be enforced for driving on the wrong side of the road?

Rights infringement without overt force. These are all the things like releasing a bunch of greenhouse gases in Iowa that causes the sea level to rise and destroy the value of somebody's property in New Orleans. There are an infinite number of examples, many involving "the commons" (see below) and some not.

This whole area is a complex mess that changes pretty rapidly with time and technology, and possibly with our degree of understanding as well. A truly satisfactory solution may not even be possible. However, it should be abundantly obvious that the solution is *not* to turn a bunch of crappy politicians loose to write thickets of laws and apply government force willy-nilly. If the intent is to maximize liberty and happiness, that might be the worst way to do it. Adjudication through courts on a case-by-case basis may be the only, though cumbersome and imperfect, solution.

Enforcement mechanisms. Some carefully defined and limited uses of force are necessary to gather evidence, not only to convict the guilty but also to be sure the innocent are not wrongfully prosecuted or convicted. Executing search warrants, serving on juries, and compelling testimony via subpoenas are examples.

Intellectual property. Patents and copyrights allow creators to derive benefits from their creations for a limited amount of time. Some argue against having patents and copyrights at all. However, without such protections, the willingness of entrepreneurs (or anyone) to assume the risk of investing their time or money in creative or experimental endeavors would certainly decrease; less creative output would be to everyone's disadvantage and result in less happiness. Others may say that if intellectual property is indeed property, its ownership doesn't have any "expiration date." Clearly, this is yet another trade-off to be optimized.

Private property ownership. This is a fundamental and crucial right. It is the primary negative right that may seem the most straightforward and simple. It certainly is a right that humans comprehend and latch onto early in their development: "That teddy bear is *mine!*"

However, far from being simple, it is a contender for the most complex and confusing of all rights. People who own a thing usually expect the following:

1. They have complete control over their thing in perpetuity without question, and no one else may use it without their express permission.
2. They may sell, rent, gift, or loan the thing to others (or even destroy it if they so desire).
3. They do not owe anyone anything for their thing, and no one can charge them for the possession or use of their very own thing.
4. If their thing were to be stolen, they would expect the help, cooperation, and support of society to regain full possession of the thing.

If all the above are true, the individual can be said to enjoy absolute ownership of the thing.

How could you (or anyone) acquire absolute ownership of something in a way that is certain not to reduce the happiness of anyone else? It would seem there are only two ways. First, create or make the thing entirely using your own labor (or the labor of others fairly purchased, i.e., through a voluntary exchange); you would also need to have had absolute ownership of any materials that were required. Second, acquire the thing in a voluntary exchange (buy it) or as a gift from someone else *who had absolute ownership of it*.

One quite important thing that people like to own is land. Can anyone have absolute title to a piece of land? No. It turns out that it is simply not possible to absolutely own land or several other things that share some similar characteristics with land.

If we sincerely want to define the right to ownership of land in a way that maximizes total happiness, a trip back to the state of nature before people showed up is a good place to begin. Looking around, we note that all the land that exists today was already present. So, quite obviously, no human has ever created or made any land using entirely their own labor. This precludes the first way that absolute ownership could be acquired. Therefore, there is no way that anybody could have ever legitimately acquired ownership of any land in the first place. Equally obviously, the only other way to acquire absolute ownership (acquiring it by gift or voluntary exchange from someone else *who had absolute ownership*) is also precluded.

But land is cool and valuable. People really want to own it. Few want to accept the fact that land just cannot be owned. Besides that, land is very useful. A situation where no one could use any land wouldn't be good. Thus, philosophers have struggled mightily (to this day) to dream up some way to justify land ownership. None has been successful, nor could they be.

The best-known attempt to philosophically support ownership of land is probably John Locke's "mixing of labor" notion. The idea was that individuals could acquire ownership of a piece of unclaimed land by "mixing their labor with it." That magical act might be accomplished by tilling the land or even simply by erecting a fence around it.

If the intent is to maximize happiness, it seems necessary to adopt the foundational proviso that no individual has a greater right to benefit from land than any other. Not to do so would create some happy people, but ultimately a much larger number of unhappy ones, not to mention sowing the seeds for much dissention. To state this proviso more usefully, all individuals should have an equal right to derive benefits from land.

Even Locke must have had this nagging concern as he added this condition to his "mixing of labor" theory: "... as long as there is enough, and as good, left in common for others." My, that's a lovely thought, but it clearly fails to take care of those who arrive upon the scene after all land is already under the control of someone else.

The optimum solution to the land conundrum is to agree that all of whatever amount of land exists is owned in common by all extant individuals. Therefore, whoever has control over a given parcel of land must pay the fair market rental for the land as compensation to all those who are not in control of it and are therefore unable to derive any benefit from it. The rental applies purely to the land itself and not to any improvements erected or placed upon it since those would presumably have been created and legitimately owned by individuals.

Note that there are other things of value to which the same logic applies. A few examples are all nonrenewable natural resources (gold, uranium, petroleum, etc.), the electromagnetic spectrum, and the possible geosynchronous satellite orbits. Taken all together, these things are known as *the commons*.

An American political economist and journalist named Henry George advocated the rental approach to the commons in the 1870s. He wrote several books that sold a few million copies. His political philosophy became known as Georgism (later Geoism) and attracted a significant following that carried on into the beginning of the twentieth century.

In contrast to how land ideally should be handled, what actually did happen?

Predominantly, assorted monarchs and dictators asserted control over the land. They claimed absolute ownership (known as *alodial title*) and backed their "ownership" up with force. This implementation of the "right" to own land obviously created a small number of happy people and a very much larger number of less happy people — a situation we hope to avoid if we are to maximize happiness.

When empirical natural rights evolved in Norman England, the situation with land certainly was better than with monarchs and dictators, but ownership of the commons by all people was not embraced. It was possible to buy and own land, but instead of an alodial title, one had a common law "fee simple" title to it. This title is a few notches down from an alodial title. Instead of absolute ownership, the owner's land is subject to (at least) taxation, eminent domain, escheat, and police powers. A fee simple title is permanent and inheritable, but an owner does not have complete control over the property. Fee simple title is still the highest title to land that anyone can hold today in the United States and other common law countries.

Securing rights. A truly magnificent set of rights may have been carefully defined, but that is of little value if individuals are unable to actually exercise and enjoy those rights a large percentage of the time. It is virtually certain that with a large and dense population, some individuals will elect to augment their own happiness by violating the rights of others. It takes very little violation of rights to result in a decrease in total happiness.

Unfortunately, it will be necessary to have some mechanism to secure rights. Unless some form of mind control becomes available (and if it were available, its use might well be a violation of the rights that have been defined), the mechanism is going to involve using force on the violators. Subjecting violators to force is bound to make them unhappy, but it creates and maintains the conditions required for the happiness of many, many others, so it is a beneficial trade-off.

Note well that the only purposes of an enforcement mechanism are to halt the abrogation of others' rights, to discourage violators from ever engaging in such behavior again in the future, and to deter other potential violators from initiating such behaviors in the first place. Reducing their happiness is counter to the primary objective, but it is a strong component of the deterrence. Perhaps this would be an acceptable application for mind control (or other creative approach) if or when it may become available. In the meantime, force, despite the concomitant unhappiness, is the go-to technique.

The consistency and uniformity of enforcement are quite important. Any unpredictable behavior of the enforcement mechanism will induce fear, doubt, and worry, which are powerful happiness killers, as is the uneven treatment of offenders. Of course, enforcement must be sufficiently effective if it is to reduce the fear of rights abrogation.

As a practical matter, it actually is the mechanism that secures rights that determines rather directly what rights meaningfully exist and which individuals can enjoy them. So is the problem really defining a set of rights, or would it be more accurate to say we are designing a force structure that guarantees some rights?

It should be readily obvious, as it was to our Founding Fathers, that such a mechanism is a dangerous thing to create. Any entity powerful enough to secure rights is certainly also capable of denying rights. Lord Acton nailed it when he said, "Power corrupts, and absolute power corrupts absolutely." Thus far, corruptible people are going to have to be the ones wielding the force of the enforcement mechanism.

How about anarchy? Some libertarians argue that happiness would be maximized by having virtually no central power structure at all. These people are known as *anarcho-capitalists* or *ancaps* for short. They'd rather not risk oppression from a power structure run amok; instead, they advocate depending solely upon a totally free, free market economic system.

The ancaps' ideas are not at all as crazy as most people think they are. Substantially all the functions that are widely considered to be only performable by "the government" can be handled, and actually are being performed today, by private entities. Clearly, *minarchists*, those who advocate a minimal state instead of anarchy, would favor something fairly close to the anarchy end of the spectrum. And we can be pretty sure that anarchy would be preferable to the oppressive, resource-consuming, wasteful, out-of-control, dumpster fire that we currently call our governments.

Ancaps frequently cite the example of medieval Iceland, which appears to have actually experienced anarchy for a couple of hundred years. It appears that Icelanders contracted with private organizations that agreed to secure their rights for a fee. There were competing protection services — a free market. It would seem that each protection service could have somewhat differing definitions of the rights it secures; this could be a source of serious conflict.

Historical records for medieval Iceland are pretty sketchy. It is clear, however, that Iceland was not comparable to a modern country. Population density was low, there was very little in the way of infrastructure, and no need for much of a defense force to protect against an invasion from the outside. The real punch line, however, is that the period of anarchy ended with Iceland asking the King of Norway to please take control of the island. So, whatever Iceland temporarily had, it must not have been paradise. A jump from anarchy to monarchy is a phenomenal philosophical reversal!

Another instance of anarchy is the aforementioned Norman England after the collapse of the Roman Empire. Rather than a state of anarchy continuing, a set of rights gradually evolved in parallel with the mechanisms and institutions needed to secure them. The result was good enough and durable enough that it persists today in the form of common law.

Although their ultimate directions were radically different, these two examples suggest that anarchy probably does not maximize happiness and *likely is not a stable form for a civilization*. It must also be noted that the two cited examples, plus a few others that have existed for periods of time, had low population densities, with somewhat isolated clans, which reduced the need for, and advantages of a centralized rights standardization and enforcement mechanism. Those days are not these days. High population density, especially combined with modern technology that virtually eliminates isolation, increases the importance of stronger, central enforcement. In addition, the capabilities of modern warfare clearly require a rather large, strong central mechanism to secure rights against external enemies who might threaten them.

Scope. The discussion thus far has focused hard on maximizing the happiness of "all" individuals by defining and guaranteeing an optimum set of rights. No mention has been made of exactly which individuals are to be the happy ones. Are we worrying about every individual in the entire universe, just those in our galaxy, or the solar system, or on planet Earth, or some even smaller group? It would seem desirable to include as many as may be feasible.

It looks like the individuals on Earth are the only ones in our solar system. The rest of our galaxy and the entire universe are so vast that it is highly probable that other individuals do exist. However, the huge distances impose delays of many years for travel and even for communications, thereby rendering meaningful intercourse completely impractical. Pending any radical revision of our understanding of physical laws, we must restrict our scope to individuals resident on Earth of which we have a working knowledge.

Unfortunately, the radical diversity of cultures on Earth, as well as the many conflicts and instabilities, augur against success for such a difficult and tricky project. Further narrowing the scope to the level of a nation-state would seem to be the largest group of individuals for which there is any hope of success. There are several candidate nations, but the United States likely is the best qualified in view of its pioneering progress in the area of securing rights. Unfortunately, stability is currently deteriorating rapidly there, as is the institutional memory of its founding principles.

Of course, it would be excellent to have competing efforts in multiple countries, but it is of critical importance to have significant success in at least one country. Assuming that a successful country understands, appreciates, expounds, and exports the reasons for its success, additional countries may follow. This would become that country's most significant and important export.

Summary and Conclusions

Defining an optimum set of rights is not nearly as simple as it may at first seem. Instead, it is challenging and downright messy. Citing simplistic rules or principles is fine, even fun and exhilarating, but it is clearly inadequate. Just defining rights, even if perfectly done, is also inadequate without some way to guarantee and secure rights so that individuals can actually enjoy and derive the intended benefits from them. There will always be some who feel free to abrogate the rights of others for their own benefit. Barring some new idea or breakthrough, the enforcement mechanism will have to employ force to be effective. Any entity able to control people using force (or otherwise) is a highly dangerous creation that itself must be *very* carefully controlled and *very* effectively limited.

There are huge numbers of complex trade-offs that need to be optimized to maximize total happiness. Perhaps the equations for rational rights provide the best insight into just how incredibly complex the situation actually is. There are the many trade-offs dealing with where the lines are best drawn in the gray or fuzzy areas of rights. There also is the critically important set of trade-offs involving the design and operation of the enforcement mechanism. This is one of those optimization problems discussed in chapter 2.

Suppose we begin a thought experiment with complete anarchy. All individuals must defend whatever they believe are their rights completely by themselves. Defending rights is a resource-consuming, happiness-reducing drag, no matter how it is done. Individuals will quickly discover that by forming groups they can achieve better defense of their rights utilizing fewer total resources. Total happiness has been increased. It stands to reason that a centralized rights defense entity could be even more efficient and further reduce the resources required, thereby further increasing happiness. There would be the additional benefit of standardizing all the lines drawn in the fuzzy areas of rights, which should prevent and reduce conflicts.

Defending rights against aggression from the outside is an obvious need in this modern world. It could be argued that, in addition to securing rights, there is an *extremely limited* set of additional truly public goods or services that should be provided by a government for the same reason — efficiency would be enough higher that the total cost would be reduced, and happiness would be increased.

However, as soon as the centralized entity requires or expends more resources than are absolutely necessary, the maximum has been passed, and total happiness begins to decline. The entity has no resources of its own, so its resources can come only from the wealth of the individuals themselves. Furthermore, if the entity oversteps and begins applying unnecessary force to those who are peaceful and honest, that's a double whammy that causes total happiness to decline very quickly indeed. This is the critical trade-off to be optimized. So far, history has emphatically demonstrated that it is exceedingly difficult to keep the centralized entity from going beyond the optimum point.

It is quite important to realize and appreciate that *it is simply not going to be possible to achieve a perfect solution!* The continuing efforts of philosophers to elegantly define some utopian system are perhaps fun but ultimately futile. It is much more worthwhile to focus hard on optimizing the many trade-offs so as to most closely approach the maximum of total happiness. To the extent that the outputs of philosophers can provide insights to guide such efforts, they are helpful.

A carefully conceived and curated document that establishes a controlled mechanism to guarantee rights would seem to be by far the best hope of tackling this assignment. Said assignment has yet to be successfully carried out, but some attempts at it have been encouraging. The most original and innovative was the US Constitution as crafted in 1787 (including its almost immediate first ten amendments).

Finally, it should be strongly emphasized that the ultimate and *overriding* objective must *only* be to maximize the liberty and happiness of all individuals. Nothing more nor less can or should be attempted. Under such an umbrella of maximum liberty, individuals have the latitude to do what they wish and collaborate with others to best solve their problems. They certainly would be free to opt into (or out of) more restrictive "local" situations as they may prefer. Freedom works. And freedom works best.

7. The Constitution of the United States

Pertinent History

Genesis of the Constitution

The Europeans who came to settle on the North American continent during the sixteenth, seventeenth, and eighteenth centuries were hardy souls who never expected any free lunches. Life was not easy, but these rugged individuals worked hard and built their prosperity over this period.

By the middle of the eighteenth century, the rapid growth in prosperity drew the attention of Scottish scholar and philosopher Adam Smith, who wondered why and how the colonies could achieve such exceptional growth in wealth. He did a remarkably good job of figuring it all out and explaining it in a two-volume work he published in 1776, *An Inquiry Into The Nature And Causes Of The Wealth Of Nations* (usually referred to simply as *The Wealth of Nations*). The great significance of his tome is that it was the first in-depth elucidation of what is now known as the free market economic system, and it also marked the birth of the science of economics.

Another party intensely interested during the same period was King George III of Great Britain, which by that time had become the supreme power of the world. The colonies were viewed as the property of the "mother country," and their existence was deemed purely for its benefit. George III had been pursuing the policies of George II, but with even more vigor. A heavy troop presence in the colonies ensured enforcement of its many laws and regulations and, later, collection of the crown's taxes.

The colonists were most unhappy about such treatment, not to mention the significant reduction in the great freedom and prosperity they had been enjoying. Things came to a boiling point with the Declaration of Independence on July 4, 1776. The American Revolutionary War ensued, ending in October 1781.

The Declaration of Independence was written by Thomas Jefferson, one of the most revered Founding Fathers of the United States of America. Along with a lengthy list of grievances and the actual declaration of independence, Jefferson eloquently set forth some significant philosophical ideas (numbering and underlining added):

1. All Men are created equal,
2. that they are endowed by their Creator with certain unalienable Rights, that among these are Life, Liberty and the Pursuit of Happiness –
3. That _to secure these Rights, Governments are instituted_ among Men, _deriving their just Powers from the Consent of the Governed,_
4. that _whenever any Form of Government becomes destructive of these Ends, it is the Right of the People to alter or to abolish it_, and to institute new Government, laying its Foundation on such Principles and organizing its Powers in such Form as to then shall seem most likely to effect their Safety and Happiness.

Several of Jefferson's ideas were especially startling in 1776, and perhaps they are still surprising to many, even today. The first is that the rightful purpose of a government is purely to secure the rights of its citizens. The second is that a government derives its powers from the consent of the governed. Furthermore, it is the right or even the duty of citizens to alter or replace any government that, in their judgment, is failing to properly so serve its citizens. These are obviously not the kinds of things your average monarch (or career politician) likes to hear.

From 1777 through March 4, 1789 (when the present-day Constitution was ratified), the central government of the United States operated under the Articles of Confederation and Perpetual Union. The document allowed for only a very weak central government while staunchly preserving the sovereignty of the thirteen states.

Unfortunately, the states did not play nicely under the Articles. They made interstate commerce very difficult. There was no standard currency. The central government had very limited taxing authority. Some farmers in Massachusetts rebelled (Shay's Rebellion) and demonstrated that the central government was powerless to quell any such uprising. It was nearly impossible to amend the Articles. Things were already so bad by 1787 that the states agreed to a constitutional convention to determine the path forward.

So, it came to pass that a very wise and well-read group of the Founding Fathers of the United States assembled in Philadelphia and hammered out the US Constitution over the summer of 1787. Their assignment was to design a more powerful central government that would remedy the problems of the Articles of Confederation. Well aware of the dangers of a powerful government, they resolved that the design had to ensure citizens' control over it and limit the usurpation of unintended powers.

Several of the states were wary that the new Constitution's safeguards were inadequate and that it did not do enough to guarantee basic rights. Thus, a second convention was convened immediately upon ratification of the Constitution, at which the first ten amendments were drawn up to further constrain the new central government. These amendments are known as the Bill of Rights, and as is now crystal clear, they were not at all superfluous and are instead a critically important feature.

The new Constitution with the Bill of Rights was indeed a groundbreaking new approach. It did, in large measure, succeed at fixing the problems with the Articles of Confederation, which was, after all, the primary objective. It launched the young nation on a trajectory of unprecedented freedom, growth, and prosperity. Many of its innovations and key features have been copied by other Western democracies. As the years have ticked by, it has completed its first quarter of a millennium as the foundational governing document of the United States.

Subversion of the Constitution

Sadly, absent a major "course correction," neither the Constitution nor the United States appears likely to survive to the half millennium point in any recognizable form. Just as surely as the relentless pressure of external groundwater eventually infiltrates an imperfectly constructed basement wall, eventually destroying it, power-grubbing politicians and their cronies have subverted the Constitution. Many of the things the Founding Fathers feared and tried hard to prevent have come true. The oft-told tale of Dr. Benjamin Franklin's somewhat ominous response to a question about what form of government had been created — "A republic, if you can keep it" — has proven especially prescient.

As has been stated, the Founding Fathers who authored the Constitution were wise and well educated. They understood their objectives as well as the problems and dangers to be avoided. Before proceeding further, we should ask why they failed.

One major reason was plain old conventional political reality and the necessity for compromise. No constitution was ever going to be ratified without near universal support from all thirteen of the states. Slavery was common in many places around the world at that time, and unfortunately, the economies of the Southern states were highly dependent upon the practice. This issue alone required some awful, painful, and difficult compromises, along with discomfort at violating fundamental principles as were so eloquently stated in the Declaration of Independence.

We are all heavily influenced by our history, upbringing, and current customs. Hence, for one example and among other things, the right to vote was not guaranteed for women.

The science of economics, kicked off by Adam Smith in 1776, was in its infancy. The laws of microeconomics were not well codified and certainly not widely known, promulgated, understood, or appreciated in 1787. Thus, it is understandable that guarantees for each of the six pillars (see chapter 11) that are required for a free market economic system did not make it into the Constitution.

It is critically important that voting and elections function well because that is the only mechanism by which citizens can maintain control. Although this would not seem to be difficult or problematic, it has turned out to be unexpectedly so and is a crucial problem.

About the time of the American Revolution, two French scholars, Nicolas de Condorcet and Jean-Charles de Borda, pointed out some of the serious and fundamental problems with the plurality, or "first past the post," voting method. Plurality is the simplistic voting method we have almost always used (and still overwhelmingly use), in which the candidate receiving the most votes is the winner, even if that candidate may have received, for example, only 27% of the votes.

More recently, it has been realized that plurality is even more harmful than Condorcet and Borda thought. In the twenty-first century, we are just now completing our understanding of the problems and the best solutions to them (see chapter 8)! Like free market economics, the Founding Fathers' knowledge in this area had to be woefully incomplete at best.

Finally, the Founding Fathers did not have word processors or fast printers. That was indeed a totally serious problem. Writing in ink with a quill pen is a horribly slow, laborious, and mistake-prone process. Whenever changes or corrections are made, the entire document must be copied over to obtain a "clean" copy (i.e., one containing only the mistakes made while copying it). This ruthlessly enforces brevity and discourages revisions, corrections, additions, or improvements. On top of that, the Fathers were under time pressure to fix the problems of the Articles of Confederation, which they did accomplish in four months.

The Constitution is a legal document of considerable importance and complexity. As such, it needs to be complete and unambiguous. Disambiguation often requires more words. The best works are rarely written — they are *rewritten*. These requirements are not compatible with quill pens and time pressure.

Following the Bill of Rights, the Constitution has been amended seventeen times (for a total of twenty-seven amendments). Some of these amendments were critical improvements, but others have weakened the Constitution and accelerated the usurpation of power by the central government.

The unresolved problems of slavery festered for half a century before coming to a head with the Civil War. Amendments XIII, XIV, and XV, passed shortly after that war, fixed some serious problems that had been compromised into the Constitution. The United States should be proud that it was able to painfully self-correct such a momentous issue. The changes that are needed to enable the Constitution and the country to survive and thrive during the remainder of the twenty-first century and beyond are at least comparable in magnitude to those already made, and they may be even more difficult to accomplish.

The lack of women's suffrage was not corrected until 1920 with Amendment XIX, but this does provide another example of a good self-correction.

In contrast, Amendment XVIII rendered it illegal to manufacture, sell, import, export, or transport "intoxicating liquors." How could a document intended to guarantee individual rights be completely subverted and used instead to blatantly deny rights? Fortunately, in this case, the blunder became quickly evident, and XVIII was repealed by XXI, which was ratified in 1933; so XVIII was in effect for only fourteen tumultuous years.

At least, it was realized that an amendment to the Constitution was required to grant the federal government the power to prohibit alcohol. It boggles the mind that no amendment to the Constitution whatsoever was thought necessary to empower the federal government to prohibit drugs, which seems entirely analogous. As early as 1848, prohibitions were placed on the importation of certain drugs. Drug prohibition really started ramping up with the passage of the Pure Food and Drugs Act in 1906, followed by the creation of the FDA.

A lot of serious damage was done under the watch of Democrat Woodrow Wilson (1913–1921), who is surely a very strong contender for the worst president. He signed the Federal Reserve Act, creating a strange central bank made up of twelve private banks, which has facilitated deficit spending, manipulated interest rates, and overseen the devaluation of our currency. The US dollar has lost more than 97% of the value it had when the Fed was created. That is, just three cents of the 1913 dollar would buy more than a whole dollar can buy in 2026! Inflation continues.

Amendment XVI was ratified in 1913. It was short, but highly significant:

"The Congress shall have power to lay and collect taxes on incomes, from whatever source derived, without apportionment among the several States, and without regard to any census or enumeration."

Prior to XVI, the federal government's taxing authority was constrained. The enumerated powers of Article I, Section 8, said, "The Congress shall have Power To lay and collect Taxes, Duties, Imposts and Excises ... ." Article I, Section 9, added the restriction, "No capitation, or other direct, Tax shall be laid, unless in Proportion to the Census or Enumeration herein before directed to be taken." Any additional funding needed (beyond import duties) had to come from the states in proportion to their populations, but it was up to the states to decide how to raise and collect the money. Nevertheless, the federal government got along satisfactorily with import duties as the mainstay, at least until the cost of the Civil War had to be paid. After Amendment XVI, the floodgates were opened, and wealth could be confiscated directly from citizens almost without limit as to method or amount.

The Founding Fathers tried to build into the Constitution many so-called checks and balances that were intended to prevent, or at least limit, the power that the central government could accumulate and wield. One of these was that laws had to be approved by both houses of a bicameral legislature and also by the president, the separately elected head of a different branch of the government.

The lower house was the people's house, with many representatives from relatively small districts (nominally comprised of one 435th of the nation's population) and elected directly by the citizens thereof. The upper house was composed of two senators from each state. Senators were not elected directly by citizens, but were instead appointed by the state legislatures, who could replace them at any time. The Founding Fathers thought that the state legislators would have a somewhat different viewpoint and were expected to be wiser and more thoughtful than the general public. Thus, the Senate would provide something of a check on the House.

Along came Amendment XVII, ratified in 1913, which removed the power of state legislatures to appoint senators and instead specified that they be elected at large by the citizens of each state. Although not a cataclysmic change, it did significantly weaken one of the checks and balances put in place by the Founding Fathers. The members of both houses are now popularly elected, and any control of or influence over federal legislation by the state legislatures has been lost.

To top all that off, Woodrow Wilson was blatantly racist, and one of the key figures instrumental in expanding the self-destructive "progressive" movement as well.

A stunningly illogical Supreme Court decision (Wickard v Filburn), rendered in 1942, misinterpreted a part of Article I, Section 8, (known as the "interstate commerce clause") to allow the federal government broad powers to "regulate" virtually anything. The precedent still stands today.

As pointed out above, some of the amendments became part of the Constitution's problems, but its subversion would have nevertheless occurred because of shortcomings present from the beginning. The degeneration got a significant shove in the early 1900s; it was perhaps paused by the world wars, but afterward, things resumed rolling inexorably downhill at an accelerating pace.

The Founding Fathers well understood that the ultimate and final check on government had to be an educated, informed, attentive, and motivated citizenry acting through the control mechanism of free, fair, and effective elections. They quite justifiably worried that this mechanism would not prove adequate, which most certainly has turned out to be the case. Eternal vigilance surely is the price of liberty.

Right before voters' eyes, the US government has been taken over by career politicians whose primary objective is to stay in power, with some percentage of miscellaneous ideologues mixed in for seasoning. Electoral politics has come to be ruled by two increasingly ruthless gangs that fight tooth-and-nail to achieve and maintain majority control.

"Good people" do occasionally make it through the party primaries or run with other parties or as independents, but their small number prevents them from accomplishing anything worthwhile. They are rendered impotent by the two entrenched gangs and the iron rule of Congressional leadership. Soon enough, they are replaced by a politician from one of the gangs, or they resign in frustration at their utter inability to effect any good change. The career politicians simply ignore them and just keep on smiling, spouting their latest talking points, raising money, buying votes with the taxpayers' own money, and working on being reelected.

Somewhat hidden from voters' eyes, a colossally huge, semipermanent, costly, and unelected administrative apparatus has grown up within the executive branch. Significantly, it is populated by a surprising number of misguided collectivist and/or one-world-government ideologues. Despite not being in any way accountable to voters, these bureaucrats enjoy tremendous power and influence. This results simply by virtue of their permanence and their direct control over the actual operational levers of government. They have a strongly symbiotic relationship with the career politicians as well.

At least as concerning and disturbing is the incestuous relationship that is hiding in plain sight between large industries and the "administrative state." Retiring military officers have jobs waiting for them on the boards of large defense contractors. Executives from these industries are appointed to positions in regulatory agencies responsible for regulating those same industries and also take administrative jobs managing large contracts. It's a busy two-way superhighway. The defense industries account for most of the traffic, but Silicon Valley, Big Pharma, and other industries are also involved. There are many, many billions of dollars of government contracts being awarded and managed by this amalgam.

Mostly hidden from voters' eyes is a very large lobbying complex whose function is to curry favor and influence with the politicians and to hijack government power for the benefit of all manner of special interests. There are many such groups; the largest and most powerful is the military-industrial complex (MIC), about which President — and former Supreme Allied Commander during World War II — Dwight Eisenhower warned in his 1961 farewell address. These lobbying groups symbiotically coexist with the politicians and the administrative state bureaucrats as one big happy family.

Moreover, totally hidden from everybody's eyes is the "intelligence community," consisting of the CIA, the NSA, the FISA Court, and connected to it, the DIA and the FBI. Their total budget obviously must be huge, but it is kept secret. Covert organizations are always tricky to control and therefore potentially dangerous. Occasional glimpses into their operations are provided by people like Edward Snowden, who risked his life to reveal pervasive and invasive NSA surveillance activities that he thought were both unconstitutional and morally wrong. The intelligence community is scary and the hands down winner of the "George Orwell Award."

"Power corrupts and absolute power corrupts absolutely" (Lord John Dalberg-Acton, 1887). Truer words were never written. Dalberg might well have included money in his pronouncement. "Crony statism" is rampant. There is plenty of corruption. As long as governments have the power to grant advantages or favors, there will be special interests happy to pay for them, and they will always find ways, direct or indirect, to reward their benefactors. Tapping into the gushing pipeline of taxpayers' money, the area around Washington, DC has become the most affluent (and recession-proof!) in the nation.

The legislative process itself has been perverted. Instead of legislation being introduced on the floor by a member of the body, then debated, amended from the floor, and voted upon (a process called "regular order"), complex bills thousands of pages in length are cooked up and negotiated behind the scenes and then introduced on the floor for an up-or-down vote. With only two or three days to consider such huge bills before the vote, no member of the body not intimately involved in the behind-the-scenes process can possibly read it thoroughly, let alone comprehend its total effect. Much power falls by default into the laps of Congressional staff members, who may attempt to follow the development of bills and advise their bosses regarding their merits.

How could voters allow their government to degenerate into such a sorry mess? Why didn't they elect better people to the various offices? The explanation derives from several compounding factors.

The first factor is the basic nature of human beings. The Founding Fathers were concerned that people would, quite naturally, be heavily involved in their personal affairs and businesses to the extent that they would pay too little attention to the affairs of their government and to electing the most qualified candidates to represent them. That concern was, of course, very well founded in nature. The advent of the Internet and especially the distractions of social media have greatly exacerbated this underlying problem. It appears that about 35% of citizens thinking reasonably rationally may be the minimum required to stabilize such a republic. We are far below that.

The second factor is that elections, the mechanism voters must use to control their government, have not functioned well. As mentioned, it has been known since the late 1700s that the plurality voting method has extremely serious deficiencies. Scores of voting methods have been proposed and extensively debated, but only in 2020 was the voting method problem clarified and sufficiently improved voting methods identified. But plurality still remains in widespread use.

Third, and in addition to the basic and pernicious problems with plurality, career politicians have found more ways to cripple elections. Drawing electoral districts to favor their own reelection, a technique known as gerrymandering, is a favorite. Although the two polarizing gangs bar no holds in the fight to the death to stay in power, they are totally willing to cooperate to suppress any "outside" competition at the polls. There are even examples of states gerrymandered to protect incumbents of both gangs in states where the gangs share power somewhat equally. The gangs have also conspired to erect barriers to ballot access. Such artificially high hurdles make it very difficult and/or resource-intensive for non-gang members to qualify to have their names appear on the ballot for any office other than small local ones.

Fourth, the art of being a successful career politician has been perfected to the point that it enables them to befuddle or neutralize most voters. Talented politicians can always appear to be concerned, thoughtful, pleasant, and sincerely interested in whatever the person currently in front of them is saying. They exude concern for doing what is best for all their constituents, and they are very careful to avoid saying or promising anything that could trip them up later or result in unfavorable publicity. On the other hand, they work hard at obtaining favorable publicity, such as showing up for ribbon cuttings, handing out awards, and conducting school groups on tours of the capitol.

Politicians know there is a high probability they will win reelection as long as they avoid the pitfall of an above-threshold unpopular statement or event that riles up a significant number of their constituents too close to an election. To minimize the chance of an "unfavorable occurrence," most are switching away from holding in-person "town hall meetings" to "telephone town halls," where many constituents on a "party line" can hear the politician making statements and answering questions. Theoretically, any participant on the party line can ask any question; but sadly, most telephone town halls are shams in which all questions are first screened by staff members, and only those the politicians wants to handle are heard during the call. ("Oops, sorry, we're out of time and just couldn't get to all of your excellent and very important questions.")

It is virtually impossible to push politicians into doing anything that they do not want to do, even if there may be tremendous pressure from an overwhelming majority of constituents. Politicians will cooperate to give each other "cover" under difficult circumstances. Sometimes, there is elaborate "choreography" to kill legislation in such a way that its death cannot be blamed on any particular politician. This could even be a bill that the politician introduced at the behest of constituents.

Obviously, fixing the problems with elections would require that the politicians legislate the necessary changes. So we have the foxes guarding the chicken coop.

The fifth factor was the progressive movement, which arose in the late nineteenth century and the early twentieth century, and from which modern progressives and liberals evolved. Modern "liberals" are quite the opposite of classical liberals. Their concept of government is the total opposite of that of the Founding Fathers. Instead of fearing the growth of government power and engineering ways to constrain it, liberals view government power as a wonderful tool to fix whatever *they* decide is a problem. They are close cousins of Marxists under another name. Amazingly, the modern liberals seem to be able to completely ignore the plethora of stark examples in countries where citizens lead miserable lives as a direct result of their all-powerful governments fixing problems.

During the 1960s and 1970s, liberals and progressives infiltrated the faculties of institutions of higher learning, eventually gaining status and tenure. From these perches of influence, they began inculcating students with their faulty philosophy. Over the ensuing decades, liberals and their acolytes fanned out into most sectors of society. Most unfortunately, many became teachers and school administrators. As a result of their influence, the teaching of basic skills and factual information — reading, writing, math, science, and history — are taking a back seat to the promulgation of progressivism. Of course, first to be deemphasized was the history of the US revolution and the foundations upon which the United States was built. The institutional memory of our founding principles and philosophy is being erased and is fading.

Crucially, understanding the free market economic system has never been taught well in public schools, if taught at all.

During the first quarter of the twenty-first century, a few batches of the poorly educated, dazed, and confused students of those liberals and progressives have become voters. Of course, liberals are also voters and run for political offices as well.

Politicians in the highest offices now make obviously false statements with straight faces. They surely know the statements are incorrect, but they say whatever they think is most likely to keep them in power, which in turn may change with time and circumstances. Thus, it is not at all unusual for politicians, without batting an eye, to state a position diametrically opposed to a position they took in the not-very-distant past — say, just a year earlier. Although members of the opposing gang may point out some of the contradictions, it is such a commonplace that it becomes just background noise to most voters. Too many citizens are paying too little attention and doing too little thinking to hold the politicians accountable.

"Vote buying" started on a fairly small scale decades ago with "pork barrel spending": through legislation, elected representatives would direct federal spending to projects in their districts. This might be a new post office or bridge, prevention of a military base closure, or something of that nature. Publicity made certain representatives' constituents knew of any such "bacon" that they brought home. Naturally, all representatives cooperated to assure passage of each other's pork barrel projects.

Congress paid some passing attention to controlling deficit spending back then, so pork projects weren't huge budget-busters. However, sometime along about the 1990s, politicians realized that they could spend money without having to anger voters by increasing taxes to pay for it (i.e., they could just borrow the money). Then the cost of vote buying exploded; so did the national debt. Politicians were perfectly fine with saddling future generations with a huge debt burden and more than willing to gamble that the country wouldn't hit catastrophic bankruptcy until they were out of office. In the meantime, they could freely bribe their constituents to vote for them by handing out expensive benefits and promising even more.

In 2022, President Joe Biden unilaterally decided to cancel some $400 billion of student loan debt at taxpayer expense. (Student loans with low interest rates had been an earlier vote-buying scheme.) This largesse would benefit predominantly those with college degrees and higher incomes, a large percentage of whom are liberals who donate to Biden's party. In addition to being another expensive vote-buying scheme, the calculation certainly had to be that some small percentage, say a paltry $5 or $10 billion, would find its way into the coffers of his party and his party's candidates via increased donations. The Supreme Court quite correctly shot this scheme down as unconstitutional.

How could the president of the United States have ever thought he had the power to do such a thing, especially without any enabling legislation whatever from Congress? Presidents (and other federal officials) don't care about legality anymore; their attitude is to just try whatever ploy they think will benefit them and see if they can get away with it. All too often, they do get away with it, and there's no penalty when they don't. When federal officials are nailed for illegal acts, they just retire, sail off into the sunset, and collect government pensions at taxpayer expense. Successful prosecutions and penalties for misconduct are extremely rare. Many, many similar (somewhat less colossal) abuses are allowed to continue unabated. Subversion of the Constitution is accelerating.

The US is careening out of control toward disaster. This cannot continue much longer. The national debt in 2026 exceeds $39 trillion, more than $350,000 per taxpayer. This debt is more than 125% of the entire gross domestic product, and the interest on it is approximately a trillion dollars per year — a large chunk of the annual budget. The credit rating for the United States has quite correctly been downgraded by all three major credit rating companies, which will accelerate the increase in borrowing costs.

In parallel with the deteriorating financial condition of the United States, civil society is breaking down. Crime and homelessness are increasing, exacerbated by more than 10 million illegal and unvetted aliens who have flooded in across deliberately open borders. Mobs ransacking and looting stores are becoming commonplace, and not just by illegal aliens. Extreme political polarization is choking off rational, constructive discourse.

The Path Forward

What does the future hold for the United States? Here are some possibilities.

Voters Implement Corrective Action

It is possible that in the normal course of events, enough voters wake up, reassert themselves, throw the bums out, and begin electing better people. Perhaps better leaders can effect reform and back away from the precipice over a period of years. Should this occur, it would be a vindication of our Constitution and the Founding Fathers' design of it.

Unfortunately, this does not seem likely. It is rendered even less likely by the deterioration of election integrity, mainly caused by increased use of mail-in ballots. There are lots of opportunities for hard-to-detect (and harder still to prosecute) fraud with mail-in ballots, but the most obvious is the lack of ballot secrecy, which enables vote buying (as is fully explained in chapter 9). Elections could become cheating contests, with the winners being the gang most skilled at cheating. If elections so degenerate, voters will no longer be able to exercise any control, even if they come to their senses and attempt to do so.

Also very importantly, there is zero indication that the pernicious plurality voting method will be replaced with a sufficiently improved method. Ditto the elimination of gerrymandering and artificial ballot-access hurdles.

Revolution

There could be a large enough number of citizens who grasp what is going on, do not believe that the normal course of events will fix anything, and are motivated enough to stage some sort of revolution. Assuming they succeed, they would force sudden reforms of a somewhat unpredictable nature and perhaps institute an improved Constitution. The probability of such a thing happening and being successful also seems rather small. (The Founding Fathers did fix the problem of the government not being able to quash a rebellion!)

Collapse

Inertia and the difficulty of making the required major changes augur continuance along the path to collapse down which the nation has been accelerating for the past century. The result might look something like the 1991 collapse of the Union of Soviet Socialist Republics. There is also the very real risk of the nation falling under the control of a hostile foreign power. Unfortunately, collapse seems to be the most probable outcome.

Engineered, Peaceful Correction

Under the right circumstances, it is possible for a small percentage, perhaps as little as 4% or 5%, of citizens to bring about significant change. Success requires a common understanding of the problem and agreement on the necessary course of action. Also required are coordination, cooperation, and the willingness to expend significant resources (time and money) sustained over a substantial period of time. History has demonstrated how difficult, and therefore how unlikely, it is for such a thing to be successful.

Those who would participate in this sort of effort are predominantly thoughtful, strong-headed individuals. Generally, this is a good thing and would seem to be a job requirement. However, it is the nature of this type of person to dissipate great energy arguing over the details of the plan. This destroys needed cohesiveness and saps progress toward the goal. The usual outcome is a bunch of small uncoordinated and ineffective splinter groups. Yet throughout history, there have been rare examples of strong and/or charismatic leaders being able to pull the troops together for such a movement and keep them on track long enough to be effective.

A Plan for Engineering a Peaceful Correction

The US Constitution was a radical, groundbreaking document in its time. The Founding Fathers did a remarkably good job despite some significant factors working against their success. The Constitution can be amended. There is a prescribed procedure for peacefully doing so. It has been amended seventeen times (following the Bill of Rights) to date. It would be logical simply to further amend the document as may be appropriate.

However, the necessary changes are many and complex. A humongous amendment or a series of somewhat simpler ones would be needed. A very hard-to-read "Frankenstein monster" of a Constitution could be the result. Significant changes would likely require some sort of organized and deliberate transition period to avoid an impossibly sudden shock.

Ratification of any amendment requires the approval of three fourths of the states. This is a high hurdle, as is appropriate for changes to the fundamental governing document of the country. Amendments may be proposed either by a two-thirds vote in both houses of Congress, or at least two thirds of the states may demand that Congress call a convention for the purpose of proposing amendments. However, Article V does not adequately define the process for either calling or conducting such a convention. Over the years, states have made more than a hundred requests for a convention, yet none has ever been called. It was a mistake to place Congress in the position of being able to thwart the states' desires for fixes or improvements to the federal government.

A more organized effort to call a constitutional convention has been underway for more than ten years. It is primarily built around instituting term limits and a requirement for a balanced federal budget. These are indeed two very important corrections that would be very helpful, but they still fall far short of what is needed. A couple of Band-Aids, even big ones, will not be sufficient. Appreciation for the magnitude of the problems and the fixes required is not widespread.

We must face up to the fact that nothing less than a from-scratch total and careful rewrite of the Constitution will set the country firmly on the right path with long-term stability. This critical task cannot be accomplished quickly or in a convention atmosphere.

To maximize the quality of the revised Constitution, the project should be controlled by a task group of a small number (say, five) of Founding Father–caliber individuals, the true "Yodas" of our time. Drafts should be widely circulated and feedback considered. There will be many revisions and tweaks. Allow a minimum of eight months, and more if the task group needs it.

The new Constitution would be attached to and made a part of Amendment XXVIII. The twenty-eighth (and final) amendment to the present Constitution would specify a hard effective date for the new Constitution and spell out a transition path leading up to it. As of the effective date and time, the new Constitution would completely replace the old one. A draft for Amendment XXVIII appears as appendix A.

The difficulty and improbability of success were pointed out in the previous section — it's a longshot. However, this plan, or a very similar one, would seem to have the best chance of success. The path to salvation is through the states. Three fourths of the states can force this to happen.

As should be obvious, a parallel, vigorous, and sustained campaign to elect the right people in at least thirty-eight states is essential. Only when "final" versions of Amendment XXVIII (including the new Constitution) are available and at least thirty-eight states are committed to support them (without further modification) could this plan succeed. Such a solid block of states would either pressure Congress to propose Amendment XXVIII or petition Congress to call a convention for the single purpose of proposing Amendment XXVIII.

The difficulty of hammering out such a carefully curated solution and obtaining agreement with it from thirty-eight or more states is formidable. However, it is more likely to achieve a good result than calling a convention first with a couple of inadequate mandates and attempting to proceed with whatever it proposes.

Fortunately, some work has already been underway for a few years to elect liberty-oriented or libertarian legislators in several states. One such organized and targeted effort is that of Young Americans for Liberty (YAL). They have made somewhat surprising and encouraging progress. The YAL program needs to be supported, expanded, and supplemented by other parallel efforts.

Once again, in the words of Thomas Jefferson in the Declaration of Independence, "Governments are instituted among Men, deriving their just Powers from the consent of the Governed, that whenever any Form of Government becomes destructive of these Ends, it is the Right of the People to alter or abolish it, and to institute new Government, laying its Foundations on such Principles and organizing its Powers in such Form, as to them shall seem most likely to effect their Safety and Happiness."

Designing an Improved and Safer Constitution

Before building or creating almost anything of significance, it is important to carefully think through, write down, and specify clearly what the thing is intended to do. Incredibly, this essential step is often skipped or glossed over. As the design progresses, it is important to keep verifying at every step that all features are consistent with and actually do support the stated objective.

The primary and overriding purpose of the Constitution of the United States is to define a set of individual rights that will maximize the total happiness of US citizens and create a safe-for-the-long-haul mechanism that will be effective, efficient, and minimally intrusive in guaranteeing those rights.

Securing such a set of rights should minimize the force, aggression, and fraud to which peaceful and honest citizens are subjected and maximize their freedom to do whatever they like, as long as it does not infringe upon the equal freedoms of other citizens. There is simply no perfect solution. It is an optimization problem. But freedom works. And freedom works best.

As discussed in the previous chapter, rights generally are not clean philosophical entities, and substantially all of them have gray or fuzzy areas that must be carefully defined. Thus, any document of a useful length can only deal broadly with rights. Fortunately, the large and detailed body of common law exists. Common law evolved over hundreds of years largely to fine-tune the dividing lines between what is a right and what is not a right in all the gray areas. The strategy for the Constitution must be to invoke the framework of common law to provide these definitions.

Some subsidiary considerations are as follows:

- All six pillars of the free market economic system must be secured.

- Both the unimpeachable integrity and the improved functionality of elections need to be spelled out and guaranteed everywhere in the United States.

- Fraud must be minimized to the greatest reasonable degree. Lobbyists will always spring into existence if there is something for which to lobby. However, if governments no longer have the power to grant subsidies, loan guarantees, tax loopholes, biased regulations, and the like, there will be little or nothing for lobbyists to seek.

- The individual must be protected from the hegemony of the majority to the greatest degree possible.

- The power of the guarantor mechanism must be very strictly and effectively limited to just what is required to secure rights.

- The cost of the guarantor mechanism must be minimized.

- While a solid basic education must be one of the positive rights guaranteed for minor citizens, all governments must be kept completely out of education, whether for minor citizens or adults.

- Parents' rights and responsibilities must be clearly delineated.

The Constitution should put up a great big umbrella over all US citizens that guarantees their maximum freedom, nothing less, but also nothing more. If freedom has been maximized, then doing any more than that would necessarily reduce freedom; all changes from a maximum are, by definition, less than the maximum.

With the primary objective clearly stated, it should immediately become obvious that it has been a significant mistake to call a mechanism that guarantees rights a "government." Merriam Webster's first definition of *govern* is "to exercise continuous sovereign authority over." That is backward! Citizens are sovereign and must have control over their government.

Anyone working in a "government" would logically conclude from the name that their job is to control citizens. While this is true in the extremely limited sense of preventing some citizens from infringing upon the rights of other citizens, it certainly misrepresents the intended and proper overall function. Instead of "government," the label should more appropriately be "individual rights guarantor." Switching to a three-word label would likely be a futile fight, so we would prefer a descriptive, easy-to-remember, one-word moniker if one exists. It may be time to coin a new noun.

Another troublesome word is "democracy." The original definition of "democracy" — and the primary definition given by Merriam Webster — is, *"government by the people : rule of the majority."* It is widely recognized and agreed that a pure democracy is a truly unworkable and horrible form of government. We do not now have, nor have we ever had, nor do we even remotely want a democracy. The word is based upon and glorifies the "rule of the majority." As we will learn in chapter 8, it is not even always best for the majority to rule in an election.

In spite of the fact that there is nothing good about democracy, it has somehow acquired and strongly holds a fuzzy but favorable connotation in most peoples' minds. Because of that, it has picked up a collection of ancillary definitions such as, *"a form of government in which the people elect representatives to make decisions, policies, laws, etc. according to law"* and, *"a country, state, etc. whose form of government is democracy : a political unit that has a democratic government."* The word is incessantly used and overused without a clear understanding of its meaning. The result is to add to the large amount of confusion that already exists. We should retire this word.

Specific Constitutional Fixes and Improvements

Appendix B contains (about the 200th draft of) an improved Constitution. Perhaps the work of the Constitutional Revision Task Force is already complete! Much more likely, appendix B may provide a good beginning that would save a lot of start-up time and supply some interesting ideas. Some of the features of the appendix B Constitution are briefly highlighted below.

Disambiguation. One immediately obvious thing is that the proposed Constitution is quite a lot longer than the original. The original is about 4,900 words, including the Bill of Rights, and about 7,500 words when all amendments are included. The replacement is more than 18,000 words. Why?

The Constitution is not some inconsequential memo, essay, or story. It is a legal document of supreme importance. As such, it needs to be both complete and unambiguous. The current Constitution is neither. The inadequately specified amendment procedures in Article V have already been mentioned, and there are worse examples. Eliminating ambiguity often requires additional words, as certainly does the insertion of missing provisions.

A more modern organization and structure supports greater depth than just Articles and Sections. This facilitates navigation, referencing, and clarity.

Philosophy and purpose. It is important to lay the foundations and provide some perspective. Certainly, the purpose of the Constitution should be spelled out, as well as the underlying philosophy. This cannot be neglected. In addition, more specific guidance regarding the document's interpretation should be provided. The current Constitution is weak in this area, providing merely a sentence in the Preamble. Some argue that this deficiency is at least partially corrected by Jefferson's general statement of philosophy in the Declaration of Independence. However, the Declaration is not a legal part of the Constitution; the Declaration is neither quoted, cited, nor incorporated by reference.

Definition of the term *individual*. If the Constitution is to define and guarantee individual rights, the definition of an individual as a legal entity is fundamental. This is the crux of the highly divisive, never-ending fight over abortion. When does a new individual come into existence and therefore acquire the rights (e.g., to life) and protections afforded by the Constitution? The appendix B Constitution provides a clear and specific definition that brings a lot of clarity (although the technology to determine the precise instant when an individual exists or ceases to exist may not be available quite yet).

Minor citizens. The existing Constitution makes no distinction between adult and minor citizens. The improved Constitution not only more clearly defines a citizen but also clearly defines a minor citizen. It also guarantees minor citizens the positive right to a reasonable standard of care (food, shelter, clothing, care, and education). Also made clear is that it is the progenitors of a minor citizen (parents) who are responsible for providing these positive rights. Parents' rights (and the limits thereof) to control what is best for their children are delineated.

Birthright citizenship. The idea that a pregnant noncitizen who sneaks across the border into the United States to birth an offspring can obtain automatic US citizenship for the child is preposterous and no longer the case in the improved Constitution. At the time Amendment XIV was adopted, it was important for the children of former slaves, but that need is long expired.

Noncitizens. The current Constitution makes no distinction between citizens and noncitizens, so does it guarantee the same rights to both? It would be nice if the Constitution could apply to the entire Earth, but it does not and cannot in the foreseeable future. Its concern must be the rights of US citizens. To best guarantee citizens' rights, it is advisable to guarantee noncitizens some, but not all, of the same rights.

Secession. Although it is to be hoped that this provision will never be used, the new Constitution specifies a path by which a state can secede in an orderly and peaceful way. Not to do so would fly in the face of the philosophy of liberty.

Elections. The entire electoral process is pinned down to the greatest extent possible. Integrity and transparency are guaranteed so that every citizen can and will *implicitly* trust election results. The pernicious plurality voting method is replaced by a new one (AADV — see chapter 8) that far more accurately and reliably identifies the correct winner of each race (the candidate whose election results in the greatest voter satisfaction). A simple five-step geometric procedure is specified by which guaranteed-to-be-impartial and compact electoral districts must be drawn, thus banishing gerrymandering. Barriers to ballot access are kept low and uniform. Politicians can no longer manipulate the system. Being the only mechanism by which citizens can meaningfully control their government, and in view of their problematic history, elections are so important that the subject warrants two chapters.

Free market economic system. All six pillars required for the proper operation of a free market economic system are protected by the improved Constitution. Government meddling in, tinkering with, and manipulation of the economy are strictly prohibited. The free market economic system is so important that it, too, warrants its own chapter.

National currency. Any economy requires sound money to function best. The existing Constitution is a miserable failure in this regard. The revised Constitution prohibits a central bank. Interest rates are the price of borrowing money and are determined normally; that is, by marketplace competition. The US dollar is reconstituted as a representative currency (no more fiat currency) that is guaranteed to be redeemable for a commodity (gold and silver at a minimum) of real intrinsic value. The dollar's value is solidly locked to the cost of living and is always worth about ten minutes of middle-class living. This seemingly straightforward topic has some confusing aspects and so deserves its own chapter.

Balanced budget. Any and every government must operate with a balanced budget. Money may be borrowed only for bona fide capital investments. Assets so purchased must be amortized over their expected useful lives in accordance with generally accepted accounting procedures.

Taxation. The sources of revenue must be specified in detail and strictly limited to a very few broadly based, simple, understandable taxes that do not require individuals to file any forms. A two-thirds vote is required to raise taxes, while a simple majority can reduce them.

Term limits. There are term limits for every federal elective office. A blanket term limit prevents making a career out of running for a chain of different offices (federal, state, and local).

Read the bill. Members of Congress may only vote for or against a bill they have personally read and comprehended in its entirety. Upon any verified violation of this requirement, the representative or senator is automatically removed from office.

Constitutionality review. Every new or amended law must pass a review by the Supreme Court. Each law must be certified as constitutional *before* it can take effect. Signing or voting for a bill that is declared unconstitutional shall be prima facie evidence that any senator or representative who voted for it or the president who signed it has violated their oath of office.

Delegated powers. The powers delegated by citizens to their government are more carefully defined and limited. Whenever feasible, powers and duties are pushed down to more local levels. Governments' ability to legislate advantages for special interests must be eliminated to the greatest possible extent. Lobbyists will exist only if there is some advantage for which to lobby.

War powers. Armed forces may engage in hostilities only when war has been declared by Congress or for bona fide emergencies, which must either be ended or covered by a declaration of war within forty-five days.

Education. No government should be involved in the education of citizens. Education services must be provided by the free market and must be subject to the normal competitive forces thereof. School choice is an important good feature that comes with the free market. "Fair" school funding is automatic because schools must earn the tuitions they charge their customers. There are many things that minor citizens should learn, but two of the most fundamental are how to think rationally and how the free market economic system functions.

Amendments. An additional path is provided by which citizens can completely bypass all politicians to amend the Constitution.

Checks and balances. Checks and balances are generally and significantly strengthened and augmented. A member of Congress or a president who verifiably violates a provision of the Constitution (thereby their oath of office) is automatically removed from office.

The "administrative state." The vast, powerful, unelected, semipermanent bureaucracy that has grown up in the executive branch must be drastically reduced and limited. Congress can no longer pass vague laws and delegate the power to fill in important details to the executive branch or the courts. Congress must write simpler and complete laws. The executive branch may not operate pseudo-courts (with administrative law judges and the like). Guilt or innocence must always be determined by a court of common law.

Immigration. Sadly, the world is a dangerous place. The country's borders must be secure. People and goods must enter or exit through normal ports of entry. Citizens' freedom to freely exit/enter (including their property and assets) must not be impeded. Immigration policy should be as liberal as serves the country's needs. However, immigrants (other than short-term visas) *must* learn English and accept all provisions of the Constitution.

Minimize Laws. A law is an authorization for the government to use force on people under some set of circumstances; it reduces freedom. Congress must pay adequate attention to repealing laws that do not work well or are no longer needed.

8. Controlling a Government

If government is to be "of the people, by the people, and for the people," citizens obviously must have effective control over it. In a representative republic, it is the elected representatives of the people who are supposed to control the levers of government. Thus, it is vitally important that "good" representatives be elected who will work hard to operate the government in the way the citizens who elected that representative prefer. If or when, in the judgment of those citizens, their representative is doing a poor job, it must be feasible and easy for them to elect a better — or at least a different — representative.

If everything is functioning as intended and desired, the vast majority of voters can be expected to be happy and satisfied with the representatives they helped elect. They should feel that going to the trouble of talking to or writing their representatives does have some beneficial effect. But instead, large majorities of voters are, in fact, not happy with their representation; they do not think their inputs are heeded, and they are frustrated by the fact that it seems to be nearly impossible to replace any elected official. Politicians remain in office until *they* decide it's time to either retire or, more likely, run for a higher office.

In order for this system to function well, it is absolutely essential that elections work well. Elections are ultimately the only mechanism voters have to maintain control. That mechanism has to be effective. The really bad and downright frightening news is that elections do *not* work at all well. Elections have never worked as well as people thought they did, and in recent decades, they have worked even less well. Career politicians have found ways to rig elections and insulate themselves from their constituents. Lately, they have been compromising the integrity of elections, thus opening the door to fraudulent manipulation.

How can that be? Elections aren't complicated, and everyone knows about elections, right? WRONG! Elections may seem to be straightforward, and that leads to a lot of complacency, but in fact, elections are quite complicated. There are many considerations, all of which need to be carefully thought through in order to "engineer" elections that work as well as they can, should, and must. Unfortunately, there are also a lot of misconceptions and bad ideas polluting the discussion and adding confusion.

The many design considerations affecting elections can be split logically into two major categories. The first, election *functionality*, deals with all the things that determine how well elections achieve their purpose — namely, choosing the "best" of the candidates for each office. Five sections in this chapter deal with this major category: Who Should Vote, Voting Methods, Drawing Electoral Districts, Ballot Access Criteria, and Other Ways to Tilt the Playing Field.

The second major category is election *integrity*, which involves a plethora of considerations necessary to ensure that election results are derived solely from the voters' inputs and cannot be affected by fraudulent manipulation. Election integrity is the topic of the next chapter.

The very first step in designing something — anything — is to clearly and specifically define what the thing is supposed to do. Write it down. That is certainly true for elections, and, inexplicably, that very first step is almost always glossed over or skipped entirely.

> **Definition 1: The primary and overriding purpose of any and every (public) election is to make the "best" choice of the candidates for the office being filled, with the caveat that decision-making power be kept "reasonably dispersed."**

That was pretty simple and straightforward but still very important. We will begin to reap the benefits of having stated such a clear and concise definition almost immediately. Note that the word "best" in the definition is in quotation marks. This is because it is a critical part of the statement that begs a more concise definition. That will surely be taken care of shortly.

With a clear definition of the purpose of elections, the engineering project can proceed.

Who Should Vote?

Maybe there is some better way than elections to choose the best candidates, but we use elections to make certain that the decision-making power does not fall into the hands of a small group (oligarchy) or a dictator.

How many must vote in order to satisfy the caveat that decision-making power be kept reasonably dispersed? Bear in mind that not all eligible citizens register to vote, and in many primary and off-year elections, as few as 20% of those registered actually vote. There does not yet appear to be any serious risk of falling into an oligarchy or dictatorship, even with those low numbers. Perhaps the caveat is satisfied safely enough if as little as 10% of eligible citizens actually vote in any given election. A question to be asked is whether the quality of decisions would be improved if virtually every eligible citizen voted.

A voter, in order to be best able to carry out the civic duty of helping to choose the best candidate for each office on the ballot in an election, ideally should satisfy the following criteria:

- Possess a reasonable level of intelligence and judgment.

- Have a good understanding of the organization and functioning of government, particularly the offices for which the voter will be helping to choose the best candidate.

- Have been paying reasonable attention to current events, especially the issues important for each of the offices being filled, and, of course, the performance of the current occupants of those offices.

- Leading up to the election, make the effort required to learn the background, capabilities, and philosophy of each of the candidates for each office.

If every registered voter met the above requirements equally well (or equally poorly, but equally), it would not matter who actually votes. All registered voters could vote, or any subset of them could vote, and the quality of the decisions made and the candidates elected would be substantially the same. It would only be important that a sufficient number vote to be sure that decision-making power remains distributed and does not fall into the hands of any particular small group.

In reality, all registered voters certainly do not have the same ability to choose the best candidates. The level of ability varies widely. The inescapable conclusion is that the quality of the choices made could be improved if only the most qualified half or third of voters actually voted. So we should prefer that only the "most qualified" voters vote so long as enough voters vote to satisfy the caveat. Whether they vote or not, it would be the best outcome for *everybody* to have the best possible choices of the candidates made. So hysterically flogging absolutely everyone to vote actually is a bit misguided. The crucial requirement is that *the right of, and opportunity for, all legally qualified citizens to vote must be absolutely guaranteed,* but whether or not they choose to do so must be entirely up to each individual.

Selecting the best-prepared voters is not a new idea at all. In fact, early on, it was thought that only landowners should vote. Later, "voter qualification tests" were employed, ostensibly to select "good" voters. Very sadly, voter qualification tests turned into a serious and embarrassing disaster when some states used them to deliberately screen out minorities. Consequently, voter qualification tests were virtually outlawed by the Voting Rights Act of 1965.

Still, there is nothing wrong with the basic idea. That it was hijacked for nefarious purposes by misguided implementations is what was wrong. If there were a test that were both relevant and unquestionably fair, impartial, and unbiased, its use would be beneficial. Well, it turns out there is such a test, and it has been in use for a long time. However, it has not been very effective because it is a multiple-choice test that doesn't often have many choices and also provides hints about the answer. This test is the voter's ballot.

The ballot "test" asks just one question: "For whom do you wish to vote for the XYZ office?" It repeats this same question for each race in which the voter is entitled to vote. Clearly, the question is highly pertinent. It is absolutely fair and not at all biased for or against any religion, race, gender identity, or anything else. It is tightly focused on what is important and even acts specifically on each race in each election.

For this test to be a reasonably effective voter qualification test, the voter shouldn't be given the answer or any hints; instead, every vote should be a write-in vote. Yes, voters may take "crib sheets" into the voting booth, but at least they will have had to do some homework in order to make up the crib sheets. Partisans handing out sample ballots outside a polling place marked as they would have voters vote is more of a problem; however, this cannot reasonably be prohibited, and no attempt should be made to prohibit it.

A more serious objection is that write-in voting is bound to slow the process down quite a lot. Another and even more serious objection is that candidates with long names and/or difficult spellings would be disadvantaged. Candidates who win elections might then mostly be those with simple, familiar names, like Jones and Smith.

Unless and until a better "test" can be devised, candidates' names should be listed on the ballot in a standard "LastName, FirstName MiddleName" format with no titles or party affiliations. The effectiveness of this as a voter qualification test would be somewhat weak but better than nothing. More candidates on the ballot for each race would make the test more effective.

It is possible that someone may be able to design a stronger "voter qualification test" utilizing the capabilities of modern technology. However, this would need to be approached extremely carefully so as to not lose impartiality, transparency, voter trust, and voter confidence.

Voting Methods

A *voting method* is the critical mechanism at the heart of an election that performs the function of gathering some specific information from each voter and then processing that data in some manner to select the "best" candidate(s) in each race. There are hundreds of different voting methods. The simplest is named *plurality* — or, as it is sometimes called, *first past the post.*

Plurality asks each voter to indicate which one of the candidates is the best. It allows each voter to vote only *for one* candidate. Plurality processes that data simply by separately adding up the number of voters who selected each candidate. The candidate indicated as best by the most voters is deemed the winner. Note that in a four-candidate race, the winner could have been chosen as the best by as few as 26% of the voters.

Not only is plurality the simplest voting method, but it is also the most widely used. It may be the only voting method most people know; some probably think it is the *only* voting method. Unfortunately, plurality is also the worst of all voting methods. It does the worst job of consistently identifying the winner with which the voters, as a group, would be most satisfied. The use of plurality is the most important single reason why elections have always worked poorly right from the beginning.

Around the time of the American Revolution, two French scholars, Nicolas de Condorcet and Jean-Charles de Borda, pointed out some of the serious problems with plurality. They proposed voting methods of their own that they theorized were superior. This kicked off a 250-year-long debate over various alternative voting methods. More recently, it has been realized that plurality is even worse than Condorcet and Borda thought.

Plurality's Problems

Polling data strongly indicate that the US presidents elected in 2016 and 2020 *were opposed by the majority of the voters who elected them*. Impossible? Unfortunately, it is not, and it has nothing to do with the much-maligned Electoral College. It's purely one of the defects of plurality.

Immediately prior to the 2016 presidential election, polling by Pew Research indicated that only 32% of registered voters said they were either "very warm" or "somewhat warm" for candidate Donald Trump, while 55% indicated they were "very cold" or "somewhat cold" toward him. On the other hand, only 36% said they were either "very warm" or "somewhat warm" toward candidate Hillary Clinton, while 53% said they were "very cold" or "somewhat cold" toward her.

Another Pew poll revealed that only 33% of voters were happy with the choice of candidates, while a whopping 63% were not happy with their choices. Other polls (e.g., Gallup) confirmed this bleak scenario as well.

Suppose that a simple "vote for or against" referendum had been held on whether voters wanted Trump to be president. The data clearly indicate that he would have lost decisively. If a similar "vote for or against" referendum had been held for Clinton, it appears that she too would have lost nearly as decisively.

So, a solid majority of voters disliked Trump, and a solid majority also disliked Clinton, yet Trump was nevertheless elected. A very similar situation existed for the 2020 election. A solid majority of voters opposed Trump, and a solid majority also opposed Biden; nevertheless, Biden was elected.

Why ever would voters elect a candidate that the majority of them oppose? They do so because plurality allows each voter to vote *only in favor of one candidate*, so the majority of voters voted (insincerely or strategically) for a candidate they didn't like because they liked the other major party candidate even less. This is called "voting for the lesser evil." It would be hard to create a more divisive situation if that were the goal!

Plurality actually fosters polarization. Why are extreme candidates nominated so often? It's largely because plurality is employed for primary elections and is nearly worthless at identifying the correct winner when there are three or more candidates. Feckless plurality facilitated Donald Trump's defeat of many competitors to become the 2020 Republican nominee, and it did so again in 2024.

Sometimes, runoff elections are used in an attempt to "patch up" plurality when no candidate has received a majority of the vote. Runoffs do help some, but even runoffs can't completely make up for plurality's deficiencies. Plurality is so bad at identifying the correct winner that it is not even guaranteed that the correct winner will be one of the top two vote-getters. So the candidate with whom the voters would be most satisfied might not even make it into the runoff election!

Nominating a highly polarizing candidate also turns out to be the best strategy for winning elections. Here is how that works.

Most presidential elections in key swing states are decided by less than five or six percentage points, frequently less than two. Since voter turnout is only in the 60% range at best, political parties believe (quite correctly) that increasing the turnout of their "base" voters is their best path to gaining those few additional percentage points needed to secure a win. After all, especially with such intense polarization, there is no hope of attracting voters from the opposite camp.

Thus, parties are motivated to nominate more "extreme" candidates that will draw their base voters to the polls. Voters are also strongly motivated to get out and vote because they mortally fear a win by the candidate at the opposite extreme.

It should be clear that plurality is harmful for any election, not just for presidential elections. Plurality is killing us and should be replaced with a much better voting method. But which one?

The states of Maine and Alaska have decided to try a method called *instant runoff voting* (IRV),[3] which has been used in France. IRV has not proved to be of any obvious

---

[3] Note: Some sloppily refer to IRV as *ranked-choice voting (RCV)*, which is a category of many different voting methods — more properly called *ordinal* methods. IRV is just one of the many ranked-choice methods.

great benefit in Maine or Alaska. That's because, although it is much more complicated, IRV is *identical* to plurality when either one or two candidates are on the ballot. Thus, IRV cannot possibly be better than plurality under those circumstances. With two dominant parties, there are, in effect, only two candidates on the ballot in many elections. The main benefit may be a somewhat higher likelihood that voters will rank their sincere first choice first instead of the "lesser evil." Some adopters of IRV are experiencing buyer's remorse and are considering reversing that decision.

There are also those who advocate approval voting, score voting, "score then automatic runoff" (STAR) voting, and others. If any of the many arguments were truly sound, convincing, and clearly superior to all others, plurality would presumably have been replaced long ago, and we would already be living happily ever after. Except for general agreement that plurality must go, confusion reigns regarding its best replacement.

Starting at the Beginning

It seems that it would be a good idea to start at the beginning and carefully engineer a really good voting method. As always, step one should be to clearly and concisely state what a good voting method should do. This will require providing a more concise definition of which candidate is the "best" candidate — filling in the definition that was glossed over in Definition 1.

Since it is the voters who will, through their ballots, choose the best candidates, there is no alternative but to lightheartedly assume that, collectively, voters do possess the knowledge and wisdom to make good decisions.

Voters use their knowledge and wisdom to develop an opinion of the candidates running for a particular office. It is the voting method's sole task to determine the opinions of the voters and translate them into a choice of the candidates that matches those opinions as accurately and consistently as possible.

When about to mark a ballot for a particular race, voters all have "opinions" in their brains about each of the candidates in that race. Sometimes, that opinion will be strongly positive for a candidate a voter considers to be very good — the voter would be very happy and satisfied if that candidate won. Sometimes, the opinion will be strongly negative, and the voter would be very dissatisfied if that candidate won. Of course, a voter's satisfaction regarding a candidate might be anywhere between strongly positive and strongly negative, including zero (no opinion). It also happens quite often that a voter's opinion of a candidate is zero because the voter is not informed and simply does not know enough about that candidate to have any opinion — elections, especially those with many candidates, will have a large number of this type of no opinion.

There are many voters, each with their own sets of opinions about each of the candidates in the race. It is possible (virtually certain with large numbers of voters) that for any particular candidate, some voters will have positive opinions, and some will have negative ones. There will also be some no opinion votes. How should a voting method process this data to identify the correct winner?

The only logical conclusion we can reach is that the best candidate is the one who has the highest (or most positive) net total of all opinions (that is, positive opinions minus negative ones).

> **Definition 2: The best possible choice is that result (chosen candidate) which maximizes voter satisfaction, net of dissatisfaction, when summed over all voters who voted.**

There is no better way to translate the collective knowledge, judgment, and wisdom of voters into the best choice. *This is the overriding and <u>only</u> objective that a voting method should have.*

Much ado has been made over the years regarding the "fairness" of elections and the "fairness" of various voting methods. The term "fair" is subjective and *depends completely on what the user of the term thinks is fair.* Therefore, the term cannot be used in any rigorous argument without accompanying detailed and objective criteria for what the user of the term considers to be fair. Note that the definitions for the primary purpose of elections and for the best choice of candidates say absolutely nothing about fairness. However, if one were attempting to define the "fairest" result, it is difficult to think of anything fairer than, in every election, choosing the candidate who maximizes the satisfaction of the voters who voted.

The remaining challenge is to find a voting method that determines voters' sincere opinions as accurately as possible, utilizes those opinions to determine the net satisfaction for each candidate, and selects the one with the highest net total. If only that were as easy and straightforward as it sounds!

A Perfect Voting Method

Suppose that we have a wonderful machine, call it a *satometer,* which is able to detect a person's brain waves and accurately measure the sincere opinion or satisfaction that a voter holds for each candidate. Our satometer is able to measure voter satisfaction with candidates on a scale of satisfaction (call the units "*sats*") with +sats of varying magnitudes corresponding to positive satisfactions and −sats mapping to negative satisfactions (dissatisfactions). The scale doesn't much matter, as we already must assume that the satometer has the correct conversion factor to map voters' satisfactions onto whatever scale has been chosen.

When each voter steps into the voting booth, we simply have the satometer grab a quick reading of the sats the voter has for each of the candidates. Then, when the polls close, all the voters' sats for each candidate are summed to obtain the net satisfactions for each. It is then a simple matter to identify the best candidate as the one with the highest (and most positive) net total. Clearly, no opinion votes must never affect the results in any way, and they do not, since they are measured as zeros. This would constitute a perfect voting method. It would reliably, without error, identify the candidate who maximizes voters' satisfactions in every election.

No such satometer yet exists. However, the fictional satometer serves to crystalize the meaning of Definition 2 and to illustrate specifically what a good voting method must achieve as closely as may be possible. Unfortunately, no real-world voting method can be perfect. Every actual voting method will make some mistakes —

that is, it will sometimes identify a winner *other* than the one that maximizes total voter satisfaction.

The Gibbard–Satterthwaite Theorem (as Extended)

Lacking a satometer that can reach into voters' brains and extract their *sincere* opinions, the only way a real-world voting method has to obtain any data from voters is to ask them for it. That is actually a rather fundamental and serious problem. There is no guarantee that voters will provide correct data. Voters can and do lie a lot. If voters believe (correctly or incorrectly) that indicating something other than their sincere opinions about the candidates will enable their ballot to have a greater impact on the election outcome in a direction that they would prefer, they will not hesitate to lie. This well-known phenomenon is called *insincere* or *strategic* voting.

It has been proven by Messrs. Gibbard and Satterthwaite that *any* and *every* voting method (other than a dictatorship where a single voter has absolute control) can be manipulated to some extent by strategic voting. No voting method can be completely immune to such degradation, but some are much more susceptible to it than others. This *must* be considered in the design or selection of a voting method.

In addition to insincere or strategic votes, there is bound to be some fraction of voters who are uninformed, careless, or, for whatever reason, unable to provide data that are useful and helpful in selecting the correct winner. Such *noise* is one more impediment to identifying the best winner with which real-world voting methods must contend.

Unfortunately, this means that *designing or choosing the best real-world voting method is always a trade-off* that must consider a method's vulnerability to strategic voting and noise or garbage inputs from voters.

The Jones Rule

The Jones rule was named for Douglas Jones (Computer Science Department, University of Iowa), who stated it so succinctly:

> **Everything about elections must be understandable by a reasonably bright high school student.**

Of course, that covers more than just the voting method, but it certainly does include the voting method. If how elections work is a deep mystery, voters may suspect that "a man behind a curtain" may be manipulating the results. And, in fact, if you don't understand what is going on, there very well *could* be a man behind a curtain manipulating the results for all you know. Under such circumstances, it will be difficult or impossible for everyone to implicitly trust election results, which is a highly important requirement. Also, no politician should vote to authorize the use of an election mechanism that they don't understand.

Designing or choosing a very good voting method may at first look like a fairly simple problem. However, it should be apparent by now that the problem is more confusing than it seemed to be. This is one of the reasons why the quest for a great voting method has gone on for so many decades and only recently has rapid progress been made toward a full understanding of the problem.

Ordinal Methods and Cardinal Methods

Voting methods can be sorted into two categories: ordinal and cardinal. This distinction is based on the information they solicit from voters. Ordinal methods ask voters to specify the *order* in which they prefer the candidates. A more popular synonym for ordinal is *ranked-choice voting* (RCV) methods. Plurality is the simplest ordinal or ranked-choice method — you only get to rank your first choice.

On the other hand, cardinal methods ask voters to rate or score candidates based upon how strongly they favor or disfavor specific candidates. The simplest cardinal method is called approval voting for which you are allowed to score each of the candidates on a two-value scale of either 0 or 1.

The amount of information a cardinal method gathers is normally greater than that collected by an ordinal method. For example, suppose a voter is allowed to specify only the order in which two candidates are preferred. There are only two options: Candidate A is preferred over Candidate B, or Candidate B is preferred over Candidate A. That is one bit (binary digit) of information. Just knowing that candidate A is preferred to B does not reveal whether A and B are both terrific candidates, with A being slightly better than B, or that A and B are both horrible candidates, with B being a bit more horrible than A, or that A is a good candidate and B a bad candidate.

On the other hand, if voters are allowed to say whether they are satisfied or not satisfied with each candidate, that conveys twice the information (two bits) on each ballot because there are now four possibilities: satisfied with both, not satisfied with both, satisfied with A but not satisfied with B, or satisfied with B but not satisfied with A.

The cardinal methods can be further subdivided into those which allow only positive scores and those which allow both positive and negative scores, with negative scores offsetting positive ones.

Suppose each voter can specify one of three opinions (satisfied, no opinion, or dissatisfied) for each of the two candidates, each ballot then conveys slightly more than three bits of information.

Quite a large number of voting methods of both ordinal and cardinal types have been proposed and debated.

Axiomatic Approach

The predominant approach for many decades has been to write down a set of axioms that a voting method should satisfy. Each axiom specifies some characteristic that a voting method should have and thereby excludes or rules out members of the set of all possible voting methods that do not comply with that axiom. It is hoped that at least one remains standing after the application of the last axiom, which would then be one or several acceptable methods. With this approach, the chosen axioms then _are_ the definition of "best possible decision," not the straightforward definition as stated by Definition 2.

Maybe this could be useful, but it seems like a rather indirect approach. Of course, the selection of axioms is crucial. Most axioms have specified various "fairness" criteria to which it has been assumed voting methods should comply. The predominant focus has overwhelmingly been on the ordinal, or ranked-choice methods, although there certainly is no fundamental reason why ordinal methods should be expected to be superior to cardinal ones. In fact, the reverse might be expected to be true.

An axiom that certainly *should* be included in any collection of axioms is simply this:

> **No candidate for whom total voter satisfaction is negative should ever be able win an election.**

A somewhat weaker version might also be acceptable:

> **No candidate that a majority of voters oppose should ever be able to win an election.**

Despite the obvious importance of this requirement, it does not appear that such an axiom has ever been a feature of the axiomatic approach. The reason may be that no ordinal (ranked-choice) method can satisfy this axiom. It also rules out many of the cardinal methods as well.

Miscellaneous Efforts

A plethora of other methods, both ordinal and cardinal, have been proposed, some of which are rather complex. Typically, multiple hypothetical election scenarios are constructed to illustrate and study how various methods handle them. Analyzing how methods deal with so-called "election paradoxes" is popular. However, there is no definitive way to extrapolate from a necessarily finite set of hypothetical election scenarios to the nearly infinite number of possible real-world election scenarios. Therefore, the "arguments" are just "hand-waving" arguments that cannot prove that one method is statistically superior to another in the many possible actual public elections with large numbers of voters.

Nevertheless, this seems to have become a sport of a sort, and the debate is never-ending.

Carefully Thinking It Through

A good voting method should work well for any number of candidates on the ballot. Think about the simplest possible election: a one-candidate election. Yes, there actually are one-candidate public elections in many states. They are often called *judge retention elections*. In every respect, these are one-candidate elections — voters vote to elect (or not elect) a single candidate to serve a term of some number of years in a certain capacity.

How does plurality work for one-candidate elections? Not very well at all! Plurality allows each voter to vote only *for one* candidate. Thus, the candidate will *always* be elected. For that very obvious reason, judge retention elections do not use plurality. They allow voters to vote either "Yes" or "No" (satisfied or dissatisfied). The "No" votes are subtracted from the "Yes" votes, and the sum has to be positive (more "Yes" votes than "No" votes) for the candidate to be elected. It's called a *referendum*. Clearly, the opinions of voters dissatisfied with the candidate are quite important and cannot simply be ignored.

However, there certainly are plenty of races in regular elections where only one candidate is on the ballot and for which the plurality voting method *is* employed! These are sham elections since voters have no ability to reject that candidate or affect the election's outcome in any way. Again, it is folly to ignore the dissatisfaction voters have with candidates. That is very important information.

Now, think about two-candidate elections in which one of the two candidates is to be elected. We wish to determine how satisfied (or dissatisfied) voters would be if Candidate A were to be elected and also how satisfied (or dissatisfied) they would be if Candidate B were to be elected. The candidate with whom voters would be most satisfied will then be designated the winner. It is certainly possible that the voters may be dissatisfied with both candidates. Just as with one-candidate elections, it is critical that voters have the ability to reject either or even both candidates; and just as with one-candidate elections, the opinions of voters dissatisfied with the candidates clearly should not and must not be ignored.

Obviously, these conclusions for one- and two-candidate elections are also true for *any* number of candidates. If a voting method is to select winners in compliance with definition 2, *voters' dissatisfactions cannot be ignored and must offset the satisfactions of other voters for each particular candidate*. This is a fatal flaw of plurality. Note that instant-runoff voting (indeed, all of the ranked-choice methods), approval voting, STAR voting, Condorcet's pairwise comparison voting method, and substantially all other generally advocated methods suffer this same flaw. The best that dissatisfied voters can do is to *not* say they are satisfied, but that is quite different. That lumps all the "dissatisfied opinions" in with all the "no opinions." That is, they do not affect the choice of the winner in any way. It is the same as not voting. That is just plain wrong.

A new voting method, called approve/approve/disapprove voting (AADV) was proposed in 2020. Each voter has the option to approve of either zero, one, or two of the candidates and also has the option to disapprove of zero or one candidate. Each candidate's approvals and disapprovals are summed separately. Disapprovals are then subtracted from approvals to obtain the net approvals for each candidate. The candidate with the most (positive) net approvals is declared the winner. If no candidate achieves positive net approvals, "none of the above" (NOTA) has "won." If NOTA should "win," all the candidates are disqualified. A new election must be held with completely new candidates.

AADV comports with Definition 2 and offers a large improvement. It works very well for any number of candidates, including just one. However, no real-world voting method can be perfect, and AADV is certainly no exception.

We know that *every* voting method can be manipulated to some extent by strategic voting and that this is a trade-off that *must* be considered when designing or selecting a voting method. AADV optimizes the trade-off by collecting the two most important data — the candidate each voter thinks is best and the candidate each voter thinks is worst — and very little more. A second approval is allowed in order to defuse any motivation to vote for a "lesser evil" instead of each voter providing their sincere first choice. Allowing any additional voter inputs would be expected to degrade performance; additional data cannot help decision-making significantly, so it could only be harmful noise or attempts to manipulate results through insincere "strategic" voter inputs.

AADV allows voters to weigh in on up to three of the candidates. No matter how many candidates there are, very few voters are genuinely concerned about more than three of them *at the time they are voting* in a single-winner election. That is not to say that only three candidates were considered. Conscientious voters will give all candidates a look, and it is fervently to be hoped that there are lots of conscientious voters. However, by the time they are executing a ballot, perhaps a third have boiled things down to just their first choice. Another half of voters are probably thinking about the candidate they most want to win and worrying about the one they least want to win. A few more may additionally have a second-choice candidate in mind. However, even if there are more than those three names on the ballot, they cannot weigh heavily in the voters' preferences by the time they are marking a ballot, so very few significant voter inputs will be ignored by AADV's limits.

We also know that *all* real-world voting methods will sometimes make mistakes (i.e., not identify the candidate that maximizes voter satisfaction). We certainly would prefer a method that makes the fewest and smallest errors and doesn't ever commit major blunders. Choosing a candidate nearly tied with the correct winner would be a small error, but electing a candidate that the majority of voters oppose would be a huge blunder.

The logic indicates that AADV is close to the best that can be done, but how good is it? This is a statistical problem. However, acquiring reliable and useful statistical data from real elections is extremely difficult, especially being able to collect data representative of "all types of elections." Furthermore, gathering the large volume of data required to have confidence in conclusions for such a huge statistical problem is very time-consuming and prohibitively daunting; the validity of the data would likely be highly questionable as well.

Simulating Elections

Fortunately, modern digital computers provide a powerful tool to model entire complex elections and quickly gather detailed statistics on any desired aspect to any reasonable statistical significance. It is entirely practical to test many voting methods and compare them quantitatively. Some forms of strategic voting can easily and accurately be simulated; other kinds can be simulated with more effort and risk. For simulated elections, we actually do have the equivalent of a satometer since each voter's opinion (or "utility") for each of the candidates is generated, therefore known. It is as though we have an X-ray or a CT machine and can see inside elections to gain a much better understanding of what is important and what is not. Of course, any such simulation requires, begins with, and depends upon a concise and correct definition for the best choice.

Surprisingly, there does not seem to have been a lot of serious effort devoted to this area. It appears that the first simulation project was done around 2000,[4] but it unfortunately had some known serious problems and shortcomings. How elections are simulated obviously does matter. More recently, there was an investigation in 2019[5] and another in 2020.[6] Yet another simulation study was carried out in 2026[7] and further expanded understanding.

---

[4] Smith, Warren D. 2000. "Range Voting"

[5] Minet, Roy A. 2019. "Election Simulation Sheds New Light on Voting Methods"

[6] Minet, Roy A. 2020. "Follow-on Election Simulation Leads to Definitive Proposal"

[7] Minet, Roy A. 2026. "Expanded Election Simulation Expands Understanding"

Those studies produced a plethora of intriguing results that certainly pass the common sense test. Readers interested in more detail can plow through the referenced academic papers.

Before further discussing election simulations, it must be emphasized that *the logic presented in the previous section is the justification for choosing the AADV method. The choice of AADV does not depend upon the veracity of election simulation results.* If AADV were to perform poorly in the simulations, it is the simulations that would be called into question. However, that did not happen.

The election simulation work was done with the objective of providing a way to *quantitatively* compare the errors that various voting methods make with varying parameters — e.g., the number of candidates — and to gain additional insights. Since the way in which elections are simulated certainly does matter, some readers may ask how the following data were obtained. The answer to that question is not short and simple, but sufficiently interested readers can find it in appendix C. Even more detail can be found in the footnoted academic papers.

The table below is a summary of some of the data obtained during the 2026 simulation project. Elections were simulated which had one candidate on the ballot through seven candidates on the ballot. One hundred thousand elections of all possible types were simulated for each number of candidates — 700,000 elections in all. Ten thousand voters voted sincerely in each election. The simulations were designed to match real-world elections as closely as possible. Without similar statistics from actual elections, there is no way to be certain how closely the simulations matched, but all the numbers on the spreadsheet certainly do appear to be entirely reasonable and understandable. There is nothing at all unexpected or surprising that would raise a red flag. The results shown are derived from a total of 28 billion voter opinions of candidates. These are just the statistics for the elections themselves and so far have nothing to do with the voting methods being tested.

The correct winner of each election was determined exactly in accordance with Definition 2 — that is, the candidate that has the highest net satisfaction of all the voters. In any election where the voters were dissatisfied with all of the candidates on the ballot — that is, all of them had negative net satisfactions — the fictitious candidate NOTA (None Of The Above) was designated the correct winner. It obviously is important to recognize and properly handle this situation as it certainly can and does occur in real-world elections (see the discussion of the 2016 and 2020 presidential elections above).

Number of Elections	100,000	100,000	100,000	100,000	100,000	100,000	100,000
Number of Voters	10,000	10,000	10,000	10,000	10,000	10,000	10,000
Number of Candidates	1	2	3	4	5	6	7
Majority Winners	100,000	99,999	92,455	84,939	77,255	69,925	62,647
Incorrect Majority Winners	49,988	25,331	10,906	4,426	1,667	640	262
Additional Condorcet Winners	0	0	7,337	14,037	20,874	26,811	33,477
Incorrect Add'l Cond. Winrs	0	0	4,539	5,647	5,534	4,722	3,973
Negative "Winners"	49,962	24,923	12,556	6,224	3,086	1,528	764
Average Winning Sats	13	22	28	32	36	38	40
Zero Opinions (millions)	152	304	459	613	763	908	1,060
No Opinions (millions)	126	253	379	505	632	803	939
No Opinion % of All Opinions	12.60%	12.70%	12.60%	12.60%	12.60%	13.40%	13.41%
NOTA "Wins" (%)	49.96%	24.92%	12.56%	6.24%	3.09%	1.53%	0.76%
Candidate A Wins (%)	50.04%	39.19%	31.18%	26.06%	22.24%	19.17%	17.28%
Candidate B Wins (%)		35.89%	30.29%	25.26%	21.70%	19.12%	16.89%
Candidate C Wins (%)			25.97%	23.45%	20.41%	18.28%	16.13%
Candidate D Wins (%)				19.00%	18.60%	17.07%	15.73%
Candidate E Wins (%)					13.97%	14.85%	14.07%
Candidate F Wins (%)						9.98%	11.79%
Candidate G Wins (%)							7.34%

First, look at the row labeled "Majority Winners." When there is only one candidate, that candidate must always be a majority winner. In the two-candidate case, one of the two candidates must be a majority winner except in the case of an exact tie (there was one exact tie in this particular run of 100,000 elections). As the number of candidates increases beyond two, the probability that there is a majority winner declines.

The next row, "Incorrect Majority Winners," is a tally of the number of majority winners that were not the correct winner. That is, the majority winner candidate was not the candidate that had the highest voter satisfaction net of voter dissatisfaction, which is the correct winner in accordance with Definition 2. For one-candidate elections, half of the majority winners aren't the correct winner. As the number of Candidates increases, there are fewer majority winners, but they are increasingly likely to be the correct winner. With seven candidates, majority winners declined to 62,647, but only 262 of them were not the correct winner. Some may find the idea that majority winners aren't always the correct winner counter-intuitive or perhaps even sacrilegious; but it is nevertheless so. This is further discussed in the next section.

A Condorcet winner is a candidate that is preferred by voters to every other candidate in a pairwise comparison with each. A majority winner must also be a Condorcet winner by definition. The "Additional Condorcet Winners" row tallies Condorcet winners in elections which had no majority winner. Condorcet winners are held in extremely high regard by many voting method aficionados. However, note in the next row, "Incorrect Additional Condorcet Winners," that well over half of the additional Condorcet winners in three-candidate elections were not the correct winner! Like majority winners, Condorcet winners are increasingly likely to be the correct winner as the number of Candidates increases.

The lower portion of the table summarizes the win percentages of the various candidates. NOTA heads the list followed by the seven "real" candidates, "A" through "G."

Look first at the column for one-candidate elections. Since all possible elections are simulated with equal frequency, one can expect that net voter satisfaction for "A" is going to be positive in half the elections and negative in the other half. Note that "A" and NOTA do split their 100,000 elections down the middle quite accurately.

In the two-candidate column, the same argument that applies to "A" also applies to "B." Just as with "A," "B" will enjoy positive net voter opinions randomly in half the elections and have negative nets in the other half. Thus, we can expect that voters will dislike both of them in 25% of elections. It is comforting that NOTA "wins" are indeed very close to 25%.

The same applies to each and every additional candidate. Thus, the probability that voters will dislike all of the candidates in the same election is reduced by half for each added candidate and NOTA "wins" are therefore halved with each additional candidate.

The 10,000 voters in the elections summarized in the above table also voted six more times in each election, once using each of the six voting methods being tested. Here is a brief description of those methods.

1. **Plurality** — Voters are allowed to specify only their first choice of the candidates. First choices are totaled for each candidate. The candidate having the largest total of first choices is the winner. Plurality is the simplest ordinal method and most widely used of all methods.

2. **Instant-Runoff Voting (IRV)** — Voters are allowed to specify the order in which they prefer up to three of the candidates. The first choices for each Candidate are totaled. If one candidate receives a majority of the first choices, it is the winner. If no candidate has a majority of first choices, the candidate having the smallest number of first choices is eliminated from all ballots. If a ballot from which a candidate is eliminated has a lower-ranked choice, it is promoted to fill the vacancy. The process is repeated until some candidate has a majority of the then-remaining first choices or until only one candidate is left standing. IRV is a considerably more complex ordinal method that has been adopted in Maine, Alaska, and some municipalities. It is too complex to comply with the Jones rule. IRV is often incorrectly called ranked-choice voting (RCV). RCV is a synonym for ordinal, which is a category of many different voting methods; IRV is just one of them.

3. **Score, Then Automatic Runoff (STAR)** — Voters are asked to score each of the candidates on a six-value scale of 0 to 5. The scores are totaled for each candidate. A runoff is then conducted between the two candidates with the top two scores. The ballots are examined a second time to determine which of the two is preferred by more voters. The more preferred of the two is the winner. STAR is a hybrid cardinal-then-ordinal method. Although it is somewhat easier to

understand than IRV, it still is in some hot water with the Jones rule.

4. **Approval Voting (AV)** — Voters are asked to score each candidate on a two-value scale of 0 to 1 (1 is an approval and 0 is no approval). The scores are totaled for each candidate. The candidate having the largest score (most approvals) is the winner. AV is the simplest cardinal method.

5. **Approve/Approve/Disapprove Voting (AADV)** — Each voter may approve of either 0, 1, or 2 of the candidates, and may also disapprove of either 0 or 1 candidate. Approvals and disapprovals are separately totaled for each candidate. Each candidate's disapprovals are subtracted from its approvals to yield its net approvals. The candidate having the largest number of net approvals that is greater than zero is the winner. If no candidate achieves greater-than-zero net approvals, all candidates are disqualified and a new election must be held. AADV is a cardinal method that scores on a three-value scale of -1, 0, and 1.

6. **Approve/Disapprove Voting (ADV)** — ADV is identical to AADV except that each voter is allowed only one approval instead of two.

The chart immediately below shows how each voting method performed in terms of its RMS (Root of the Mean Square) error. There are many ways to compare voting method performance and the RMS error probably is the best single measure. That is because the RMS error is much more sensitive to large errors than it is to small ones. Thus, voting methods are penalized more severely when they make big blunders than when they make small mistakes, just as they should be.

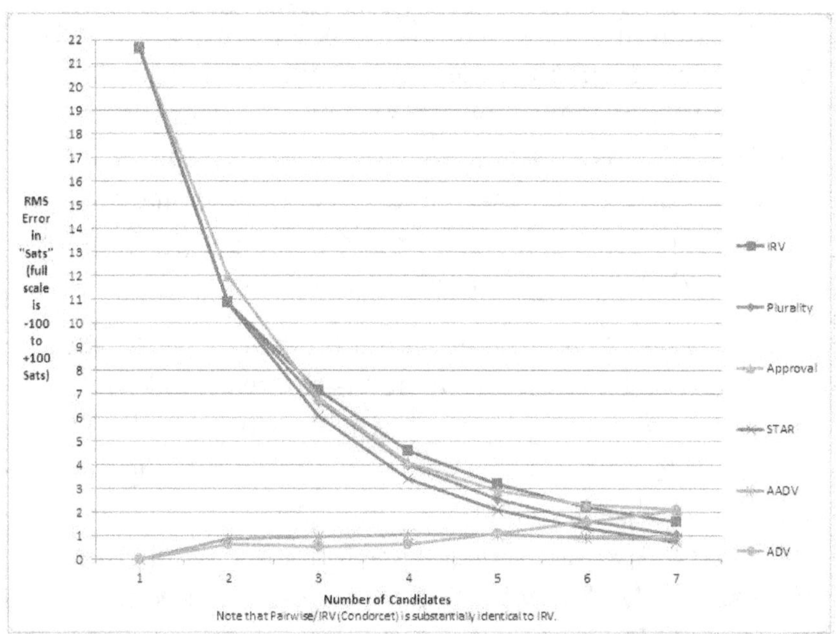

For a perfect voting method, which unfortunately is impossible, the RMS error would be zero for any number of candidates. The errors relate to a full scale of -100 sats to +100 sats. Thus, a one sat error is only 0.5% of the full scale.

The voting methods clump rather dramatically into two groupings. The methods that empower voters to express both satisfaction for candidates they like and dissatisfaction with candidates they do not like have much lower errors, while ones that restrict voters to only positive inputs have higher errors.

Perhaps the easiest way to think about AADV and ADV is that they conduct a separate "yes or no" referendum for each of the candidates. When there are multiple candidates, the candidate who wins their referendum by the largest (positive) amount becomes the overall winner of the race. Voters are allowed to vote "Yes" in the referendum of the candidate(s) they think is best, and they also have the option to vote "No" in the referendum of the candidate they think is worst. As with any referendum, "No" votes subtract from the "Yes" votes. The ability of ADV and especially AADV to consistently identify the correct winner for any number of candidates (at least for 1 through 7) reduces the need for runoff elections.

It is important to remember that the accuracy of _all_ voting methods will be degraded to some extent in real-world elections because of strategic voting. AADV has been designed to optimize resistance to strategic voting and should be expected to be the least degraded. Although AADV and ADV are similar in performance when voters vote sincerely, AADV is the strongly recommended method. AADV is very easy to generalize to handle multiple-winner elections (e.g., electing four school board members out of ten candidates). The generalized form is called generalized approve/disapprove voting (GADV).

Although there is no valid reason to do so, if one insists that one of the "real" candidates has to win (there is no NOTA), AADV is still the clear choice. It most consistently identifies the candidate that has the highest voter satisfaction or, when voters don't like any of the candidates, the one that is least disliked.

Appendix D contains detailed instructions for voters and tally instructions for election officials, as well as important notes that apply to AADV and GADV. Note the "2% rule" that is included to preclude a win by a virtually unknown write-in candidate who has garnered only one or a few votes. This would otherwise be possible in the somewhat unlikely but completely possible event that all candidates on the ballot have a zero or negative result. A win by such a write-in candidate may indeed be the best outcome in such a sad situation, but most people would find it disquieting for the winner of a large election to have been chosen by a small handful of voters, while being unknown to most voters.

It was learned from the simulations that the single datum most helpful in choosing the correct winner is (no surprise) the voters' choice of the candidate they think is best. However, coming in a very close second is the voters' choices for the candidate they identify as the worst. It was also learned that, after those top two data, very few voters have additional information to offer, and when they do, the additional information only very slightly improves the accuracy and consistency of identifying the correct winner.

The technique of simulating elections enables peering inside complex elections to understand what is going on. It was expected that errors would increase with small numbers of voters for virtually all types of voting method. That was confirmed. It requires about 1,000 voters to approach the lowest error rate of which a voting method is capable. That is why reported simulation data were acquired with 10,000 voters. There are many other aspects of elections that could be probed. It is hoped that more work (perhaps by others) will be carried out in the future.

As long as this section is, it explains only the most relevant results of the election simulation projects and does not even explain all of the data shown in the above spreadsheet. Complete information certainly is available in the papers footnoted above.

Returning now to one-candidate elections, let's consider whether it might be possible to improve accuracy by increasing the "resolution" of the strength of each voter's opinion. When voters use "Yes" and "No" or "Approve" and "Disapprove," they are using a three-value scale:

> +1 Yes or Satisfied
>
> 0 (Abstain, Don't Care, or No Vote)
>
> −1 No or Dissatisfied

Our hypothetical perfect voting method described above used a satometer to read voters' minds so as to obtain accurate and sincere information, presumably with a much higher resolution (the 201 values from −100 to +100). Until such a satometer is developed, voters will have to register their opinions on some sort of scale, just as is done for many surveys:

> +3 Extremely satisfied
>
> +2 Satisfied
>
> +1 Mildly satisfied
>
> 0 Neither satisfied nor dissatisfied (no opinion— the same as not voting)
>
> −1 Mildly dissatisfied
>
> −2 Dissatisfied
>
> −3 Extremely dissatisfied

The above seven-value scale enables voters to express more nuanced opinions than did the three-value scale. The candidate's score is the sum of the weighting numbers (shown next to each opinion level) for each voter's opinion. Of course, further increasing the resolution (using a scale with even more values) would further improve performance, but not very much. It turns out that most of the improvement that is possible can be obtained with only 5 or 7 values.

> **Example 1:** Suppose five voters voted: +3, +2, +2, −1, −3 = +3 (the candidate is elected).
> **Example 2:** Suppose five voters voted: +2, +2, +1, −3, −3 = −1 (the candidate is not elected).

Notice that there is something that might be considered strange about the second example: The majority did not rule! Using the Yes/No three-value scale, the first three of the voters would have voted "Yes," and the last two would have voted "No" (the candidate would have been elected). This demonstrates how additional information regarding the strengths of voters' opinions can sometimes improve decisions.

If a five- or seven-value scale can improve decisions, why, then, does AADV utilize only a three-value scale? It is because of insincere or strategic voting. It will not take the vast majority of voters long to figure out that if they want a certain candidate to win, they can make their ballot help that candidate most by always selecting the strongest satisfaction level, whether or not that truly represents their sincere opinion. Similarly, voters who don't want a candidate to win can most strongly weaponize their ballot against that candidate by selecting the strongest dissatisfaction level, whether or not that is their sincere opinion. Thus, in practice, many-value scales will strongly tend to function like three-value scales, so we may as well put all voters on the same footing and just use a three-value scale. Fortunately, the statistics of a large number of voters somewhat smooths over, or compensates for, the coarse granularity of the rating scale.

Is there any way (without a satometer) to obtain *sincere* opinions from voters on a scale having more resolution than a three-value scale provides? Maybe. It is worth discussing, but it might be very difficult to come up with a solution that would be widely acceptable. For that reason, anyone interested can find that discussion in appendix E.

Is it a problem if the majority does not always rule? (See example 2 above.) No. It is entirely consistent with the definition of the correct winner, which rightly depends only on the voters' net satisfaction. The "majoritarian rule" must be abandoned, at least as far as voting methods are concerned.

Accepting that there are instances where the majority should not rule is bound to cause many people severe heartburn. We are all inculcated from early childhood that, for a system to be "fair," the majority must rule. To provide some antacid for these people, it can be pointed out that many exceptions to the majoritarian rule are widely accepted. Most especially, we do not allow a majority to abrogate individual rights — the majority may not vote to execute someone just because the majority doesn't like a particular individual.

Furthermore, routine real-world decisions are made every day in which the majority does not rule, and everyone is completely cool with that. Look back at example 2, in which a two-voter minority prevails over a three-voter majority. Suppose that instead of being voters, the five people are friends deciding whether or not to have dinner at a fairly new restaurant. Three of the five friends have not been there and favor trying it, but they don't feel super strongly about it (+2, +2, and +1). The other two have already tried it once — one of them found a hair in the salad, and the other had a fly in the soup, so their opinions are strongly opposed (−3 and −3). The decision is made not to have dinner there, and all five are happy and comfortable with the minority overruling the majority! Majoritarian rule is generally a good thing, but it is overrated.

In Example 2, we saw a minority of 40% overrule a majority of 60%, but that was with only five voters. Majority rule diehards can take some solace in the fact that a 60% percent majority will substantially *never* be overruled when there are more than 1,000 voters. With the statistics of large numbers of voters, it is extremely unlikely that a minority of 48% would ever overrule a majority of only 52%.

Quite a few people realize that plurality is a horrid voting method. Most of them understand that one of plurality's fundamental limitations is that it does not collect sufficient information from voters for it to make good decisions. This has led many of them to advocate throwing open the floodgates and collecting as much data as possible from voters. But that, too, is a mistake.

As explained above, the Gibbard–Satterthwaite theorem proves that *no* voting method can be completely immune to manipulation and disruption by strategic or insincere voting, but attention can and should be paid to minimizing its susceptibility. It's always an important trade-off. One dimension of this problem (the strength of voters' opinions) was addressed just above. Another dimension concerns the number of candidates for which each voter may express an opinion. Some methods (AV, STAR, Score, etc.) accept voters' inputs for as many candidates as they wish — even all of them. That is too much data. Beyond an optimum point, additional data does not significantly improve decisions and can only be noise or strategic manipulation attempts which degrade decision making more than it helps.

With plurality, the most serious strategic voting problem is voting for the lesser evil, which means voters then cannot vote for their true first choice; therefore, the most important single piece of information needed to identify the correct winner is often missing. AADV removes that problem by allowing two approvals, which virtually guarantees that the voting method will receive that most critical datum — the voter's sincere first choice. If there is a "lesser evil," the voter can also vote for it with the second approval. Note that such a vote for a lesser evil may well be a strategic datum, but it is not as damaging as not having the voter's true first choice. When there is no lesser evil or when the lesser evil is also the second choice, the voter can use the second approval sincerely. The second approval also improves the method's ability to identify the correct winner when there is a large number of candidates.

AADV's disapproval can and should be used for the candidate the voter considers to be the worst. With this datum, the horrible blunder of electing a candidate opposed by a majority of voters can virtually always be avoided. Of course, a voter might deploy the disapproval to defeat the candidate believed to be the most serious threat to the voter's favorite. If that candidate is not also the one the voter thinks is worst, it would then be a strategic input. Remember that *no* voting method can be completely immune to strategic voting.

Conclusions

Continued use of the plurality voting method for public elections is causing far more damage than is generally realized; it needs to be replaced as soon as possible with a very much better method. No voting method can function adequately unless it allows voters to vote both for and against some candidates. The specter of strategic voting is the main spoiler that renders a perfect voting method impossible and degrades the performance of all voting methods; its effect must be minimized. All things considered, AADV is the best replacement for plurality that is known.

AADV provides such a large improvement that it can *qualitatively* improve elections. No longer will parties nominate highly divisive candidates, as they will garner lots of disapprovals and not fare well. Winners will be candidates with broad appeal and few negatives, which is far healthier. Thus, AADV will tend to reduce polarization instead of exacerbating it as plurality does. The election of candidates the majority of voters dislike will be a thing of the past. It will be a pleasure to vote sincerely for *the better candidate* instead of having to vote strategically for *the lesser evil*. The "playing field" should become more level, resulting in all candidates being able to receive reasonable media coverage and serious voter consideration. AADV continues to work extremely well when there are many candidates; this eliminates or greatly reduces the need for runoff elections and should be expected to elect more widely acceptable, less polarizing candidates in both primary elections and general elections.

Drawing Electoral Districts

States entitled to more than one representative in the US House of Representatives must subdivide their areas in some manner to define the electoral districts for each representative. The same is true in most states for the districts of their state houses and senates. The manner in which such districts are to be drawn could and should be a reasonably straightforward and well-defined procedure. Unfortunately, it is far from that. Although specifications and limits governing how districts may be drawn have been somewhat tightened over the years, including by the Voting Rights Act, numerous court cases, and state requirements, enough flexibility remains to be problematic.

It is the legislators in each state who have the primary responsibility to define districts. They have roundly abused that power to draw districts in a way that favors their own reelection or the election of another member of the same political party. This helps insulate politicians from their voters and is another problem that prevents elections from functioning as intended.

Gerrymandering versus the rules

Gerrymandering is the corrupt practice and process of drawing the boundaries of electoral districts to intentionally cause the election of candidates from a favored faction to be easier and more likely. The "favored faction" normally is a political party. The practice is not unique to the United States and is centuries old. Its use and notoriety increased in 1812, when it received its name. Governor Elbridge Gerry of Massachusetts approved a redistricting map of oddly shaped districts. A media cartoonist thought one of them resembled a salamander and dubbed it a "Gerrymander." From that came the process name, "gerrymandering," which stuck and quickly gained widespread acceptance and use.

"Packing" and "cracking" colloquially describe the process. First, draw as few districts as possible to contain the maximum possible number of opposition voters (packing). Second, distribute the remaining opposition voters so as to keep them in the minority in as many districts as possible (cracking).

The favored faction depends upon the party controlling the legislative body. Disputes are usually decided by state courts, which should be scrupulously neutral but frequently turn out not to be. Gerrymandering has been done to favor Democrats, to favor Republicans, and occasionally even to favor incumbents, with Democrats and Republicans actually cooperating to accomplish that.

Some restrictions on drawing districts

The oldest, most common, and most often obeyed restriction is that districts should be *contiguous* (connected). Surprising though it may be, municipalities and even voting precincts (the smallest jurisdictions) are not always contiguous themselves. This obviously can be at least a complication, if not an outright problem, when districts are drawn.

A more recent restriction is the *one-person-one-vote* opinion of the US Supreme Court (SCOTUS), which held that Congressional districts must have equal populations. The one-person-one-vote descriptor would lead one to think that this means an equal number of voters so that each vote would carry substantially the same weight. Many still argue that position, but SCOTUS clarified in *Evenwel v. Abbott* (2016) that it is the populations that should be equal, not the voters. This is derived from interpreting the equal protection clause of the Fourteenth Amendment to mean equal representation in Congress. The practice has been to use the total population. However, it would seem that the "population" should include only US citizens. The difference may not have been large in the past, but with the millions of illegal aliens that have flooded across the southern border, it may well become a highly contentious issue for the 2030 decennial redistricting, if not sooner!

Just how equal the district populations have to be is another issue. Guidance from SCOTUS is that a 10% error would clearly flag a problem. One might take from that that 5% might be acceptable. Some have taken it to the ridiculous extreme of attempting plus or minus one person. That is totally absurd since considerable change and shifting of population is a certainty over the ten-year period between redistrictings. If plus or minus one person were to be achieved as of a given census, it would be wrong a day or two later. Targeting a plus or minus 1% or less population error for redistricting should be more than sufficiently accurate.

The population of the United States is about 331,449,281people (2020 census). Therefore, the target population for each of the 435 congressional districts should be 761,952. Consider that the state of Wyoming has one Congressional district for its entire population of 576,851. That is a 24% error below the target population. Wyoming residents are *very* overrepresented in Congress, and there is absolutely nothing to be done about it! Thus, it would seem silly to be upset about a 1% error.

Very recently, SCOTUS ruled in Louisiana v Callais (2026) that race cannot be a consideration for defining districts. One would think that should have been obvious, but it wasn't. As is normal, the opinion was narrowly tailored to the case, but it surely could have been a giant step forward if the Court had pushed the envelope a bit and held that the number of citizens must be the *only* consideration.

State guidelines often say that district boundaries should be drawn to *minimize the division of political entities*, especially counties. However, satisfying the hard requirement for equal populations almost always necessitates the splitting of quite a few political entities. Apparently, it is acceptable to divide some political entities but not others.

Guidelines also usually state that districts should be *compact*. There are several ways to measure "compactness," but no standard has been adopted. True compactness can be hard to achieve along with all the other requirements. Since district boundaries must in some cases follow the boundaries of political entities, and those can be quite irregular, the application of a hard compactness measure tends to be problematic. Nevertheless, a lack of compactness is considered a strong indication that a district has been gerrymandered. The map below shows Pennsylvania Congressional District 7 as it was defined for the decade from 2011 through 2020.

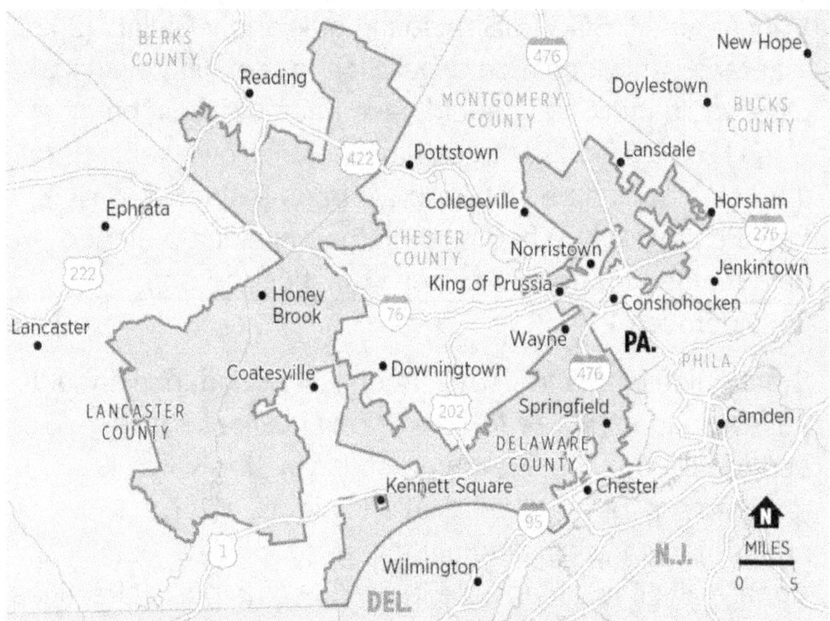

This district is obviously quite the opposite of compact and clearly appears to be a gross gerrymander job. It was so ridiculous that it was described as "Goofy kicking Donald Duck." It may be an extreme example, but it actually has plenty of serious competition all around the United States. Clearly, the current rules have not prevented gerrymandering.

If one of your takeaways from this discussion is that the proper drawing of electoral districts is a slippery and messy problem, you would be correct. It gets worse.

The impact of digital computers

Copious data bearing upon the definition of electoral districts are now readily available in digital form. This includes, but is certainly not limited to, the geocoded boundaries of all political entities with their populations, voter registrations, and voting history. There is a remarkable level of additional detail. Modern digital computers can quickly manipulate, analyze, and present such data in limitless ways and have had a major impact upon all aspects of drawing electoral districts.

Those who wear the black hats and gerrymander have been able to utilize these tools to achieve a new level of sophistication in their "art." They are able to do their packing and cracking more quickly and accurately. Also, it is usually possible to achieve the desired result while avoiding such grossly obvious district configurations as "Goofy kicking Donald Duck."

However, the guys who (claim to) wear the white hats have been able to use the same tools to detect and measure gerrymandering. It is possible to easily compute various indices of "compactness." Several such indices are based upon the ratio of the district's area to the square of the length of its enclosing boundary. There are others. Of course, analyzing the composition of each district in terms of voter registration, ethnicity, and many other parameters is also possible. Predicting and comparing how various districts would vote in future elections based upon voting history is another capability.

Some white hats advocate drawing districts so as to minimize the difference in "wasted votes" between factions. Wasted votes are defined as those over and above the votes that were required to elect a candidate plus those cast for losing candidates. This is a good and clever idea theoretically and in paper examples, but in practice, it would turn out to be based entirely upon Democrat and Republican registration and/or voting history. This completely disregards other parties and all those who have made it clear that they do not affiliate with either the Democrats or the Republicans. The non-Democrat/non-Republican "faction" is growing, is nearing a majority, and is much larger than either one of the two old, declining parties.

The white hats have been proposing various ways to rein in the black hats by deploying the tools they have developed. No such "controls" have yet been adopted. As we will learn later, that probably is a very good thing.

Finally, it has occurred to some that computers might be programmed to draw electoral districts automatically. Stay tuned.

Why Gerrymandering Has Not Yet Been Banished

Polling data regularly shows that more than 80% of citizens strongly want the practice of gerrymandering to be eliminated. That is just about as near to unanimity as polls ever get. Citizen organizations boasting more than 50,000 members have leaned hard on their legislators to fix the problem without success. How could gerrymandering still be alive and well across this country?

There are four main obstacles to banishing gerrymandering.

Those responsible for fixing gerrymandering do not want it to be fixed. The most obvious and difficult-to-surmount problem is the simple fact that the career politicians who populate the various state legislatures would need to take some action to abolish the practice. Despite what they may say, precious few of them are willing to give up the power to bias elections in their favor that drawing districts affords them.

Politicians are superbly skilled at making sure that things they don't wish to have happen never do. They are perfectly willing to help each other out with "cover" when needed. A representative under heavy pressure from constituents may even sponsor and introduce a bill to appease them, but the bill "so, so unfortunately" never makes it out of the committee to which it is referred — in spite of the sponsor's strenuous efforts, of course. In extreme cases, such a bill may be discharged from committee, but "unfortunately," the legislative session ends before it can be scheduled for a vote. Such bills have even been voted on and actually passed by one house of a bicameral legislature, only to meet a planned demise in the other chamber. This provides those who voted for and passed the bill "hard" (but false) evidence to demonstrate their great and sincere intentions to their constituents.

This is important information for anyone endeavoring to influence politicians; it can save many frustrating and fruitless years of work before a realization and understanding of how politicians operate is gained. There certainly may be some exceptions, but they are far too rare to have any beneficial effect. (Of course, *your* representative is one of the exceptions; just ask, and they will gladly explain why that is so.)

The remaining three reasons conspire to preclude a truly on-target solution for gerrymandering from ever being proposed.

A persistent bad idea: Citizens' commissions. It is a perennial proposal that an "unbiased" citizens' commission be assigned the responsibility for defining electoral districts. No one with the intelligence to define electoral districts is going to be completely unbiased. So the selection of commission members is problematic. Shielding them from nefarious "influences" is difficult at best. Even if they could be guaranteed to be absolutely impartial, does it make sense to put together a new group of people every ten years and have them reinvent the redistricting wheel? There likely would be next to no transparency into how they went about doing their work. If their work is disputed, it ends up back in the legislature or in the courts, with hard-to-predict and sometimes arbitrary results. Courts are not necessarily politically neutral. However, if we can't devise a better solution, such a commission might be some improvement over leaving the responsibility directly with the politicians.

An even worse misconception: Communities of interest (CoI). Many redistricting guidelines discourage having district boundaries divide political entities, such as counties. Not dividing political entities stems from a desire to not divide so-called "communities of interest," which are blithely presumed to coincide with political entities. There are two fundamental and *fatal* problems with the notion that communities of interest should be kept together: one is practical, and the other is based upon principle.

The fatal practical problem is that CoI is a very nebulous and hard-to-define concept. Different people will have radically different definitions. CoIs can be based on religious beliefs, political philosophies, single hot-button issues, and countless other criteria. CoIs as defined by different people can and will differ and overlap. Whose definition is to be adopted? CoIs can shift and change considerably from one election to the next, depending on the hottest issues of a particular election. Not dividing CoIs is a poorly defined and completely insoluble problem of impossible complexity. It's an exercise in futility that obviously cannot be solved by mere mortals, whether they are state legislators or citizens on a commission.

The fatal problem of principle is that the only possible valid reason anyone would want to keep a CoI together in an electoral district is so that a representative who "truly represents their interests" can be reliably elected. The only way that can happen is if the members of that CoI can outvote a smaller number of those in their district who do not share their same interests. That is the very definition of gerrymandering, which presumably we are trying to prevent! Oops.

We have lived for decades with districts that slice and dice counties in all manner of arcane ways. We have suffered *zero* harm caused by the division of political entities. However, we *have* suffered harm, *all* of which was caused by contriving districts to keep communities of interest together, where the communities of interest are those who share the philosophy of a specific political party!

In order to accurately achieve equal population districts, the splitting of many political entities is unavoidable. If splitting some is OK, it shouldn't be a problem to split others. One might validly argue that if some must be split, it would be fairer to split all.

An incorrectly stated objective: Electoral districts must be fairly drawn. The word "fair" should never be used in this context. It is highly subjective and means different things to different people. If the word is used, it is necessary to spell out in considerable detail the objective criteria to be used when judging fairness or unfairness.

This is rarely done, so confusion reigns and progress becomes impossible without agreement.

The correct statement of the objective should be that *electoral districts must be <u>impartially</u> drawn*. "Impartially" has an objective definition. In this context, it means that districts must be drawn in such a way that *does not confer any systematic advantage or disadvantage to any particular faction* (or community of interest, if you prefer).

All the muddled thinking surrounding redistricting has made it even easier for politicians to stay in the driver's seat and keep right on gerrymandering.

The Precinct-Preserving Splitline Procedure

Suppose it were possible to write down a clear and concise procedure to define electoral districts that is guaranteed to be completely impartial. Such a procedure could be followed by anyone, or even a computer, and the identical impartially drawn districts would be the result. And suppose that the same straightforward procedure could be used to quickly and impartially draw equal-population districts very accurately for any number of districts and for any state. The procedure could be enshrined in the Constitution, and there would be no need to reinvent the redistricting wheel every ten years. Redistricting could be done quickly, at a very low cost, and without all the strife. The process would be completely transparent, and anyone could independently verify that districts have been correctly drawn.

The good news is that such a procedure has already been written down and is available for use at any time. It is called the *precinct-preserving splitline* (PPS) procedure. It has just five steps. It will never divide voting precincts and always produces equal-population districts that are maximally compact. Here is the PPS procedure:

In all cases in which a political entity (e.g., a state) is entitled to elect multiple representatives, the procedure defined here must be used to determine the electoral districts for such representatives. Voting precincts will never be divided. The geographic boundaries of political entities (states, counties, municipalities, and precincts) and the total number of citizens for each voting precinct are the *only* data to be utilized. Note that party affiliation, voting history, race, gender, etc. may never be considered.

If the population of the political entity is *p,* and the number of districts to be drawn is *n,* the following (sometimes iterative) procedure is to be used.

1. If *n* is 1, no subdivision is necessary, and this is a final district. If *n* > 1, then define two new numbers, $i = n/2$ rounded up and $j = n/2$ rounded down. (Note that $i + j$ always equals *n,* and if *n* is even, *i* obviously will equal *j.*)

2. Draw the shortest possible (great circle) line dividing the area into two sections so that one section has a population equal to *p* multiplied by i/n, while the other section has a population equal to *p* multiplied by j/n. If there is more than one equally short line, use the line closest to a north-south orientation, and if there is still a tie, use the westernmost line. For irregularly shaped entities, it is possible that a line could exit and then reenter the entity; the length of the line is defined as the total distance between the two most distant points of intersection that lie on the boundary of the area being subdivided.

3. Make a list of just the voting precincts that have parts of their area on both sides of the great circle line just drawn in step 2. If 80% or more of any split precinct's area lies on one side of the line, assign each such precinct entirely to that same side of the line and remove it from the list. Sort the remaining list in the order of the largest population precinct to the smallest population precinct.

4. If there are any precincts on the list, assign the first (largest) entirely to the side of the line that needs the most people to hit its target population. Repeat this step until all precincts have been assigned.

5. The division of the original large area into two sections has now been completely defined. For each of the resulting two sections separately, go back to step 1 using the section's population for p and either i or j (whichever was associated with the section) as n.

Those not mathematically inclined will prefer to have a visual illustration of how the procedure works. The state of Pennsylvania will be utilized as an example.

If Pennsylvania had just one representative, there would obviously be nothing to do, and the entire state would be the one required district.

The map below shows Pennsylvania with two districts. The procedure draws them simply by finding the shortest possible line that divides the state into two sections, each having half the population. Nothing could be simpler or more impartial. If that line splits any voting precincts, a simple rule determines on which side of the line each split precinct is to be placed so as to maintain its integrity. Those familiar with this state will quickly understand that

the very heavy population density associated with
Philadelphia in the southeastern corner of the state causes
the splitline to occur (perhaps surprisingly far) toward the
eastern end of Pennsylvania.

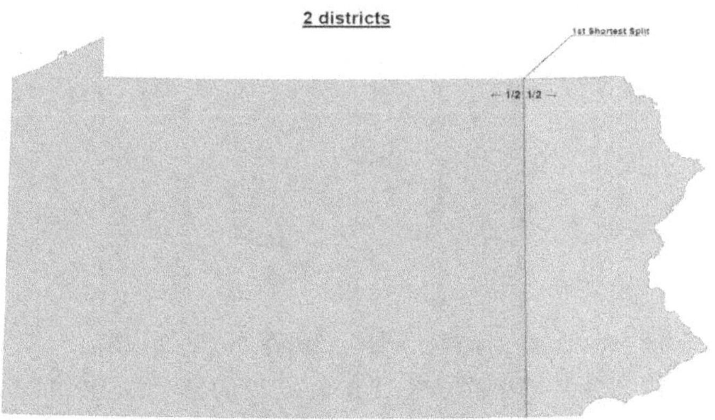

The next map (below) shows Pennsylvania with three
districts. The procedure tells us to first draw the shortest
possible line that divides the state into two sections, one
having 1/3 of the population and the other having 2/3 of
the population. Finally, the shortest possible line is drawn,
which divides the larger section into two districts, each
having 1/3 of the population. After each line is drawn, any
voting precincts that would have been split are placed
entirely on one side of the line or the other, as determined
by the simple rule that is part of the PPS procedure.

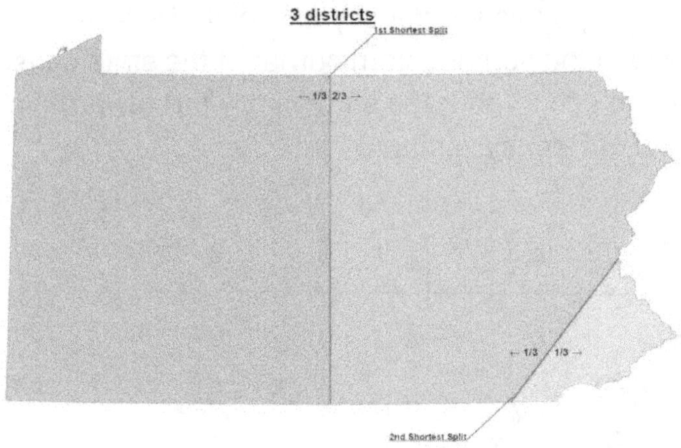

The next map (below) shows Pennsylvania with four districts. First, draw the shortest possible line that splits the state into two sections, each having half the population (the same line as drawn for the two-district case). Next, draw the shortest possible lines that split each of those sections into two districts, each having one-fourth of the population.

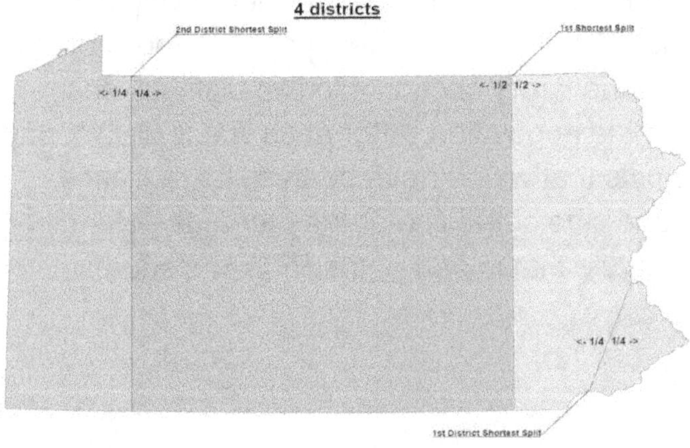

For *any* number of districts, just follow the procedure, and the required number of equal-population districts will be impartially drawn.

Now that the basic operation of PPS should be clear, we jump to the case of Pennsylvania with the seventeen districts that it actually has (map below).

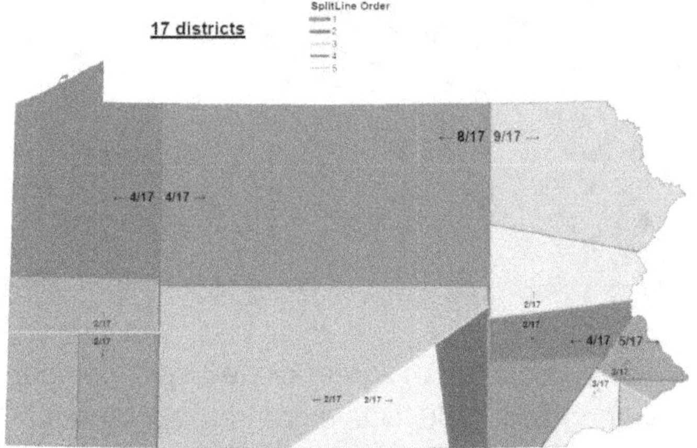

Notice that for seventeen districts, the first splitline now divides the state into two sections, one having 8/17 of the population and the other with 9/17 of the population. This is the first step in defining eight districts to the west of that line and nine districts on its east side.

Finally, just for pretty, below is a clean map of the seventeen districts without all the notations.

Drawing straight (geodesic or "great circle") splitlines can achieve equal population districts extremely accurately. However, preserving the atomicity of voting precincts will necessarily introduce some errors in population equality. Is this a problem?

Voting precincts are the smallest political subdivisions. They are normally defined by county governments for the purpose of facilitating and managing voting in elections. Their configuration depends upon the availability, location, and size of a polling place that can conveniently service the number of voters in the precinct. This will nominally range from 500 to 2,500 voters. Populations will be somewhat larger since not everyone is a registered voter.

Setting up voting precincts and maintaining them as populations grow and shift over the years and the availability of desirable polling locations changes is a lot of work for counties. Chopping up a large number of them all at once in a redistricting would be highly disruptive, and that is why PPS is designed to avoid doing that.

The procedure PPS uses to preserve precinct atomicity is designed to be simple, understandable, and easy to follow.

It also must not stumble when precincts are encountered that are not formed as a single contiguous area, because those do exist. It does attempt to minimize population errors, but an optimal solution in that regard is not guaranteed. Population errors should be less than half the population of the smallest precinct that a splitline divides. Thus, the population error percentage will depend upon the number of precincts contained by the district.

A large district, such as a congressional district, will contain on the order of two hundred precincts. Population errors for districts this large are completely inconsequential. Looking for a worst case, the Pennsylvania House has 203 representatives, requiring very small districts containing nominally thirty precincts. Here, the population errors should be less than plus or minus one percent. As previously reasoned, even this worst case should still be quite acceptable.

To summarize the advantages of using PPS for redistricting:
- PPS draws maximally compact equal-population districts — any number for any state.
- PPS is guaranteed to be absolutely impartial (renders gerrymandering impossible).
- PPS completely eliminates the influence of politicians (indeed, all people) from the process.
- PPS can be done by people or by computers.
- PPS is completely transparent — anyone anywhere can verify that districts are correctly drawn.
- The PPS procedure could easily be amended into the US or state constitutions.
- PPS provides a weak term-limiting effect as a byproduct.

- PPS turns decennial redistricting into a low-cost nonevent lasting about half an hour.

Acknowledgements. The basic splitline procedure was invented circa 2002 by Warren D. Smith. Basic splitline is ruthless and splits anything and everything in its path. Voting precincts are sliced and diced. At the lowest level, rules are provided for locating a split residence entirely on one side or the other of a splitline.

The PPS procedure was independently invented by Roy Minet circa 2009. PPS employs basically the same underlying splitline process but includes the precinct-preservation feature that renders it a practical solution.

The excellent map work was graciously contributed by geographic information systems professional Stephen Kruzik. His contribution is greatly appreciated.

Ballot Access Criteria

The Democrats and the Republicans fight each other intensely to obtain and retain political power. However, they happily cooperate to minimize any "outside" competition. They justify artificially high ballot access hurdles for others in the name of limiting "ballot clutter." Eliminating ballot clutter for them means eliminating their competition, but for voters, it means eliminating their choices. This is yet another example of how politicians in power have jimmied the functioning of elections to make it easier for them to remain in power. Not only do onerous requirements keep some candidates off the ballot, but they also sap the limited time and resources of those who do qualify, making it more difficult for them to mount an effective campaign.

Each state sets its own requirements that a candidate must meet in order to appear on the official general election ballot. Some charge a filing fee, some require a candidate to obtain voters' signatures on a nominating petition, and some require both. Nomination signatures can number as high as 60,000 and even more, depending upon the state and the office being sought. In substantially every case, ballot access requirements are considerably more difficult for any candidate other than those of the Democratic and Republican parties.

Pennsylvania goes to the trouble of setting up classes of political parties. Qualifying as a "major" party requires 15% of statewide voter registration, a ridiculously high hurdle. Even the Democrats and Republicans can't clear this hurdle in some other states. It is reasonable to require a modicum of public support to screen out hundreds of fifty-member organizations that flicker into and out of existence, but a tenth or even a hundredth of a percent of registration would accomplish that (0.1% is approximately 9,000 voters); 0.05% would be a good choice.

Voters should normally expect to have plenty of choices. Historically, there have been three or four candidates only in the higher profile races, but just two in many others, and one or even none in smaller local races. With a good voting method, five or seven candidates would be fine. More choices could be expected to strengthen the ballot's function as a voter qualification test.

All political parties should be treated equally. Ballot access requirements should be low and uniform for all political parties. The barriers should be lowered until six or more candidates begin to appear in a significant number of races.

Other Ways to Tilt the Playing Field

If a candidate is to have any chance of winning an election, the candidate's "message" must be gotten out to the voters. That inevitably requires money. The Republicans and Democrats have used their power to funnel taxpayer dollars into their parties' coffers, thus freeing up dollars to help their candidates.

In excess of $100 million of taxpayers' money goes to subsidize their gala quadrennial national nominating conventions. The media exposure their candidates receive at these conventions is also a big bonus worth a lot of dollars.

In states that have primary elections, more millions of taxpayer dollars are spent to pay for them. Candidates gain media exposure through these elections as well. Primaries are part of the nominating processes of private political organizations.

No taxpayer dollars should ever go to the support of any private organization, especially not a political party.

The League of Women Voters (LWV) has long performed a valuable public service by sponsoring free, fair, and open debates among all candidates for various public offices. Prior to 1988, this often included a much-watched series of televised debates between the candidates for President of the United States. However, the LWV withdrew when the Republican and Democrat candidates signed a memorandum of understanding dictating which candidates would participate (only the Republican and the Democrat) and who the moderators asking the questions were to be. The LWV released a statement saying, "The demands of the two campaign organizations would perpetrate a fraud on the American voter."

Since 1988, the Commission on Presidential Debates (CPD) has largely taken control of presidential debates. The CPD is a nonprofit corporation established by and completely controlled by the Democrat and Republican parties. "Third party" presidential candidate H. Ross Perot was allowed to participate in the 1992 debates and walked off with 19% of the popular vote. Since then, the CPD has set rules that have excluded all but the Democrat and Republican candidates from the debates. No one is expecting any candidate(s) other than Republicans and Democrats to appear in any presidential debate with either the Democrat or the Republican candidate for the foreseeable future.

The LWV still strives to organize fair and impartial debates for lower-level contests and to include *all* candidates who are running. They are to be commended for those efforts.

Much needs to be done to ensure free and fair elections that function as well as they can, should, and must.

9. Guaranteeing Election Integrity

What on Earth is wrong with the United States of America? Millions of people do not trust the results of elections. Worse, there seems to be no way to convince them that there was no fraud. Even if there were absolutely no fraud at all, this is nevertheless a serious problem. All the turmoil is highly disruptive and exacerbates polarization. It is also prima facie evidence that election integrity is inadequate.

It is critical that election integrity be so airtight that no one would think it necessary or worth their while to question the results. Citizens must be able to *implicitly* trust election outcomes. In the event that there should be any question, it must be possible to conclusively and rather quickly prove that the results are correct. One would expect this to already be the case here in the modern "cradle of democracy." Sadly, and dangerously, it is not.

Chapter 8 worked through the problems of designing elections to function as best they can. This chapter deals with the challenge of engineering all aspects of elections to guarantee airtight integrity. Integrity is, to a large extent, independent of functionality, but it is equally important.

Almost needless to say, if elections become cheating contests where the faction that cheats most effectively always wins, the republic is lost — perhaps permanently.

Pertinent History

Beginning with the nation's founding and continuing until the late twentieth century, the overall trend was toward improving election integrity. Concern for integrity was virtually universal. When problems were identified, serious attempts were made to remedy them. A seminal event was the realization in 1880 that it was quite important to guarantee a completely secret ballot to prevent coercion of voters and outright vote buying.

The high point of integrity was achieved during the several twentieth-century decades during which nearly all voters voted at polling places using hand-marked and hand-counted paper ballots, which ensured ballot secrecy. But since then, integrity has declined at an accelerating rate.

The decline, beginning in the late twentieth century and continuing into the twenty-first century, was initially caused by attempts to improve efficiency through the use of modern technology. Many such "improvements" were ill conceived and/or poorly tested and implemented. Examples are the famous "hanging chads" in Florida and the direct-recording electronic (DRE) voting machines that had no audit trails, so results could not be verified. It is dismaying that the DRE machines were ever put into service and a very good thing that they have been phased out.

Much more alarming is that the decline in integrity has accelerated in the twenty-first century, primarily caused by measures ostensibly intended to make it easier for people to vote and thereby increase participation. Chief among them are a radical expansion of absentee and mail-in voting, early voting, and the use of ballot drop boxes. All of these things not only add time, cost, and complexity to the administration of elections but also open the door for hard-to-detect and harder-to-prosecute fraud. Complete secrecy of the ballot is a casualty.

There is no indication that voter participation or turnout has actually been increased by such reckless measures, yet any attempt to tighten up procedures is met with howls of "voter suppression." The State of Georgia enacted some fairly minor improvements after the 2020 election and was accused of passing Jim Crow laws that would crush minority voter turnout. However, voter turnout for the 2022 election set all-time records, so obviously, there wasn't *any* suppression of voters.

It would be dead wrong to think that other modern democracies pay even less attention to the integrity of their elections than does the United States. Generally, the opposite is true. A very high percentage require positive (photo) ID for voters and either do not allow absentee voting at all or have extremely tight controls on it.

Mexico is a particularly interesting case because it had a history of election fraud but fairly recently implemented very strict reforms. Absentee voting was eliminated entirely. Voters are required to show an ID with a photo *and* their thumbprint! To prevent people from voting more than once, the thumbprinted digit is coated with indelible ink. Those crying "voter suppression" may be surprised to learn that instead of decreasing, Mexican voter participation actually increased from 59% to 68%, which exceeds the turnout for almost any US election. Evidently, more people made the effort to vote when they had high confidence that their votes actually were the only thing that determined the outcomes of elections.

Requirements for Airtight Integrity

The difficulty of achieving the necessary level of integrity must not be underestimated. The overall process and every part of it must be carefully thought through. Every step must be engineered to make fraud substantially impossible. It must be extremely difficult and highly unlikely that election results could be nefariously controlled or influenced by any special interest group. If fraudulent manipulation should nevertheless somehow occur, its detection, correction, and prosecution must be virtually certain. Furthermore, the evidence required for the successful prosecution of the perpetrators should be readily available.

It is not sufficient just to eliminate fraud. It is also critical that substantially all citizens have high confidence in all results — especially the losers of elections. Even if no fraud has occurred, it is still highly disruptive if some nevertheless question election outcomes. Citizens need to be able to understand how elections work. A lot of transparency is necessary to maintain high levels of confidence.

It is not terribly difficult to write down the essential requirements for solid integrity. All of these must be solid; there can be no weaknesses.

1. **List of registered voters.** An accurate, current, and complete list must be maintained of citizens who are eligible to vote and have registered to do so. The list must, of course, show the voting precinct to which each voter is assigned.
2. **Positive voter identification and control.** There must be positive control mechanisms and procedures which ensure that only those on the registered voter list are allowed to vote, and only once in each election. It must be guaranteed that the positively identified voter actually is the person who votes.

3. **Guaranteed secret ballot.** A completely secret ballot must be guaranteed for each and every voter. There are two aspects of ballot secrecy: 1) If voters wish to keep how they voted a secret, that certainly must be possible; 2) If voters want to prove to anyone else how they voted, that must *not* be possible.
4. **Durable audit trail.** There must be a durable audit trail (e.g., paper ballots) that forms the legal record of voters' intents and enables audits that can verify results quickly and with certainty.
5. **Transparency, supervision, and control.** Other than for any brief time when voters handle their own individual ballots, any and all handling of ballots (even including simple access to them) and/or official ballot tallies must be done *only* under the supervision of election officials and while observers from opposing factions are present and able to closely observe. In order to have confidence in elections, the public needs to have a good general understanding of how elections work and have as much visibility into them as possible. Remember the Jones Rule from chapter 8.
6. **Machine verification.** If any output of any machine can affect the election results, each and every such output must actually be checked and verified as a part of, and in the course of, normal operating procedure.

Managing Voter Registration Rolls

Airtight election integrity begins with accurate voter rolls. The Help America Vote Act (HAVA) of 2002 requires states to maintain a database of eligible voters who have registered to vote. The basics are elementally simple. When they register and after each voter's eligibility is verified, they are added to the database. Registered voters are removed from the database when they die or move to another state. Voters' records are updated when they move to a different voting precinct within the same state, and they are updated to indicate in which elections they have actually voted.

Registration

When someone applies to become a registered voter, it obviously is important to verify all of these things:

- Name: A living person by the name given actually exists.
- Citizenship: The applicant is a citizen of the polity.
- Age: The applicant is old enough to vote.
- Address: The address is not fictitious, the person actually is currently living there, and it is that person's permanent legal address.
- Uniqueness: The person is not already in the database (e.g., at a different address or under an alias).

It is a mistake to shortcut or hurry the verification process. Furthermore, accurate, current, and complete information must be available at each polling place on election day. Therefore, voters need to register a safe period (say, at least ten to fourteen days) before an election in order to be able to vote in that election.

Some advocate accepting registrations up to, and sometimes even on, election day; that is, someone could register and then vote essentially immediately. It should seem obvious to anyone that such a policy risks compromising integrity. Furthermore, there simply is no compelling need or problem that would be solved by allowing this. Timely registration is just one very minor additional requirement of good citizenship.

Purging.

Even if voter registration is under perfect control, registration rolls can still be incorrect. Voters do relocate occasionally, and they also die, sometimes without notice. Consequently, the database must be carefully purged and/or updated, either continuously or at least in advance of each election. (HAVA prohibits purging within 90 days of an election.) Historically, purging has sometimes been neglected, and there certainly are examples of fraud, in which impersonators have shown up to vote claiming to be voters who had recently passed away or moved.

One method of purging is called *voter caging*, in which registered US mail is posted to voters, and any returned as undeliverable is taken as evidence that the voter should be purged. Often, this was done by political parties for voters of opposing parties. When such voters did appear to vote, they were challenged. Voter caging is now illegal in several states.

It can be especially difficult to detect voters who have moved outside a state. To cover that base, a nonprofit organization called the Electronic Registration Information Center (ERIC) was formed with the sole mission of assisting states to improve the accuracy of America's voter rolls. ERIC maintains a database consisting of voter and motor vehicle registration data from all member states. Membership grew quickly at first, but then shrank leaving primarily "blue" states. Clearly, participation in a trusted service that reliably performs this function is important for all states.

Purging is not going to be perfect, but it needs to be very, very good if citizens are going to trust elections implicitly.

Occasional mistakes are inevitable. HAVA requires that any voters who appear at a polling place and find that they are not on the voter rolls be allowed to complete a provisional ballot. Provisional ballots are then counted or not counted based upon confirmation of voters' eligibility. This is a good solution, and very few provisional ballots should be needed.

HAVA also prohibits purging voters solely on the basis of their voting history. However, it does not seem at all unreasonable that, as a catchall, voters who have not voted in any election for, say, more than four years, be purged and mailed a notification that they must reregister. Ohio implements this policy but combines it with other checks to comply with HAVA.

Positive Voter Identification and Control

It is an obviously basic and critical integrity requirement that only registered voters be permitted to vote and that each be limited to one vote per election. When voters check in at a polling place, their names are looked up in the voter rolls to be certain they are entitled to vote. As soon as a voter is approved to vote, the records are marked to show that he or she has voted in the current election.

It is equally important to verify that voters are, in fact, who they say they are. The simplest, easiest, and most widely acceptable way to accomplish that is for the voter to show a photo ID (e.g., a driver's license). Requiring a photo ID to vote is nearly universal among all modern democracies. The United States, where only about half the states require a photo ID, is a glaring exception.

A blue-ribbon commission, known as the Carter-Baker Commission, was formed in 2005 to study US elections and recommend changes and improvements. It was jointly chaired by former president Jimmy Carter (a Democrat) and former secretary of state James Baker (a Republican). Chief among the commission's very sensible recommendations was the universal use of photo IDs.

Polls consistently show that over 80% of citizens believe that a photo ID should be required to vote. That is as close to unanimous as polls ever get. Wherever this has not been made law, it clearly is the fault of the elected politicians. Their specious excuse is that this would place an unnecessary burden on voters and result in voter suppression!?

States are beginning a transition from the traditional bulky paper "poll books" of registered voters to electronic poll books. A possible alternative to a photo ID might then be simply to snap a picture of each voter as they check in. The photo would be stored in the voter registration database and compared to photos of the voter from previous elections that would appear on the screen. This would be fast and painless, and it would place absolutely no burden on voters. It would be interesting to hear what the excuse would be for not implementing it.

Wherever photo IDs are not required, the predominant fallback mechanism employed is some form of signature verification. *Signature verification cannot be relied upon for positive voter identification.* Worse, it creates a false sense of legitimacy and security. It is worth thinking about this carefully to understand why this is so.

The first problem is that people simply do not always sign their names the same way. Signatures can change radically as people age, suffer from arthritis, or perhaps undergo injury or surgery on their writing hands or wrists. The appearance of someone's signature can be significantly affected by the texture of the surface upon which they are writing, the position they are in, whether they are hurrying, how they feel, how much Starbucks coffee they have drunk, and many other similar factors. Trained handwriting experts sometimes have difficulty and, in any case, require some time (at least 20 or so seconds of scrutiny) to determine whether two signatures match.

During an election, voters frequently must be processed quickly. The poll workers certainly are not trained handwriting experts. Poll workers who would even have the confidence to challenge a voter's signature for a mismatch are few and far between. This alone renders the process unreliable, and that assumes that the poll worker actually attempts to verify the signature. The next time you check in to vote, watch the poll worker and see if any effort at all is made to compare signatures. It is a rather safe bet that zero time will be spent verifying the signatures of the majority of voters.

Thus far, we have assumed that voters are voting at a polling place. There, it is at least possible to implement positive voter identification. *It is also possible and easy to be sure that the voter who checked in is actually the person who votes.*

But suppose mail-in ballots are being used. Since voters are not mailed in along with their ballots, positive voter ID is simply not possible. As we already know, signature matching is a crap shoot. Imagine tabulators processing thousands of ballots as quickly as possible; not much time to study signatures. Even if signature verification were not a problem, there still is no way to know for sure that the person who signed the ballot is the person who marked the ballot.

Consider also that workers verifying signatures in a large processing operation could be a vulnerability. A strongly partisan worker processing ballots from a municipality known to vote heavily for the opposition might (consciously or even subconsciously) reject more signatures. Of course, when processing a municipality known to strongly favor the worker's party, it might be a lot harder to find any problems with signatures. Such a subtle bias could never be reliably detected, let alone successfully prosecuted. Whether it ever actually happens or not, some will worry that it may have. It is the kind of fuzzy vulnerability that just cannot exist if citizens are ever going to trust results implicitly.

Clearly, there is no way mail-in voting can be made to satisfy this requirement. That should be sufficient reason to prohibit its use. However, we will learn later that mail-in has even greater problems with some of the other requirements.

Durable Audit Trail

There must be a durable audit trail that forms the legal record of voters' intents and supports audits that can verify results. The customary, and still quite satisfactory, way of accomplishing this is with a paper ballot that is a record of each voter's choices. Citizens need to be confident that, if there is any question about the results of an election, there is a guaranteed way to resolve it. An audit or recount will either verify the original result or provide a way to correct it. Audit trails (including all pertinent or related records) should be sealed and saved for at least two years after each election.

It is extremely difficult to audit an entire election at one time; it's hard to manage, and there is a high probability of mistakes occurring during the audit. It will be hard for everyone to have complete confidence in the audit. This is yet another strong reason in favor of voting at polling places where only about 1,000 or so ballots must be handled. Such a small, isolated unit can be audited quickly and with very high confidence. The total time and effort to audit all polling places likely would not be more than would be required to *accurately* audit the entire election as a whole unit.

Even if election outcomes are not challenged, it is a good standard practice to audit a small number of randomly selected precincts. If significant problems are discovered, the audit can be expanded, perhaps to a total recount. Another similar approach is a risk-limiting audit (RLA). The statistical basis for RLAs is beyond the scope of this book but is readily available elsewhere. The concept is to audit a small number of randomly selected ballots to gain an acceptably high level of confidence that the outcome of a given race is correct. Close races will require a larger ballot sample than races with large margins of victory in order to achieve the same confidence level. If the ballot sample does not support the results of the race, additional ballots need to be examined, which may lead to a complete recount. RLAs are now required in a few states.

Of course, suspicions or accusations of fraud should be decisively resolvable by audits. Audits assure election integrity, discourage fraud, and their availability builds citizens' confidence. One of the worst blunders in this regard was the (one has to believe thoughtless) adoption of the previously mentioned DRE voting machine. The only good thing about the DRE is that it resulted in the nearly universal passage of laws requiring durable audit trails.

Guaranteeing a Completely Secret Ballot

Of course, *all* of the requirements are essential to attaining adequate election integrity. However, guaranteeing a completely secret ballot is both critically important and quite difficult to achieve in practice. It must not be possible for any person other than the voter to know for sure how that voter voted. The easier part is making it possible for voters who do not want anyone to know how they voted to keep that information secret. The hard part is making it impossible for voters to prove to someone else how they voted, *even if they want to do so.*

Everyone readily agrees that they should be able to keep how they voted a secret if they wish. However, the second equally important secret ballot requirement tends to be forgotten. The reason voters must not be able to prove to anyone else how they voted, *even if they want to do so*, is that being able to prove how they voted exposes voters to possible coercion to vote a certain way, and it flings the door wide open to vote buying. And yes, those things can and do happen if it is possible.

Coercion could be as simple as a domineering spouse dictating how their mate should vote or just standing over them, watching as they fill out their mail-in ballot. Vote buying, however, is a greater threat and has myriad variants. South Carolina was the last state to recognize the importance of the secret ballot and adopted it in 1950 because of significant vote buying. The percentage of people voting dropped by about 12% when the gravy train ended, strongly suggesting that fraud had been even more widespread than thought.

France banned absentee ballots completely in 1975, when rampant vote buying was discovered on Corsica. It should be totally obvious that voters can easily prove how they vote with absentee or mail-in ballots simply by showing someone their ballot or by photographing it. There is no way this can be effectively controlled. Although there are many other very good reasons for not allowing mail-in voting, the lack of ballot secrecy is the most obvious and dangerous. Mail-in voting renders vote buying both extremely easy and very hard to detect. A completely secret ballot is the only way to stop vote buying in its tracks. No one is going to pay someone else to vote a certain way if it is impossible to verify that the vote was actually cast as agreed.

When voters vote at a properly staffed and managed polling place, there is at least a good chance that a completely secret ballot can be guaranteed. When voters vote in the privacy of a voting booth and then directly drop their ballots into a ballot box, each voter is the only one to see his or her own ballot. If voters wish to keep how they voted secret, they are certainly able to do that. But what if a voter *wants* to prove to someone else that they voted a certain way? Thanks to progress and modern technology, that's a lot easier to do and harder to prevent than it used to be.

Imagine a vote purchaser intercepting voters in the parking lot on their way into a polling place. After negotiating the price, the purchaser hands the voter a cell phone containing instructions on how to vote or just a picture of a sample ballot filled in the way the voter is to vote. The voter uses the same phone to snap a pic of their actual completed ballot while in the voting booth. The voter returns the phone to the buyer, the buyer verifies that the voter voted as promised and hands the voter a cash payment. This type of operation might be relatively easy to detect and prosecute, but individual voters using their own cell phones clearly would not.

It must be illegal for anyone to possess any device capable of capturing and/or transmitting an image or facsimile of a ballot while in the voting booth or ballot box area of a polling place. Penalties must be stiff, even for first offenses, and enforcement must be taken seriously. Notices should be prominently posted. Provisions could be made for people to check their phones at the door and reclaim them on the way out. Alternatively, each voter's phone could be locked inside a bag that the voter carries along while voting, and the bag would be unlocked after the voter's ballot has been deposited into the ballot box

Note that federal and state laws in all fifty states already prohibit vote buying. There are stiff penalties for both the buyer and the seller, but these laws alone are not going to prevent this type of fraud, especially with mail-in ballots. When political organizations are willing to spend more than $100 million just with the hope of influencing one senate race, the motivation to buy votes as a more surefire and lower-cost alternative is obviously intense. Vote buying needs to be made as impossible as possible or it is going to happen, regardless of its legality. The lessons learned in the past need to be remembered and heeded.

Transparency, Supervision, and Control

Everything about elections should be as transparent as possible — except, of course, how any specific voter voted. Such transparency would be of little value, however, if voters did not understand how elections work. Therefore, it is important to comply with the Jones rule explained in the previous chapter: ***Everything about elections should be understandable by a reasonably bright high school student.*** Voters cannot be expected to trust anything they cannot understand.

Every step of every process must be carefully designed to make fraud substantially impossible. It must be extremely difficult and highly unlikely that election results could be nefariously controlled or influenced by any special interest group. If fraudulent manipulation should nevertheless somehow occur, its detection and correction must be virtually certain. Furthermore, the evidence required for the successful prosecution of the perpetrators should be available.

Every operation (other than voters' brief handling of their own ballot) that could affect an election's outcome must be supervised by trained election officials and must be closely observable by observers from opposing factions — also, preferably, the public. It should be obvious that there must be no exceptions to this because even one exception provides opportunity for fraud and is enough to engender doubt and destroy trust. The following are some of the operations that must be so controlled and observable:

- Identification of voters and verification of their eligibility to vote
- Guaranteeing that the voter who checked in is the person who completes the ballot

- Any handling of ballots, including counting and verification
- Any in-process transportation or storage of ballots between operations
- Any handling, transportation, or storage of ballot tally information prior to its publication

Achieving and maintaining the required level of supervision, control, and transparency is difficult. The difficulty increases rapidly as the time period over which controls must be maintained is made longer. The difficulty also increases rapidly as the spatial area, the number of people, or the complexity of the operations increases. It follows that all such critical operations should be carried out in a small area, with the fewest people, and over the shortest possible time period.

This requirement, as is true for some of the others, is best met by having a manageable number of voters vote in a properly staffed and managed polling place: The physical setup is prescribed, and carefully thought-through procedures are followed as established by law. An official judge of elections is in charge. Poll workers assist. Watchers from opposing factions can watch. Polling place personnel are trained on the correct procedures.

Video surveillance of polling places is a good idea — the video could even be livestreamed and recorded — and a copy could be sealed and preserved with the ballots. Obviously, it must not be possible to read the choices on any ballot, but observing the movement, flow, and activities of people could be quite helpful evidence in the event of audit discrepancies or suspected fraud. Video surveillance also is a strong deterrent to any would-be fraudsters and provides a way to guarantee that polling place procedures are adhered to.

Although it should be unnecessary to restate, it must be strongly emphasized that mail-in voting *cannot* meet these requirements. Mail-in ballots float around the countryside for at least days — more likely weeks. They are handled by an unknown and unknowable number of unknown people. When returned, they are handled by more people who validate and count them. The opportunities for serious problems are too numerous to discuss. Some of the ways to manipulate elections that are possible when perpetrators have plenty of time and no one is looking are very hard to detect and harder still to prosecute.

Difficulties with transparency, supervision, and control explode with mail-in ballots and with large mail-in ballot-counting operations, especially ones spanning multiple days and requiring safe overnight storage and lots of handling of ballots. Even if, miraculously, no fraud occurred, fraud would often be suspected, and there would be no conclusive way to prove that it didn't happen. Citizens could not *implicitly* trust their elections, which would be endlessly disruptive — exactly as it now is.

Machine Verification

People do not trust machines. They are quite correct to not trust them. No one can guarantee that any machine at least as complicated as a paper stapler will work correctly 100% of the time.

Modern machines are far more complex than staplers. They almost inevitably depend upon a digital computer for their operation. Digital computers are extremely complex, and worse, they are controlled by complex software (or firmware) that can be modified fairly easily. Software can be defective; that is, contain bugs (mistakes), which can cause malfunctions. Bugs are accidents, but software can also be intentionally modified in subtle and hard-to-detect ways that could fraudulently affect election results.

The customary way to ensure that machines used for voting have a very high probability of working correctly through an entire election day is to rigorously test them before approving them for use. State agencies are responsible for certifying voting machines. Such certification processes may have been satisfactory for the older and simpler electromechanical voting machines.

However, certification in advance is not at all sufficient for modern computer-controlled equipment and can only create a false sense of security. Of course, somewhat rigorous reliability testing in advance is still necessary to avoid the possibility of disruptive system failures on election day. However, it can no longer adequately assure integrity for two reasons.

First, it is possible to engineer a system that will pass testing with flying colors and yet still manipulate voting on election day. Recall the fairly recent case in which Volkswagen scurrilously engineered the software that operated its vehicles to detect when its emissions were being measured. The software tweaked engine operation to minimize emissions during testing. At all other times, the software operated the engine to achieve maximum performance, even though the emissions then exceeded legal limits.

Second, and more likely, a machine's software could be secretly replaced or modified at any time after certification testing. This could happen during machine storage, transportation, or whenever it is connected to a network, either before or even on election day. (Network connections can be wireless and invisible.) There would be no obvious evidence of such a software modification. Of course, it should be possible to develop rules and procedures that could minimize the opportunities for fraud and provide some reasonable assurance of machine integrity. However, a significant number of voters are bound to question machine integrity, and there is no quick and conclusive way to prove to them that all machines were indeed functioning properly during an election.

Unfortunately, there is yet one more problem standing in the way, and it's a serious one: the Jones rule. There simply is no way that a large majority of voters are ever going to be able to understand these highly complex machines. A lack of understanding is a lack of transparency that inevitably engenders a lack of trust.

Does all this bad news mean we have to forego the huge advantages that modern complex machines can provide? No. It just means we have to be extremely careful to properly engineer the overall election system and process of which machines are a part. We need a new rule to govern this situation.

> **Each and every output of a machine that could affect the outcome of an election must actually be checked and verified routinely as a part of normal operating procedure.**

If every machine output is indeed verified, we can guarantee that any mistake, whether just a machine malfunction or an attempt to fraudulently manipulate the election, definitely *will* be caught and can be corrected.

This is something that all voters can understand and trust. It takes the machine's complexity (and all its unavoidable risks and inscrutability) right out of the picture and renders it irrelevant.

Checking and verifying each and every machine output (that could affect election results) sounds so onerous and burdensome that it could obviate the advantages of machine automation. That is not necessarily so. One system complying with this new rule already exists: Election Manager. It awaits further testing and acceptance into service, but here are the basics of how it works:

Voters vote in the customary private voting booth, choosing and selecting candidates for each race using a computer touch screen. After making, changing, and checking their selections (as often as desired), voters tap a "Cast Ballot" button to finalize their ballots. An image of the ballot appears on the screen for an "Are you really, *really* sure?" final check. When the image is approved, a clear and simple plain paper ballot is printed showing the candidates that were selected in each race. It looks just like the ballot as it was displayed on the screen. There is nothing on the ballot that the voter cannot read and understand.

Voters are instructed to read and carefully re-check their ballots. If there is any problem with the ballot, voters can tap a "Ballot NOT Printed Correctly" button, which will summon the judge of elections and a poll worker to immediately resolve whatever the issue may be. If the ballot is correct, the voter taps the "Ballot Printed Correctly" button. Each voter then takes the paper ballot that they have verified to the customary ballot box and deposits it there on the way out of the voting booth area.

When the polling place closes, the computer produces
both totals of all ballots for the polling place and a text file
that is a list of every ballot cast but in a random order,
including the selections made on each ballot. The text file
is in a well-known, widely understood, and widely used
format called Extensible Markup Language (XML). XML
files can be read by both humans and computers. The
specifications for this file are published information. The
XML ballot list has triple redundancy for reliability and
quadruple tamper protection. There is no way to prevent
someone from tinkering with or modifying such a file, but
the tamper protection means that any modification(s) *will*
be obvious and easily detected as a matter of routine
procedure.

Each polling place posts its list of ballots publicly on the
Internet ASAP after closing. There is no way anyone can
tell which voter cast any particular ballot; there is no way
any voter can prove which ballot is theirs; so complete
ballot secrecy is guaranteed. A computer anywhere can
read and tally the ballots from all polling places. Election
Manager can tally results and produce complete reports.
Anyone anywhere can verify the tally, even by a tedious
hand count, if desired. Complete and final election results
are almost immediately available when the polls close —
including tallies of all write-in votes.

There are only three outputs from the machine that can
affect an election outcome. The first is the paper ballot that
was printed for each voter. Each and every one of those is
immediately checked and verified by the voters
themselves. The second is the totals report for the
precinct; it can be verified by totaling the ballots from the
ballot box. Third is the list of ballots (and the selections on

each). If necessary or desired, the ballot list can be positively verified by matching each ballot on the list up one-to-one with the ballots from the ballot box. (Election Manager can help expedite this process.) This can be done immediately upon closing by the polling place crew before sealing a copy of the file with the ballots, or it can be done later or repeated as part of an audit.

This system has many advantages:

- Every machine output is actually checked and verified as part of the normal procedure. Therefore, anything incorrect can and will be detected and can be corrected. That is true whether the problem was caused by attempted fraud or just a plain old bug or machine malfunction.
- Voters can easily understand the overall procedure. Thus, they are able to implicitly trust election outcomes without having to understand anything about how the machine functions internally.
- The complete secrecy of every ballot is guaranteed.
- Transparency is maximized. All polling place procedures are simple and understandable. Every choice on every ballot from every polling place is made publicly available immediately after the polls close. Therefore, election results can be verified by anyone anywhere using any method. There are no large or lengthy counting operations to control and supervise.
- Efficiency is greatly improved by automation, and the window of opportunity for fraud is minimized. Complete and final election results, including a tally of all write-in votes, can be available a half hour after the polls close.
- The currently available system supports a choice of voting methods. Either the plurality or the far superior

AADV (Approve/Approve/Disapprove Voting) method can be selected for each race (by officials when setting up the election, of course; not by voters). More detail regarding the Election Manager system can be found in appendix F.

Note also that Appendix G provides a one-page summary of the three most important election functionality fixes and the three most important election integrity fixes. This is a perfect outline for discussions with your state and federal representatives! Leave a copy with each of them. Brandish a copy of this book. Repeat visits often.

Many mistakes have been made that were caused by the improper use of technology for voting systems. However, there is every reason to utilize the most modern technology if it is carefully and properly done. In fact, elections could have and should have been benefiting from such automation for the past quarter-century. Properly done, it can improve not only election efficiency but also election transparency and integrity.

10. Feeding a Government

A government of any size and for any purpose will require resources to sustain its existence and fund its activities. Governments do not possess or create any wealth of their own, so their only alternative is to confiscate some of the wealth earned, owned, and possessed by their citizens (i.e., taxes). That's tantamount to theft. It is a clear violation of the NAP.[8]

Ancaps argue against any and all forms of government for two reasons. First, taxation is theft and violates the NAP. Second, there is a serious risk that any centralized power structure will eventually break free of restrictions and controls placed upon it and become an oppressor of the citizens.

One has to grant the ancaps that the evidence to date certainly supports their concerns rather strongly. However, hope springs eternal. A lot has been learned since the first and somewhat successful attempt in 1787, both in terms of fundamental knowledge and understanding and from observation of the failure modes and weak points of the current US Constitution. It seems a good, or at least reasonable, bet that a fresh attempt can be successful *if it is well and properly executed*. The highly risky bet is whether it can be accomplished under the current deplorable and deteriorating state of affairs.

---

[8] See chapter 6, the Non-Aggression Principle (NAP): Nobody may deal fraudulently with anybody else, and nobody may *initiate* the use of force (or the credible threat of force) against anybody else for any reason, excepting that minimum amount of force which may be necessary to enforce this non-aggression principle.

It is the task of this chapter to dispel the first of the ancaps' objections: the taxation bugaboo. The perhaps obvious first step will be to identify significant sources of revenue that can be obtained without theft or violation of the NAP. That should knock the problem down to one of a much smaller magnitude. If the acceptable revenue sources must be supplemented to some extent with (ugh) more traditional taxes, we can select the least objectionable of them and then explain how they, too, may be justifiable.

It should be clear that the numbers in this chapter are rough order-of-magnitude estimates only. The numbers are not the point. The purpose is to show how the problem of funding government can be approached and most acceptably resolved.

Usage Fees

The most innocuous revenue source is payments for goods or services rendered by the government. However, fees can only be levied for goods and services that do not suffer from the economic free rider problem; that is, the users of the goods or services need to be separately identifiable, and usage can be denied without payment. The fee-for-service opportunities are limited because the bulk of justifiable government services do suffer from the free rider problem. The poster child free rider service is national defense. Defending the nation defends everyone, and there is no way to deny national defense to someone who does not wish to pay for it. Unfortunately, it is one of the largest costs.

Transparency requires that governments furnish data and documents relating to their activities upon demand. This certainly is a service for which governments can and should charge a fee. Such charges should be set to recover only governments' reasonable cost of producing documents. Compared to the total revenue required, it is hard to even justify this short paragraph to mention these fees.

Fees for the use of public parks and facilities should also be levied. In these cases, the pricing should be set to match the demand to the capacity of the facility. This revenue stream will also be quite small compared to the total revenue required.

A much larger budget item is the construction and maintenance of roads, bridges, and tunnels. Fuel taxes have been a reasonable approximation of a user fee for those using roads. Especially considering the uncertainty as to what will power vehicles of the future, a more direct approach is to be preferred.

Vehicles wishing to use the roads should be assigned a "dollars per kilometer" rate proportional to their gross vehicle weight. Technology is readily available that can track in detail how many kilometers each vehicle has traveled and on precisely which roads. However, governments must be prohibited from gathering such details about citizens' whereabouts and travel without first obtaining a warrant. It would be better to just collect the fee periodically (annually or semiannually) for the total miles traveled by each vehicle, then allocate it among the appropriate governments based on a formula adjusted to properly cover their costs.

US federal, state, and local road budgets total approximately $300 billion annually, so this is a very substantial usage fee.

Land Value Tax

The concept of the commons was developed in chapter 6 in the discussion of the right to private property ownership. The commons comprises all things of value to which it is impossible to hold an alodial title. The most prominent example is land. The term *commons* is derived from the fact that all parts of the commons are owned in common by all currently living individuals.

A tax levied on land, a *land value tax* (LVT), is therefore not a tax on owned property. Actually, it is not a tax; it must be viewed instead as a rental for the land. The rental is due to all the common owners of the land for the privilege of allowing its current possessor temporary control of the land and the benefits of using it. An LVT is assessed *only* on the value of the *unimproved* land. Improvements thereon are never taxed. As such, a land value tax is a usage fee that is entirely justifiable and certainly not theft.

In order to discuss the mechanics of an LVT, we need to think of the value of land in terms of the free market rent it would fetch. This is because imposing an LVT will affect the price for which the land can be sold. The price is determined by capitalizing the rent. That is, the price equals the amount of capital required to generate an amount of interest equal to the rent.

For example, if a parcel of land can be rented for $900 per year and the current interest rate is 3%, the price the land would fetch is $30,000 (3% of $30,000 yields $900 of interest per year). But if the owner of this land is liable for $300 per year in taxes, the net rent left for the owner will be only $600. Thus, the price for which it can be sold will be only $20,000 (capitalizing the $600 at 3%). Clearly, it would be disruptive to collect too high a percentage of the land rent as a tax. Prices would collapse, and some land might even remain unutilized. To maximize the benefit to its owners, all land should be put to the most productive possible use.

How the value of land is to be determined is worth considering carefully. If all the rent were to be collected as tax, land prices would collapse to zero, and there would be no free market for land. Land values and rents would need to be set by government assessors based on — what? That plainly is not a good plan! The best way to establish land values is certainly through healthy free market mechanisms of supply and demand.

Setting an LVT at the proper rate actually can produce some significant economic benefits. Holding land out of productive use would be discouraged, while investing in improvements would be encouraged, rather than discouraged, as is the case with conventional property taxes. The proper rate is much debated. Some say that the possessor owes the entire rent. Philosophically, that may be true, but to preserve the advantages of a normal, stable, and orderly real estate market for land, it is advisable to target a collection of only about half the rental.

As explained, the LVT rate, the interest rate, and the price of the land are all interrelated. That relationship can be stated mathematically in two useful forms:

i = Interest rate as a decimal fraction

p = LVT rate as a decimal fraction of the land price

r = LVT rate as a decimal fraction of the land rent

$$ r = \frac{p}{p+i} \qquad\qquad p = \frac{ir}{1-r} $$

If the plan is to collect half of the rent, we can plug in 0.5 for the r parameter in the second equation. Simplifying, we have $p = 0.5i / (1 - 0.5) = i$. That is, the LVT rate will be equal to the current interest rate, which is convenient.

An interest rate of 3% has been used in the examples because it is a typical "real" interest rate. We are used to higher actual interest rates because we lack sound money. The value of the dollar has been shrinking (losing value) at rates that have typically varied from 2% to 10% per year for decades. Misleadingly, this is called *inflation*. No one can loan money at 3% interest when the loan will be paid back with dollars that are worth less, so inflation must push up interest rates, and it certainly has done so. Economies function best with sound money, and for the purposes of this discussion, we will assume that the inflation problem has been solved and we have sound money (see chapter 12).

There are about 2 billion acres of land in the United States. Some of it is in downtown Manhattan and valued at millions of dollars per acre, while much of it is in vast expanses valued at $100 or $200 per acre. Guesstimating an average value of $15,000 per acre and applying a 3% LVT rate would yield in the neighborhood of $900 billion per year of revenue. All land should be subject to the LVT.

Unfortunately, the defense budget is currently about $900 billion. Even cutting everything possible back to "minimal state" levels likely would leave us a bit short of revenue, and, of course, the state and local governments will need to be funded as well. Some economists advocate higher LVT rates, and some estimate higher average values per acre. However, limiting LVT to a safer, more reasonable rate strongly suggests that we will need additional sources of revenue.

So far, we have considered only the most obvious part of the commons: land. There is a fixed amount of land that existed prior to the arrival of people and that can neither be created nor destroyed. But there are some other resources that meet these same criteria; the electromagnetic spectrum and the number of geosynchronous earth orbits for satellites are good examples. A rental can be charged in the same way for the use of these resources. A guesstimate is that this could add perhaps $200 billion per year.

Severance Taxes

There are nonrenewable natural resources in the ground (oil, gold, uranium, methane gas, etc.). These were not created by the labor of people and so constitute part of the commons. However, there is no way to charge rental fees for natural resources. They are extracted and used. They are divided up and dispersed in many directions that are impractical to track, and/or they are chemically changed or combined with other elements to form new compounds.

The best that can and should be done is to levy a *severance tax* on such common resources. Severance taxes on the depletion of such resources can be justified by the same reasoning that applies to land. As before, we need to limit this tax to a reasonable rate, say, 36% of the amount of the first sale to an end user, to be paid upon sale. Employing the SWAG[9] technique, suggests this could provide about an additional $350 billion per year of revenue.

Gambling

Most states currently operate lotteries, with total profits of about $35 billion annually. Although perhaps small potatoes, there is no reason not to include this source of revenue. Participation is, of course, entirely voluntary.

Donations

It may be amusing to think of a government GoFundMe page, but why not? It's obviously voluntary. There is really no way to know how much revenue might be raised; even the SWAG technique fails. With a minimal state and far lower taxes, well-off people may be more willing to contribute, and this would definitely encourage and facilitate their doing so. They may have a more favorable view of their government when it is limited and strongly focused on doing only the things it properly should do.

A more significant positive factor is the free market economy. The rate of wealth creation will increase substantially when the drag of all government meddling is removed. Citizens will have more wealth, but they very well may prefer to support private charities rather than the government.

---

[9] Scientific wild-assed guess.

Rights Infringement Through the Commons

When an individual or group infringes upon the rights of another individual or group, it is altogether fitting and proper that the infringers be required to pay restitution or compensation for damages to the infringees. Increasingly in our modern complex world, it may happen that an infringer harms infringees through the commons in an indirect way that can harm many. It may even be difficult to clearly and specifically identify those harmed and the value, significance, or magnitude of the harm done. A clarifying example might be the emission of some substance into the atmosphere at a location that harms the health of people over a wide area and possibly at a great distance; or the substance might cause the climate to warm, eventually flooding properties thousands of miles away.

Perhaps penalties on infringers might provide a revenue stream to help fund government operations. It might be justifiable as compensation for those harmed by relieving them of some of their burden of funding the government. Proposals such as a carbon tax have already been widely discussed and even implemented. Anyone for an environmental impact fee?

It is the purpose of this section to disqualify this messy area as a potential revenue source. As attractive as it may initially sound, it would be a very bad idea.

Such cases are virtually always at once complex and nebulous. Things change fairly rapidly with time, technology, and knowledge. Opinions differ. It is difficult to define a stable and clearly justifiable revenue stream. This description should make it quite obvious that this is the antithesis of the kind of thing that politicians should be allowed to tinker with and create a thicket of laws.

The universe provides no guarantee that every problem has a good solution, or even any solution at all. The best that can be done is to leave this area to the courts. Those harmed will have to bring suit in court. Where a preponderance of evidence supports a claim, the perpetrator can be identified and the harm quantified, courts should award damages.

The "Score" Thus Far

Significant revenue sources have been identified that even hardened ancaps will have to agree are justifiable. But would they be sufficient? Here is what has been discussed thus far:

Road Usage Fees	$300 billion
Land Value Tax	$900 billion
Other Commons Rentals	$200 billion
Severance Taxes	$350 billion
Gambling	$35 billion
Total	$1,785 billion

Assuming that governments are ruthlessly pared back and strictly limited to their proper role as guarantors of rights, plus providing an *extremely limited* number of truly public goods (principally roads), the required annual revenue (again with liberal application of the SWAG technique) is guesstimated as follows:

U.S. Government	$1,400 billion
State Governments	$ 500 billion
Local Governments	$ 500 billion
Total	$ 2,400 billion

Unfortunately, there remains a $615 billion annual revenue shortfall. Furthermore, it would be wise to have some strong "backup" revenue options available in case of emergencies.

It appears that some more conventional revenue sources will need to be tapped. That being the case, it is important to employ only the least objectionable of those. Here are some characteristics that those taxes should have:

- **Efficient:** The cost of collecting and enforcing the tax must be a very small percentage of the amount collected.
- **Clear and simple**: Taxpayers must be able to understand the tax, be able to tell how much they owe, and know when it is due.
- **Broadly based and not burdensome**: The tax should affect all or most citizens reasonably uniformly and should not unduly burden anyone (including citizens' cost of compliance).
- **Hard to evade:** This might be considered an aspect of efficiency.
- **Pay as you go**: No large lump payments due at some deadline.
- **Noninvasive of citizens' privacy:** No financial forms or information returns to file.
- **Taxes consumption:** Taxing consumption is generally preferable to taxing production.

There are two good candidates.

Import Duties and Imposts

Although difficult to imagine today, the young United States got along just fine for decades with only import duties and imposts as the primary source of funding for government operations. In the past, one could argue that these are voluntary taxes insofar as it is voluntary to buy imported goods; now, not so much, as nearly everything has some imported material and/or labor content.

This tax checks all the boxes for a "good tax." Rates should be kept low and uniform in the interest of maintaining reasonably free trade. Perhaps a rate of 12% for friendly and trusted nations would be appropriate and 30% for entities unable to qualify for that list. This revenue source could be expected to raise approximately $450 billion annually.

Broadly Based Sales Tax

A broadly based sales tax on all goods and services sold to an end consumer or user also checks all the "good tax" boxes. There should be no rebates, prebates, exclusions, or other complexities or funny business. It is better to tax consumption than production, and we prefer a simple tax that we can hope to keep politicians from converting to a tool for misguided socioeconomic engineering. Except for bona fide emergencies, the rate would be expected to be fairly low. From a pragmatic standpoint, almost any tax can be tolerated if it is small enough. A two-thirds vote should be required to increase the rate, while a simple majority could lower it. A maximum rate limit (say, 9%) should also be imposed. Such a tax can be a powerful revenue generator if/as/when needed.

Some screech that a sales tax is "regressive." It really is not. The wealthy spend more than the poor and therefore pay more taxes. It is true that no taxes would be paid for money sitting in a bank, but the only way to derive benefit from money in the bank is to eventually spend it and pay the sales tax. However, if necessary to ameliorate the screeching, basic food, clothing, and tuition for education could be exempted from taxation so as to make it more progressive.

A 4% rate is guesstimated to raise $250 billion, and that should more than cover the guesstimated requirements.

Business Taxes

There should be no taxes specifically targeting businesses. To the extent that a business owns land, buys imported goods, uses roads, etc., it is liable for the corresponding taxes. The sales tax would be owed on items for which a business is the end consumer but not, however, on goods purchased for resale or materials used to manufacture products that the business sells.

Justifying the Sales Tax and Import Duties

Even though these two meet all criteria for "good taxes," they are nevertheless just plain old conventional taxes, perhaps with no philosophical justification. Ancaps will claim they are theft, although certainly the magnitude of the theft has been very drastically reduced.

The following paragraph is reproduced from the conclusions section of chapter 6:

Suppose we begin a thought experiment with complete anarchy. All individuals must defend whatever they believe are their rights completely by themselves. Defending rights is a resource-consuming, happiness-reducing drag, no matter how it is done. Individuals will quickly discover that by forming groups they can achieve better defense of their rights utilizing fewer total resources. Total happiness has increased. It stands to reason that a centralized rights defense entity could be even more efficient and further reduce the resources required, thereby further increasing happiness. There would be the additional benefit of standardizing all the lines drawn in the fuzzy areas of rights, which should prevent and reduce conflicts.

If the optimum point described at the end of chapter 6 can be closely achieved, where governments are simply performing their legitimate function as guarantors of individual rights — just providing necessary enforcement of the NAP — and performing that service more efficiently than could otherwise be done, then any taxes required to support those government operations are legitimately "usage fees" for the guarantor services.

One small rub remains. Because of the economic free rider problem, taxes cannot be optional. Normally, usage fees are thought of as optional. You voluntarily agree to use the service, and then you are obligated to pay for it. Is there any way these taxes could be viewed as voluntary?

Presumably, the citizens responsible for setting up the system did so through some democratic process — "consent of the governed" or some such. So in that sense, they can be considered as having voluntarily opted in. Anyone not happy living under the setup surely must be free to opt out by leaving the country. Anyone immigrating after the government is in place clearly is opting in voluntarily. That would leave only those who are born into the system.

"Parental oppression" likely is a far greater concern for minor citizens than government taxation. Furthermore, they are guaranteed reasonable care and education (positive rights provided by parents). Upon reaching adulthood, the same ability to opt out by leaving the country is available as it always is to any citizen. See Article 15 of the Constitution in appendix B for rights guaranteed to minor citizens; also parents' rights and responsibilities.

See Article 9 of the appendix B Constitution for government revenue details. Whether or not these revenue sources and the justifications for them fully satisfy all ancaps, this would seem to be about the best that can be done.

11. The Savior of the World

We begin this chapter with a quote from the end of chapter 2: "The *real* beginning for Homo sapiens on Earth was the advent of rational thinking. This could occur only after suitable and sufficiently complex structures had evolved to enable it." When was that exactly?

The best estimates are that a reasonably modern version of Homo sapiens had evolved by approximately 300,000 years ago. Even the ancestors of Homo sapiens had some more limited capacity for thought, but we will begin this story with the appearance of Homo sapiens. Rational thinking did not suddenly take off at that point like the runners in a race at the crack of the starter's pistol.

The Progress of Rational Thought

The first "rational thinking" was just gaining an understanding of things in the immediate environment that could improve the chances of staying alive. Existence for all living things was a constant and full-time struggle for survival at that time. There was plenty of sustained "evolutionary pressure" to develop anything that could help keep an organism alive, at least long enough to reproduce.

"Natural selection" is perhaps a more descriptive name for this harsh process than "evolution." Random mutations in a species are most often setbacks that reduce the likelihood of survival. Some may propagate forward for a generation or a few before dying out. Rarer favorable mutations do propagate forward, perhaps after some failed attempts, and become permanent improvements.

Thus, over many thousands of years, brains gained some additional size, complexity, and processing power. However, save for a few things learned from parents, every new member of the species had to start from very close to the very beginning deducing how their world worked. Although there was some progress over the millennia in figuring things out, it was necessarily rather severely limited.

Homo sapiens was a successful species, and its numbers grew. Small groups formed that enabled some cooperation and somewhat better sharing of information, both among contemporaries and forward to later generations. Increasingly clever weaponry both for hunting and defense chronicles the progress, as do other artifacts from each period.

The development of agriculture about 12,000 years ago enabled further progress, initiating a major shift away from nomadic hunting and gathering and toward more permanent farming settlements. Still, survival was more than a full-time job, and those less capable didn't survive.

Roughly 5,000 years ago, an event of very considerable significance occurred: the development of language and writing. This greatly improved the efficacy and fidelity of information transfer, especially forward to subsequent generations. It also facilitated greater collaboration among thinkers, thus amplifying the capabilities of minds over those thinking in isolation. Further progress was enabled. The human condition, although experiencing some ups and downs, continued its gradual improvement.

Moving now into more modern times, though greatly improved, the human condition as late as the 1700s was still far below what would be considered abject poverty today. At the most fundamental level, rational thinking has to be credited with enabling the progress that had been made. Yet, rational thinking was still very far from achieving its full potential.

Today, we measure and track "the human condition" or "the standard of living" quantitatively. Although other factors may sometimes come into play, the best measure of the standard of living is the amount of wealth a person possesses or has access to for their own benefit. Two dimensions of the standard of living are of interest: The first is the average standard of living. The second is its distribution — that is, how much above the average are the wealthy and how much below the average are the poor.

As a good proxy for the average standard of living, we use the gross domestic product (GDP) per person. This is the total wealth (goods and services) output of an entire economy in one year divided by the number of people participating in that economy. To measure distribution, we usually look at the annual incomes of people or families. For example, the average annual income of the bottom 20% of the population compared to the top 20% or the percentage of the population having incomes below or above a certain dollar figure. Since we do not have sound money (a "hard" currency), we must always be careful to correct for the changing value of money (usually inflation, which is a decrease in the value of money) when we are comparing data for different years.

Getting back to the 1700s and the gripping saga of human progress, we see that something dramatic and truly phenomenal happened in the late 1700s. Following approximately 299,000 years of painfully slow and incremental improvement of the human standard of living, rather suddenly, the standard of living began to increase at an astonishingly rapid rate. We are not talking about the standard of living for a small group somewhere; we are talking about the standard of living for most of the world's population. It is as though the savior of the world appeared on Earth and began dispensing copious quantities of wealth. The chart[10] below depicts this graphically.

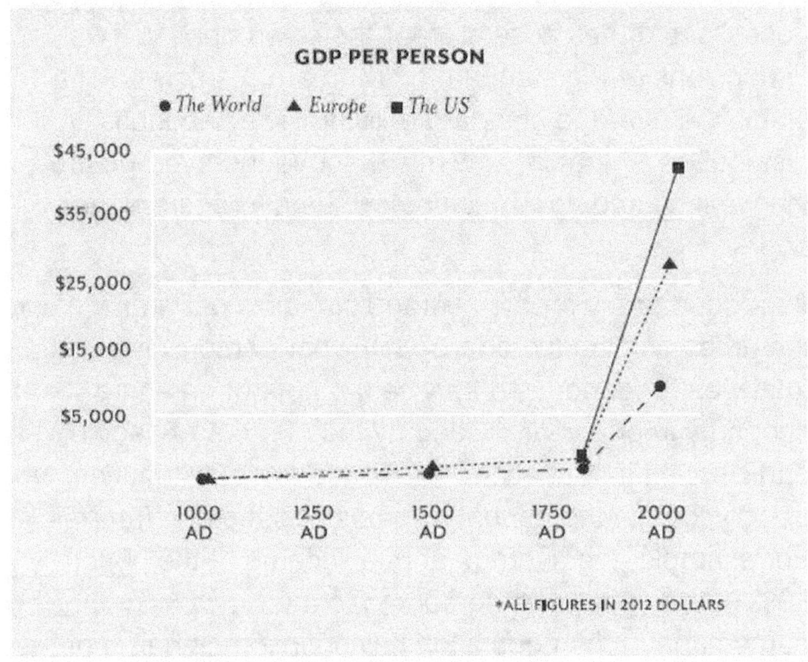

Credit: Economic Growth: Unleashing the Potential of Human Flourishing

Before allowing ourselves unqualified, delirious happiness, it would be good to check the distribution of all this wealth; perhaps only some people were helped, while many others

---

[10] Chart from *Economic Growth: Unleashing the potential of human flourishing* by Edd S, Noell, Stephen L. S. Smith, and Bruce G. Webb reproduced with permission.

still wallowed in abject poverty. This work has already been done by the World Bank and others.

In 1820, approximately 84% of the world's population survived on \$1.90[11] per day per person. According to the World Bank, this was still true for 42% of the world's population in 1981. Today, less than 8% (about half of whom live in sub-Saharan Africa) still suffer in such extreme poverty. That's dramatic. Billions of people have been lifted out of poverty. Clearly, the extremely poor benefited greatly, perhaps the most, from this phenomenon.

The increase in wealth per person was indeed truly remarkable but does not tell the whole story. After thousands of years of very gradual growth, the earth's population shot up by at least eight-fold over this same period. Not only did the average person enjoy much greater wealth, but this was so for many, many more people.

The total amount of new wealth that materialized is mind-boggling. Even Santa Claus couldn't distribute that much valuable stuff if every day were Christmas. It certainly behooves us to understand as thoroughly as possible what happened and why. Did rational thinking uncork a really good one in the late 1700s? No, not exactly, but rational thought certainly did play an important role.

---

[11] These World Bank statistics use 2011 "international dollars." These are adjusted for currency variations, inflation and/or deflation so as to allow valid comparisons over long time periods. That is, the \$1.90 would purchase the same goods and services in any year as it would in the base year, 2011.

Actually, the progress in rational thinking has been disappointing in some ways. It has, of course, been crucial to progress, but there is so much more unrealized potential. What has been the holdup? As explained, progress for the first 297,000 years was understandably severely limited, but what has been the holdup, say, for the most recent 3,000 years? During that more recent period, there certainly has been an increasing number of thinkers doing a whole lot more thinking, and significant progress definitely has occurred. Two primary things have been gumming up the works.

The first deterrent is plain old mistakes. Understandably, thinkers don't always get it exactly right. Mistakes can cause trips up blind alleys and wasted time and effort — sometimes a lot of it. But mistakes can be found and corrected. They are a continuing nuisance that will likely always be with us, but they are not the main showstopper.

The second and largest problem is that rational thought must always fight its ever-present archenemy and nemesis: irrationality. Irrationality comes in numerous forms: superstitions, myths, religions, customs, and sometimes just refusal to accept valid new deductions for no rational reason. Irrationality has been a major headwind against progress. As decried in chapter 3, irrationality is still kicking today. It appears that it will still be some time before rational thinking is able to vanquish its archenemy.

In the latter part of the seventeenth century, a particularly brilliant and prolific rational thinker contributed greatly to human knowledge and understanding. That was English mathematician and physicist Sir Isaac Newton (1642–1727). He, in parallel with Wilhelm Leibnitz, independently completed the formalization of calculus, an extremely important branch of mathematics. He formulated Newtonian mechanics (laws of motion and gravity), constructed the first useful reflecting telescope, and advanced science in many areas.

A particularly notable accomplishment of Newton's was the formalization of the scientific method, which was introduced in chapter 2. This was the result of employing rational thinking to understand rational thinking itself. Rational thinking is not something that applies only within some segment of reality called science; rather it is generally applicable to all of reality. The scientific method stuck, but we are still waiting today for that very important generalization to permeate much of society.

Of course, Newton was not able to achieve such progress entirely by himself working in isolation. There were other contributions by other thinkers, precedent and contemporary, feeding into his efforts. Although Sir Isaac was not the savior of the world, his work, more than that of any other single person, enabled technological developments that would significantly amplify the rate of wealth creation that was soon to begin ramping up.

Individual Rights

It was an entirely different type of thinking that was more directly responsible for fomenting such radical change. These thinkers became known as Enlightenment thinkers. Chief among them was Englishman John Locke (1632–1704), whose main thinking was based upon his idea that human individuals had "rights," especially the three primary libertarian rights of life, liberty, and property ownership. He thought nature provided for a set of built-in basic rights, and he spent considerable effort trying to back that notion up with clever arguments (an effort that continues to this day). Other Enlightenment thinkers postulated various sets of rights. Most argued that rights were bestowed upon people by a deity. Monarchists, of course, continued to insist that rights were determined and granted by the government — which, under a monarchy, is de facto true.

The Enlightenment thinkers failed to comprehend that it was they themselves who conceived the idea of individual rights. That they wrongly understood the origin of the concept of rights did not diminish the impact that these ideas were to have. Their ideas were propagated fairly widely, were adopted by influential people, and caused considerable rethinking of the relationship between citizens and their governments. As a result, large numbers of people began to enjoy more individual rights, which is tantamount to having greater freedom.

Meanwhile, over in the New World, the settlers had always enjoyed quite a lot of liberty. Indeed, many of them had come to the New World seeking greater freedom. Clearly, the Founding Fathers of the United States were strong subscribers to the principles of individual rights and liberty. As population density increased through the 1700s, so did economic activity and wealth. Especially with the peace following the Revolutionary War and with the US Constitution in place, the GDP per person in the United States sustained a remarkably steep increase.

A similar growth in wealth happened to a somewhat less explosive extent in England and spread to other nations. Apparently, the savior of the world had quietly sneaked in with no fanfare at all and started dispensing increasing amounts of wealth. Of course, the increasing wealth was noticed, but its cause was not understood.

The Free Market Economic System

The savior of the world is the free market economic system. It is the most prolific creator of wealth known — by far. Who invented the free market economic system? Nobody! When a community of people is predominantly free, honest, and peaceful for a sufficient period of time, a free market economy will automagically self-organize. It is a 100% natural thing. It is just free people voluntarily cooperating to satisfy their wants and needs.

Throughout history, people have not, by and large, been predominantly free, honest, and peaceful. As civilizations evolved through emperors, pharaohs, monarchs, feudalism, mercantilism, and so forth, conditions began to improve somewhat, but it was the Enlightenment thinkers who finally focused attention on individual rights. Securing a decent set of individual rights is absolutely necessary for creating an environment in which a free market economy can form and flourish. The New World provided a large-scale environment in which a very strong set of individual rights was secured over an extended period of time. That is why a free market economy was most spectacularly successful there.

As mentioned earlier, Scotsman Adam Smith was the first to put all the pieces together and grasp the big picture. His *Wealth of Nations* was a great gift of understanding as to how the free market economic system functions and works its magic. Smith introduced the famous metaphor of an "invisible hand" that consistently allocates scarce resources to the uses that create the most wealth.

The free market economic system is the goose that lays golden eggs. But incredibly, it has haters and enemies. They wish to supplant the free market system with crazy schemes such as socialism or communism — even though such systems have been tried time and time again, only to fail and cast millions into poverty and worse.

How can the enemies of free market economies ever succeed in forcing their destructive schemes onto so many people? It is purely because of ignorance. The enemies of the free market economic system can only gain support if people do not understand how and why free markets work so well. Anyone who understands the free market economic system will immediately be able to grasp why other systems fail so miserably.

Why is ignorance of free market principles so widespread? It is not commonly taught in public schools, and when it is, it is not usually taught well, because few teachers truly understand the concepts. Some of the concepts are a bit counterintuitive until that "Aha!" moment when the big picture snaps fully into focus.

A great way to gain this crucially important knowledge is to take a good Microeconomics 101 course. Everyone (especially those in Congress) should take one and earn at least a B+. Such a course is normally a full college semester of study that some may find difficult. What causes eyes to glaze over is usually mastering concepts like supply curves, demand curves, marginal cost, and marginal utility. These topics certainly *are* important, but they absolutely *are not* necessary for gaining a perfectly fine understanding of and appreciation for the crucial core principles.

Anyone with a good grasp of how the free market system works its magic will forever be inoculated against ignorant collectivist pitches. They will be able to instantly spot the many idiotic statements and proposals that bombard us daily about economic issues. Such statements spew forth from those in both high and low places. It is important to be able to authoritatively and confidently explain why these ideas are not only wrong but also counterproductive and destructive to everyone's welfare.

By this time, some may be wondering, "What about capitalism?" or "What is capitalism?"

The term *"capitalism"* originated during the 1860s as an alternative name for the free market economic system. Karl Marx and Friedrich Engels used the term *capitalist* (*Kapitalist*) in *The Communist Manifesto*. However, the term capitalism was primarily popularized by Karl Marx in his writings *Das Kapital* and *Theories of Surplus Value*. The fact that the term came into widespread use has enabled an avowed enemy of the free market economic system to saddle it with a less descriptive and less appealing label.

Do not use the term "capitalism." Instead, always say "free market economic system." Yes, it's more words, but it's far more descriptive and harder to paint as an evil thing.

Take, for example, the often-heard knock, *crony capitalism*. That surely does sound like capitalism is a really sinister thing. What this term actually means is that someone has hijacked the force of government to gain an unfair economic advantage. That has nothing whatever to do with capitalism. Cronyism is a degradation of capitalism. A more accurate term would be *crony statism*.

If the term were instead "crony free market economic system," it would immediately be recognizable as the oxymoron that it is!

Consequently, this is the *only* place in this book where you will find the term capitalism.

The Science of Economics — Allocating Scarce Resources

Many people think economics is just about money. Money certainly is involved, but *the primary concern of economics is how certain kinds of decisions are made.*

> **Definition: Economics is a science that studies how people, acting individually and in groups, decide to allocate and use scarce resources to satisfy their wants.**

A resource is deemed scarce whenever wants for the resource exceed the amount of the resource that is available. Whether a specific resource or commodity is scarce can depend on many things.

In the middle of a desert, water is a scarce resource, but there is a whole lot more sand available than there are wants for it, so sand is definitely not a scarce resource. No one is worrying about how to allocate sand in a desert. However, at a New Jersey beach resort far from any desert, water may be plentiful, but sand very well may be a scarce resource, and it may be important to allocate available sand to various uses. Many, many tons of sand may be needed to replenish that eroded from beaches by the ocean and storms. A nearby concrete plant may use considerable amounts of sand for its operations. Smaller quantities may be wanted for lots of fish tanks and

sandboxes for children in homes and parks. At that
location, sand is a scarce resource.

There are three basic types of economic decisions that
need to be made for the operation of an economy:
1. What goods and services are to be produced?
2. How are they to be produced?
3. For whom are they to be produced?

Based upon how these decisions are made, there are only
two fundamentally different kinds of economic system:

> **Free market economy:** In a free market economy,
> people are left alone and free to make these
> decisions for themselves in any way they see fit. It
> is assumed that people will always make decisions
> based upon their *rational self-interest* when free to
> do so. This is a very solid assumption since
> examples of people intentionally making decisions
> contrary to their rational self-interest are
> exceedingly rare! Note that the decision-making
> power stays distributed and diffuse.

> **Command economy:** In a command economy,
> many, most, or substantially all of these decisions
> are made by some central authority. They are
> sometimes called *managed economies* or *centrally
> planned economies*. There are many command
> economy variations, such as socialism,
> communism, fascism, and dictatorships. No matter
> what "sales pitch" is used to justify the use of force,
> all command economies end up with power
> concentrated in a small group that uses and
> depends upon force to make and implement at least

some of the most important economic (and other) decisions.

In a pure free market economic system, everything is voluntary. It is the *only* economic system that functions entirely without the use of any force or coercion and

therefore comports with the libertarian Non-Aggression Principle.[12]

There are no pure command economies and no pure free market economies in the real world. All actual operating economies are *mixed economies*. Each occupies some spot on the spectrum between predominantly free toward one end to predominantly command toward the other.

Free market economies are dynamic and prolific creators of wealth, while command economies definitely are not. Despite this, economies have a dismaying tendency to drift toward the command end of the spectrum. The cause of the drift is the application of force to the economy through increasing government meddling. When command economies collapse, a free(er) version may eventually replace it. Much more rarely, an intentional reset toward the free end of the spectrum may be carried out in order to rejuvenate wealth production.

We are going to focus here on understanding free markets with the objective of arresting the drift of the US economy (indeed, *any* economy) toward a less free and less

---

[12] The Non-Aggression Principle or NAP was discussed at some length in chapter 6. It states, "Nobody may deal fraudulently with anybody else, and nobody may initiate the use of force (or the credible threat of force) against anybody else for any reason, excepting that minimum amount of force which may be necessary to enforce this non-aggression principle."

productive command economy. In the interest of simplicity and brevity, some of the finer and/or more advanced economic concepts have been omitted.

Finally, it should be explained that the science of economics has two main branches. The first is called *microeconomics*, which deals with understanding the basic and immutable underlying laws of economics. The second branch is called *macroeconomics*, which attempts to understand the operations, aspects, and behaviors of an entire economic system. An entire economic system is an incredibly complex entity with many moving parts, almost all of which interact with each other in various ways, and those interactions change with time, conditions, and technology.

Substantially all economists agree with the basic tenets of microeconomics — the laws of economics. However, within the field of macroeconomics, conflicting opinions and theories abound. It is a land of computer models (which can be tweaked to confirm favored hypotheses) and maybe even Ouija boards and astrologers. The reader is warned to view macroeconomic pronouncements with a healthy dose of caution and skepticism.

The Six Pillars of the Free Market Economic System

Six distinct "pillars" are required to support a free market economy. Each and every one is essential for the proper and effective operation of a free market economy. We will examine each pillar in some detail and thereby begin to build an understanding of how free markets work.

Pillar 1: Private Property

It is essential that the right to own and control private property be well secured. This is one of the three primary individual rights (life, liberty, and property) that people widely agree should be guaranteed. Without private property, there can be only chaos. It's hard to be peaceful if everybody is stealing everybody else's stuff, so maintaining peace requires respect for private property.

Pillar 2: Specialization

People must be free to specialize in whatever they do best. Some may be very good at farming. Others may be great at making shoes. People are happiest doing what they like and are skilled at doing; their productivity will be much higher. Not only can each person spend most of their time doing what they are best at doing, but they can also further hone their skills and knowledge, as well as justify making or acquiring specialized tools to further boost productivity.

Pillar 3: Voluntary Exchanges

People must be free to voluntarily exchange goods and services with each other. This may sound ridiculously trivial, but it is absolutely crucial.

Suppose you specialize in farming. Presumably, you would have lots of food available to you, more than you could consume yourself. But you would lack all the other things you need. You would have to trade some of your excess food with other specialists for the things you need that they have produced. Of course, the same applies to everyone else who would need to trade some of whatever they have produced for food.

When you need a new pair of shoes, you reach an agreement with a cobbler to trade, say, three bushels of corn for a pair of shoes. Each such transaction is called a *voluntary exchange*. Many such trades form a *barter economy*, in which various types of goods are swapped for all manner of other goods.

Each and every voluntary exchange is a powerful, almost magical thing that is grossly underappreciated. As long as the exchange is completely voluntary on both sides, *both parties to the exchange must come out ahead*. Were this not true, the exchange simply would not occur.

Consider that the value of three bushels of corn is less to the farmer than to the cobbler. Since it is his specialty, the farmer can produce three bushels of corn a lot more easily (at a lower cost) than the cobbler can, plus the farmer has lots of corn, while the cobbler has little or none. On the other hand, the value of a pair of shoes to the cobbler is less than to the farmer for the same complementary reasons. As long as the value of the shoes to the farmer is higher than the value of his three bushels of corn *and* the value of three bushels of corn to the cobbler is higher than the shoes, the exchange will take place; otherwise, it will not. If a voluntary exchange does occur, then it is guaranteed that *the wealth of both the farmer and the cobbler has been increased*.

Such exchanges must never be forced, because any exchange that did take place would obviously not be voluntary. Nor can they be prohibited, because then there would be no exchange at all. In either case, the guarantee that wealth must increase for both parties would be voided.

There is another aspect of the voluntary exchange that needs to be more widely understood and appreciated. The value that the person on each side of the transaction assigns to the things being exchanged depends upon many complex factors that are almost always unique to the circumstances of the person and sometimes even to the circumstances surrounding each specific exchange. One individual may value something highly, while another may place a much lower value on the exact same thing. Circumstances, and therefore valuations, will change with time. *Valuations are subjective.* All parties to any exchange must make the value determinations for themselves; specifically, it is just not possible for someone else or an outside entity to assign these values as accurately. This is one fundamentally important reason (among others) why central planning systems cannot possibly work well.

Voluntary exchanges (billions and billions of them) are the beating heart of a free market economy. Some may hesitate to accept that a simple exchange can increase wealth, but it is absolutely true. Consequently, it would be a good idea to reread this section until the concept is crystal clear and you are entirely comfortable with it.

Pillar 4: Price System of Resource Allocation

A price system is one of the things that distinguish a free market economy from a simpler barter economy; it boosts the creation of wealth dramatically by assuring that scarce resources are allocated to their highest and best (most productive) use; that is, the use that creates the most wealth.

In order to function, a price system must have money. There are three functions that money needs to perform well:

A. **Provide a convenient medium of exchange:** Money needs to be available whenever and wherever you need it. In the past, that meant it was easy to carry around in any reasonable amount, but technology is now in the process of obviating that need. Money needs to be divisible to a fine enough level so that amounts exactly matching the value of any transaction can be easily transferred. Money should be durable and difficult to duplicate or counterfeit. It would also be nice if money were difficult to steal.

B. **Act as a standard of value:** Just as a meterstick (or a yardstick) measures distance, money should establish a measure of value. It provides an easy way to compare the values of disparate things, such as bushels of corn, pairs of shoes, houses, and cows. The scale on a meterstick is fixed and enables distances to be measured reproducibly and accurately at different places and at different times. Just as stretchy rubber would not make a good meterstick, something with a varying value calibration does not make good money. A standard that changes is not a good standard.

C. **Provide a mechanism to store value:** As a farmer, you harvest your corn in the fall, but you may not need a new pair of shoes at that time. Money enables you to sell your corn when you harvest it, store its value as money, and buy shoes (as well as other things) later whenever you need them. Thus, the use of money decouples the two ends of a transaction and enables them to happen at different times; it also facilitates saving and lending. Obviously, money's ability to store value is seriously impaired to the degree that money does not act as a good standard of value.

A currency that performs all three functions well is called *sound money*. A free market economic system needs sound money, and its operation will be degraded to the extent that its money is not sound.

Pillar 5: Market Competition

There must be free and open competition among multiple sellers and multiple buyers for each commodity (a commodity could be either a product or a service). Sellers compete with each other to sell their products and services, while buyers compete with each other to buy scarce commodities.

Active market competition always causes the price of each and every commodity to automatically seek what is known as the *market-clearing price*. At the market-clearing price, the quantity produced is equal to the quantity consumed (purchased). Supply and demand are balanced. There will be neither a shortage nor a surplus of a commodity at its market-clearing price.

It is not hard to see how this works. If there is a shortage of a commodity, intensified competition among buyers will tend to drive its price higher. Higher prices will reduce the amount purchased and also encourage suppliers to produce more of the commodity. On the other hand, if there is a surplus, intensified competition among sellers will tend to push prices lower. Lower prices encourage more purchases while at the same time discouraging production.

At any particular price, there will always be some who place a higher value on the commodity than its current price; these are the ones willing to buy it. And there will always be some who place a lower value on that commodity than its price; these are the ones willing to sell it if they have it. But *the market-clearing price is the best overall representation of the current value of a commodity in the overall economy.*

Prices are crucially important signals that regulate market competition and keep everything running as smoothly as possible. The purpose of a business is to make a profit (we will learn more about why profits are so important a little later). Prices tell a business what products and services their customers most want and which will be most profitable to produce and offer. Prices also tell a business what goods and services to buy in the operation of the business to minimize costs and maximize profits. It is prices that automatically allocate the use of all scarce commodities to the uses that will create the most wealth!

We most often give examples of and think of scarce commodities being allocated to the best productive uses; that is, when they are used to produce or provide other goods and services. But the price system is a "double (good) whammy." It also makes sure, on the consumption side, that goods and services go to the end users who value them most highly.

Clearly, it would be a very bad idea to interfere with the important functions of prices; there are so many things that would be disrupted. Yet that unfortunately does happen.

During the 1970s, Middle Eastern oil producers reduced their exports to the United States. The reduction in supply was about 5%. When gasoline prices began to rise, the government ordered a price freeze, which prevented prices from adjusting to the market-clearing price. This very predictably created a shortage, with gas stations running out of product and vehicles lined up waiting for hours hoping to buy a few gallons.

Contrast that unfortunate episode with another one in the early 2020s, when our own government caused a reduction in domestic oil production. This time, the government refrained from freezing prices. Gasoline prices rose significantly to the market-clearing price. Nobody liked higher gasoline prices; there was lots of grumbling and squawking, but there were no shortages or cars wasting time (and gasoline!) waiting in lines. The available quantities of gasoline were smoothly and automatically allocated to the highest and best uses (greatest creation of wealth).

There are other examples of (always counterproductive) interference with prices, such as minimum wage laws (the price of labor). Do not mess with prices. It just causes scarce commodities to be misallocated to less productive uses, which *reduces the rate of wealth creation and harms everyone.*

Pillar 6: Entrepreneurship

The amazing number of choices of products and services that our economy offers us certainly does not happen by accident. People have to create them. Someone has to decide 1) what goods and services are to be produced; 2) how are they to be produced; and 3) for whom they are to be produced. Also, and very importantly, *such people must be willing to assume the risk of investing money to produce the goods and services with the hope that they can be profitably produced and sold.*

The intrepid, creative, and valuable individuals or groups who perform this highly essential function are called *entrepreneurs.* If things don't go as expected, much of — or even all of — an entrepreneur's investment could be lost. Just as with everything else about free markets, there is no central control or force involved in entrepreneurship; it is distributed and voluntary. In the event of a failure, no bailout is available, and it is critical that there be no forced bailouts.

Without entrepreneurship, nothing happens. Without entrepreneurship, there can be no free market economy, just as there can be no free market economy without any of the other five pillars.

Comprehending the Big Picture

Understanding the foundations (six pillars) of a free market economy should have brought the big picture into at least fuzzy focus. In this last section, we will paint it more fully and clarify several aspects of it that may be somewhat counterintuitive. We will pay special attention to debunking some of the fallacious and scurrilous attempts that are regularly made to discredit the free market economic system.

Commodity Substitutes

We learned that an increase in the price of a commodity always results in less of it being purchased (and vice versa). Depending upon the commodity, this may be a small or a large change. For example, in the case of a gasoline price increase, part of the reduction may come from drivers simply skipping some less important trips, combining errands for greater efficiency, or traveling in carpools. *Only individual drivers or businesses (not some central planner) can accurately determine which trips are less important.*

However, there is almost always another possibility that can have a larger effect: switching to the use of a substitute. The substitution of 10% ethanol for gasoline is an example of a *direct substitution*. There are also lots of *indirect substitutes* for gasoline. Instead of driving, one can carpool, ride a bicycle, or take public transportation. Higher gasoline prices may even result in increased sales of hybrid or all-electric vehicles.

There are substitutes for virtually any commodity. One result of this is that nothing happens in isolation. A change in the availability and/or price of one commodity affects others, sometimes in hard-to-predict ways. A major economic event or shock in one sector of the economy will ripple into other sectors, sometimes immediately and sometimes after a delay. The price and sales volume of any given commodity can be affected by changes in the price or availability of its substitutes.

An economy is an incredibly complex web of constantly changing and interacting entities, all driven by billions and billions of voluntary exchanges. Each such exchange is based upon the rational self-interest of the participants and must increase the wealth of both. Thus, a free market economy will always adapt to changing conditions to maximize the creation of wealth under the new conditions.

It is this complicated mess that macroeconomists attempt to understand and predict. That they frequently fail to get it right is not at all surprising.

That Which Is Seen, and That Which Is Not Seen

As has been explained, a free market economy will self-organize and flourish when people are free, honest, and peaceful. Such a free market maximizes the creation of wealth. The proper role of a government, then, is to secure citizens' rights by deterring and punishing those who would engage in fraud or use force on others and to ensure that all six pillars of a free market economic system remain solidly in place — nothing more.

Unfortunately, governments seem to have a hard time sticking to their proper role and can't resist interfering in the economy by applying the only thing a government has: ham-handed force. Examples are excessive taxation (for wealth redistribution schemes, aid programs, or myriad other boondoggles), regulations, subsidies, loan guarantees, and more. Yet another disruption is the Federal Reserve manipulating interest rates and inflating the dollar. Interest rates are the price for borrowing money and, like all prices, should be set by marketplace competition. Inflation (or deflation) changes the standard of value, interferes with the ability to safely store wealth, and makes it harder to plan for the future. All such things throw sand into the gears of the economy.

A free market economy is resilient and will find a new equilibrium to optimize wealth creation under the new conditions imposed by force. However, *the rate of wealth creation will be lower than it would have been without government meddling.* With enough forceful meddling, we approach a command economy, and wealth creation really grinds to a crawl.

Why does the voting public not object strenuously to governments screwing up the free market? It is because of the aforementioned ignorance of how free markets function and also because of an unfortunately misleading phenomenon.

Suppose the government levies a tax on "the wealthy" to feed "the poor." The benefit to the poor is seen by the public as a good thing; the politicians make certain of that. What is not seen are the delayed negative effects that result from confiscation of taxes and ripple out diffusely through the economy. There are inevitably many unseen things that now cannot be done because wealth was confiscated for taxes. The nearly invisible diffused and hard-to-track bad effects more than offset the good, so total wealth is reduced.

A French economist named Frederic Bastiat very clearly explained all of this in two seminal works published in 1850. One was a book titled *The Law.* The other was an essay titled *That Which Is Seen, and That Which Is Not Seen.* These works are easily understandable by anyone and are highly recommended reading: https://fee.org/media/14951/thelaw.pdf and http://bastiat.org/en/twisatwins.html.

Businesses and Profits

Businesses are created by entrepreneurs for the purpose of providing goods and/or services that people want. A business is the mechanism by which the means to produce the goods or services are assembled, organized, and managed; it also facilitates measuring and tracking how well the business is succeeding at its endeavor. Small businesses can be sole proprietorships or partnerships. Large businesses are usually set up as corporations, with shareholders as the owners. A business — especially a corporation — is a structure or a mechanism that facilitates the cooperation of many people to create value in ways that are too large or complex to be handled by individuals.

When rights are properly secured, businesses may not engage in fraud and may not use force to compel anyone to do anything. Therefore, a business's employees work there voluntarily. Each employee and the business believe they are gaining from the employment relationship, or it would not happen (or would soon be terminated by one side or the other). It is a voluntary exchange. Similarly, each customer who purchases the business's goods or services does so voluntarily. Each customer and the business must believe their wealth is increased, or the transaction will not occur.

Note that the conditions just described are violated to the extent that crony statism exists. It must not be possible for any business (or individual) to benefit from the use of government force to warp the free market economy in their favor. By this point it should be obvious that the use of force to benefit some does even greater harm to everyone else. Overall, it must be counterproductive.

In a free market economy, businesses must be completely benign entities. Yet, they are frequently characterized as villains. We often hear them referred to as "greedy corporations," as though their pursuit of profits makes them evil. Well (duh!), of course they are "greedy," and that is a very good thing. The overriding objective and measure of success for any business is to make a profit. *Profits are always good for everyone*, not just for the business.

Consider that the total cost of operations (material, labor, etc.) for a business measures the total wealth that the business has consumed in creating the goods and services it has sold. The total sales measures how much wealth the business has created. The total sales minus the total cost equals the profit. Therefore, the profit is the amount of *additional* wealth that the business has created and contributed to the economy. Profits contribute to raising everyone's standard of living! Large profits are good things to be celebrated, not villainized.

There is no guarantee that a business will be able to earn a profit. If it does not and instead loses money, the business will be consuming more wealth than it creates and *lowering* everyone's standard of living. That is why it is very important that any business that consistently loses money must go out of business. That is also why it is folly to subsidize such a business to keep it going! It is an extremely important feature of free market economies that unprofitable businesses must automatically shut down (without the use of any force) so remaining assets can be redeployed to more productive uses. This highly important process is sometimes called "creative destruction."

Most people have an inflated idea of how much profit businesses make. Having something left on the "bottom line" isn't easy in the face of marketplace competition. On average in a reasonably good economy, companies are only able to make a profit of about 3.8%[13] of their sales. Of course, the hope/expectation of making a profit is the only incentive that entrepreneurs have to undertake the considerable risk of starting a company. An entrepreneur with a world-beater new idea might be able to make big profits for a few years until competition develops, but there are also plenty of cases in which entrepreneurs lose money.

Politicians often beat up on large corporations, claiming they are making huge profits because they are "price gouging" their customers. They complain about, say, a $15 billion profit. Of course, the politicians neglect to mention that this still is only a small percentage of sales and that the company may have lost almost that amount in an economic downturn year. (Has anyone ever heard a politician urging a company that is losing money to raise its prices?)

As we have learned, prices are set by marketplace competition, so businesses don't actually have much flexibility to control their prices. If they want to make more money, they must instead work as hard as possible to reduce their costs; reducing costs is overall a more beneficial thing, of course. Since we know that business

---

[13] This information is not readily available. It was provided by a US Internal Revenue Service analyst for the year 2004. Total sales of all US businesses were about $20 trillion that year. The US economy was reasonably good in 2004. The 3.8% certainly fluctuates from year to year, but not by a lot.

profits average only about 3.8% of sales, if every business gave up all their profit and cut prices until they just broke even, it would mean only a 3.8% average reduction in prices — a far smaller decrease than the politicians would like you to believe. We citizens need to think things through carefully and not fall for ignorant rhetoric.

One final observation: Businesses cannot pay taxes. Only people pay taxes. There are always three sets of people associated with any business: its employees, its customers, and its owners (or shareholders). When governments levy taxes on businesses, they are using them as tax collectors and hiding the tax from those who actually pay it. When dollars are confiscated from a business, the loss *must* pass through to the people connected with that business, either through higher prices for customers, lower wages/benefits for employees, a lower return on the investment of the owners/shareholders, or some combination of all three. The next time a politician tells you he or she is going to cut your taxes and instead raise taxes on greedy corporations, don't fall for it, and don't vote for such politicians!

Wealth Distribution

The enemies of the free market economic system incessantly criticize it for fostering an unequal distribution of wealth. *Unequal wealth distribution is absolutely necessary and required for the proper functioning of a free market economy.* It actually is the motive force that drives wealth production. Never apologize for it.

Suppose for the moment that there is an economic system that makes the distribution of wealth substantially equal. (Despite any and all claims, there is no such system, by the way.) The sixth pillar would be wiped out by such a system. There will be no entrepreneurs. Who would decide to take the considerable risk of investing to create new or better goods and services if there could ultimately be no reward for doing so? No one. The "American dream" of becoming wealthy by "building a better mousetrap" would be dead.

Critics say or strongly imply that the wealthy have become wealthy by somehow taking wealth that rightfully belongs to poor people. In a pure free market economy, that simply is not possible. No one can engage in fraud, and no one can force anyone else to do anything they do not want to do. Everything is voluntary. The only way to become wealthy is to do a better job than the competition at providing goods and services that other people want and voluntarily purchase. Remember that each such voluntary exchange increases the wealth of both the seller <u>and</u> the buyer. The wealthy get their wealth by creating new wealth, not by taking existing wealth away from anyone else. They deserve everyone's admiration and thanks!

Command economies always devolve into a wealthy elite class that calls all the shots backed up by force. They are able to accumulate wealth through the use of force (taking it from others), not by creating it. This leads to people fighting for power instead of peacefully earning their wealth. The production of new wealth is much less, so everyone else is very poor. Essentially, there are just two classes: a very small, very wealthy elite class that wields the power and a very large, very poor lower class. There is virtually no middle class.

In contrast, in a free market economy, there is a continuum of wealth, including a large, robust, and healthy middle class that possesses the bulk of the wealth. Think of the bell-shaped "normal distribution" or Gaussian curve. Only small percentages are on the very wealthy and very poor ends of the distribution. The average wealth is far higher.

As previously explained, the United States does not have a pure free market economy, and as a result, there is an accumulation of too much power at the top. Crony statism does exist because some are able to hijack government power to unjustly obtain economic advantages and enrich themselves. The enemies of free markets point to such inequities as an argument against free markets when these actually are the things that a pure free market economy would prevent. The only effective solution is for governments to not have the power to grant such favors as loan guarantees, subsidies, and tax and regulatory loopholes. They are not necessary to guaranteeing and securing rights, which is the rightful function of governments.

A few years ago, it was noticed that the middle class seemed to be shrinking. Some loudly proclaimed, "Our economy is not working for everyone," adding, "The middle class is taking a beating." Presumably, middle-class folks were falling into poverty. It would have been wise to first look more carefully at the statistics.

In 1967, 53.2% of U.S. households had incomes between $35,000 and $100,000 per year; call them the middle class. (All data are in terms of 2016 dollars to remove the effects of inflation.) By 2016, the middle class had declined to 42.1% of U.S. households. The middle class did shrink, at least over that time frame. We should look at the low-income households with less than $35,000 income to see if they are ending up there.

In 1967, 38.7% of households had incomes below $35,000. However, by 2016, only 30.2% were in this category. Nope, the middle class surely wasn't crumbling into the low-income group; that category was shrinking, too.

In 1967, 8.1% of households had $100,000 or more of income. By 2016, 27.7% of households were in the high-income category. So it looks like the economy actually has been working very well for substantially everyone. Consider this information along with the worldwide data cited near the beginning of this chapter.

A question to be asked is this: Do we want to reduce poverty, or do we want to equalize the distribution of wealth? It is not possible to do both. One would hope the choice is to reduce poverty. In that case, people need to stop whining about unequal wealth distribution and start encouraging everyone to take advantage of the many opportunities a free market economy provides to create more wealth for themselves. The sky is the limit.

The Safety Net

Another perennial criticism of laissez-faire free market economies is that they do not provide a "safety net." No matter how many opportunities there may be, there still will always be some small percentage of people who are, for a variety of reasons, just not capable of supporting themselves. Most will agree that having some sort of safety net to catch and support such people is preferable to letting them starve in the gutters.

Currently, the safety net is provided by a combination of government programs, private charities, and individual acts of kindness. Many believe that the government's involvement is necessary. However, it is highly likely that private charities could do this job better themselves if government force were completely eliminated. There are many powerful reasons, both philosophical and practical, to curtail the use of government force:

- We have learned how the application of government force reduces the rate of wealth creation in the free market economic system. Forced wealth redistribution schemes are but another example of this. Ending destructive meddling in the economy would increase wealth production, lift more people out of poverty, and reduce the load on the safety net.
- Forced "charity" cannot be called charity at all. Confiscating wealth from those who have earned it and giving it to those who have not earned it is philosophically repugnant; it is purely and simply theft.
- Private charity is more personal. There is a much closer coupling between donors and beneficiaries. Donors can derive some pleasure from helping others, and recipients tend to feel grateful and appreciative. With the government in the middle, donors are no longer donors and instead become victims who resent the confiscation of their wealth. Recipients know that benefits received from the impersonal government are not voluntarily offered; feelings of entitlement and victimhood are fostered.
- Private charities are way much better than governments at making sure donations actually are getting to those most in need (as opposed to going to overhead and/or grifters).

As a purely practical matter, the "bang for the buck" is *incredibly awful* for government welfare. On top of apparently inevitable government inefficiency, bloated bureaucracy always grows, and controls are poor, leading to waste, fraud, and abuse. A reasonable guesstimate would be that at best, only twenty cents of each taxpayer dollar collected for the purpose actually reaches and helps the intended beneficiaries. Some estimates are as low as thirteen cents!

Government is so horribly inefficient and wasteful that, based on this fact alone, it makes no sense at all to have government do *anything* other than those very few things that it absolutely *must* do, like national defense!

The statistics for private charities are much better. About seventy cents of each donated dollar actually reaches and helps the intended beneficiaries.

Charitable donations during 2023 totaled $593 billion. *This total does not include the additional value of the 5 billion labor hours that volunteers donated.* To achieve the same benefit through the government would require more than 2 *trillion* taxpayer dollars. Furthermore, the figures just quoted are for organized charities only and do not include informal neighbor-to-neighbor assistance, people directly caring for other sick or poor people, etc.

Bear in mind that Americans donated $593 billion in spite of the fact that governments confiscate more than a third of their earnings as taxes. Donations are likely also somewhat suppressed by the knowledge that plenty of taxpayer dollars are already being spent on welfare by governments. It seems entirely reasonable that private charity could and would provide an adequate safety net if governments stopped screwing up the economy, got out of the welfare business, and reduced taxes accordingly. It would be a more principled, humane, charitable, ethical, voluntary, and effective solution to the problem.

The Bottom Line

A free market economy is based on simple, understandable principles. It facilitates the peaceful and voluntary cooperation of many individuals to most effectively satisfy their needs and wants. Such cooperation can be local or it can even be at a distance with unknown people. Apparently, the hardest thing to understand is that it has to be left alone to function best.

You should now feel good about your grasp of these key concepts. However, the additional knowledge to be gained in a Microeconomic 101 course would still be a worthwhile endeavor.

Go forth and spread truth and enlightenment. But be aware that the free market economic system is an optimization solution. As pointed out in chapter 2, such are the most difficult to defend against attackers. It will always be possible to find and point out something that is a problem. This is one of the reasons for the frustrating success of its enemies. No system can prevent all possible problems. However, you can be confident that messing up the free market economic system to fix whatever problem has been cited will cause worse problems somewhere else.

Finally, do not miss seeing the forest while focusing on the trees. A free market economy can form and flourish only when people are left free to collaborate and solve their own problems. Freedom works, and freedom works best.

12. Money, Good and Bad

In our modern society, almost everyone deals with money in some way on a daily basis. Thinking about transactions or exchanges in terms of money is so normal and routine that few people ever think about the nature of money itself, what things would be like if money didn't exist, or what problems could possibly arise with money. Well, money has not always existed, and many problems — some of them quite disruptive — have occurred since money has come into use.

As common and familiar as money may be, precious few people comprehend the various types of money and what is required for a truly sound currency. Since sound money is essential to the proper functioning of a free market economic system, it is worth a chapter to gain a thorough understanding and to figure out what needs to be done to implement a sound currency.

Background

Millennia ago, there was very little of anything that could be called economic activity among people. That is, individuals and families were pretty much isolated economic entities and had to produce for themselves substantially everything they needed: food, shelter, clothing, and so on. Just surviving was more than a full-time job. Plenty of the less fit were unable to support themselves and perished.

Over time, people learned that they could be more successful (achieve a higher standard of living) through peaceful cooperation. Cooperation was facilitated by banding together in communities. It's hard to be peaceful if everybody is stealing everybody else's stuff, so maintaining peace required respect for *private property*.

It was realized that some people were much better hunters than others, while other people were better at farming, building shelters, making clothes, or other occupations. Therefore, much higher overall productivity could be obtained through *specialization*. Not only could each person spend most of their time doing what they were best at doing, but they could also further hone their skills and knowledge as well as justify making specialized tools to further boost productivity.

With specialization came the need to exchange commodities. If you specialized in farming, presumably you would have lots of food available to you, more than you could consume yourself. But you would lack all the other things you need. You would have to trade some of your excess food with other specialists for the things you need that they have produced. Of course, the same applied to everyone else who would need to trade some of what they had produced for food.

Each such transaction is called a *voluntary exchange*. Many such trades form a barter economy where various types of goods are swapped for all manner of other goods.

A barter economy surely works, but the exchanges tend to be a bit clumsy and inconvenient. Money might help. In order to best facilitate exchanges, there are three key functions that good money needs to perform well.

The Functions of Money

Although presented in chapter 11, no discussion of money could be complete without stating its purpose. The three functions money should perform are restated here:

A. **Provide a convenient medium of exchange:** Money needs to be available whenever and wherever you need it. In the past, that meant it was easy to carry around in any reasonable amount, but technology is now in the process of obviating that need. Money needs to be divisible to a fine enough level that amounts that exactly match the value of any transaction can be easily transferred. Money should be durable and difficult to duplicate or counterfeit. It would also be nice if money were difficult to steal.

B. **Act as a standard of value:** Just as a meterstick (or a yardstick) measures distance, money should establish a measure of value. It provides an easy way to compare the values of disparate things, such as bushels of corn, pairs of shoes, houses, and cows. The scale on a meterstick is fixed and enables distances to be measured reproducibly and accurately at different places and at different times. Just as stretchy rubber would not make a good meterstick, something with a varying value calibration does not make good money. A standard that changes is not a good standard.

C. **Provide a mechanism to store value:** As a farmer, you harvest your corn in the fall, but you may not need a new pair of shoes at that time. Money enables you to sell your corn when you harvest it, store its value as money, and buy shoes (as well as other things) later whenever you need them. Thus, the use of money decouples the two ends of a transaction and enables them to happen at different times; it also facilitates saving and lending. Obviously, money's ability to store value is seriously impaired to the degree that money does not act as a good standard of value.

Money that performs its functions well (especially points B and C) is known as *sound money*, *good money*, or a *hard currency*. When more than one form of money is circulating, people prefer to hang onto and accumulate (or save) the sound money and get rid of (spend) the bad money. If the bad money is bad enough, it loses value and eventually falls into disuse.

Commodity and Representative Money

It appears that barley may have been the first thing to be widely used as money. The *shekel* was a specific weight of barley that became the currency unit. Other things were valued in terms of shekels of barley or fractions of a shekel. Later, but still several hundred years BCE, gold and silver coins came into use and have demonstrated remarkable staying power. Different weights of precious metals performed the above three functions better, and they are still used today. These types of money are called *commodity money* because a designated commodity that itself has intrinsic value is used as money.

For improved convenience, *representative money* eventually came into use. A commodity (e.g., gold or silver) was deposited with a dealer or a bank for safekeeping. Receipts were issued for which the commodity could later be reclaimed or withdrawn. The receipts, frequently called *bank notes*, were used as currency (primarily for larger amounts) in parallel with circulating coins to handle smaller amounts. Although the receipts or bank notes themselves had little or no intrinsic value, any holder was guaranteed to be able to convert them to something that did have value at any time upon the request of the bearer. It was far easier to carry bank notes around than large amounts of precious metals.

The immutable laws of economics tell us that the value of any and every commodity in an economy is always set by the availability (supply) of the commodity relative to the demand for it. There have been many and continuing foolish attempts to force the value (price) of various commodities to some desired amount, but those who attempt to defeat the laws of economics inevitably lose.

Of course, it is possible that the supply and/or demand for a commodity (therefore its price), especially one traded in small volumes, could be manipulated. Someone could sell large amounts of a commodity at an artificially low price or buy large amounts at an artificially high price. Obviously, either would be to the disadvantage of the manipulator and could not long continue before the manipulator's resources were depleted. Scurrilous promulgation of misinformation, either to increase or decrease demand, might be more cost-effective, but such lies will become evident fairly quickly. Thus, any manipulation, if successful at all, is bound to be short-lived, so any advantage to be reaped from manipulation needs to be nailed down quickly. However, since the supply of and demand for anything can validly change over time, it is entirely possible, even probable, that the value of any given commodity *will* change over time.

Thus, commodity money has the disadvantage that the value of everything is measured relative to the value of the chosen commodity, which is not always constant. To the degree that a commodity's value relative to other commodities is not constant, that commodity's ability to act as a standard of value and a store of value is necessarily impaired.

Gold has performed the three functions of money amazingly well over a remarkably long period of time. An important reason for this is that gold is durable and its supply is fairly inelastic. More gold cannot be created without significant cost and effort. Another reason is that despite short-term fluctuations, the value of gold relative to everything else has remained surprisingly constant over the long term. Of course, there is no guarantee that this will always continue to be true in the future.

On the other hand, commodity money does have one very big advantage: it has a definite intrinsic value that is never zero. Representative money also has this advantage, although there is some added risk that the dealer or other depository may not actually still have the commodity that was supposed to be in safekeeping when someone shows up to reclaim it.

Fiat Currency

Soon after the end of the first millennium CE, the "innovation" of fiat money burst onto the scene. Like representative money, fiat money consists of bills or tokens that have substantially zero intrinsic value (or the intrinsic value is far below the face value). Unlike representative money, fiat money does not represent anything at all. There is no guarantee that it can be redeemed for any amount of anything of value. Its value is simply decreed by law or fiat.

Suppose you made up some paper bills in your basement with a "1" or "One" and a nice headshot of yourself printed on them. You then declare that each of your bills is worth one ounce of silver. Now you boogie on down to the store and exchange some of your fiat bills for groceries and clothing. That is all there is to a fiat currency. The only difference is that it is normally a government that prints the currency and decrees its value, not an individual. Unless the individual happens to be the dictator of record, they will not be able to use force to back up their decree or fiat.

The first fiat currency was attempted approximately a thousand years ago by the Song Dynasty in China. Paper bills were issued and decreed to be exchangeable for certain amounts of gold, silver, or silk. However, there was no way to actually redeem the bills for these commodities or anything else of intrinsic value. This realization, combined with the printing of many bills, caused people to lose confidence in the currency. The government attempted to force the use of the currency by insisting that taxes be partially paid with the bills, but nevertheless, rampant inflation (loss of perceived and functional value) completely killed the currency.

In view of the abject failure of the first fiat currency, no one would try that again, right? Wrong. Many fiat currencies have been attempted, and many have failed when the currency collapsed to its true value: zero. Considering its nature, it is not at all surprising that there have been, and continue to be, so many fiat currency failures. What is shocking is that there actually are examples of fiat currencies that have been made to work somewhat well for periods of several decades. How could something like that ever be pulled off?

In a totalitarian society, extreme oppressive force works pretty well. But even there, barter, black markets, and the use of precious metal coins still creep in "under the table" when people have no confidence in a fiat currency.

In freer societies, one fairly effective trick is to start out with a sound currency that is actually redeemable for something of real value — a representative currency. Then, in the face of some "emergency," currency redeemability is "temporarily suspended." It works best if redeemability is suspended and restored a few times before "temporarily" suspending it permanently. People have by then been conditioned to continue to think their money is "as good as gold" since its redeemability is to be restored. Someday. Maybe.

If nothing disruptive occurs for a period of time following the last suspension of redemption "privileges," the "currency levitation" becomes self-perpetuating. It appears that a period of just a few decades without serious problems is all it takes to lull most people into a profound state of ignorance and complacency regarding their money.

In the final analysis, a person is willing to swap something of real value for a worthless piece of paper today if and only if they have confidence that they can swap the paper for something of reasonably equal value tomorrow. When this has been happening for an extended period, people become more confident that it will continue to happen in the future. However, if and when this confidence is shaken, the collapse of a fiat currency is usually rapid and highly disruptive. The image comes to mind of the cartoon character that runs off a cliff but doesn't fall. After a suitable comedic interval, he looks down, realizes that absolutely nothing is holding him up, and then quickly crashes to the hard earth below.

Comparison of Characteristics

The first thing to note is that fiat money is created by force — an edict or fiat. On the other hand, commodity money comes into use voluntarily among free and peaceful people. Thus, a fiat currency is monopolistic and entirely controlled by a government entity. Commodity money is the antithesis of this as it cannot be monopolistically controlled. Through the expenditure of work and effort, anyone can mine, grow, or otherwise create more of the commodity, but it cannot be limitlessly created for next-to-no cost.

Fiat money is political. If you move out of one political entity into another, you must change to using the fiat money demanded by the new political entity. Commodity money has intrinsic value and, therefore, can transcend political boundaries. Your gold coin will have substantially the same value (relative to other things) in any country, no matter whose likeness may have been stamped onto it.

Commodity money came into use and has been successfully used for thousands of years. Fiat money has been around for about the last thousand years. Fiat currencies tend not to last. There are a few examples where fiat currencies have been abandoned and phased out by the political entity that created it, but most have collapsed when people have lost confidence and reverted to using commodity money and/or barter.

The characteristic most critical to a currency's ability to perform the functions of money well is the *elasticity* of its supply. The supply of any commodity money tends to be quite inelastic. There is a definite cost to creating more of any commodity, and that turns out to be a good thing when it is used as money. Fiat money, with substantially zero intrinsic value, is almost completely elastic. Governments can create additional fiat money at near-zero cost and essentially without limit.

Any sound money begins with something of value. You can exchange that thing for other things of value or for representative tokens (physical or electronic) with the guarantee that tokens can always be redeemed for something of equal value. A fiat currency starts instead with worthless tokens and attempts to hoodwink or force people to value them.

Inflation

With representative or commodity money, the value of everything is measured in terms of, or relative to, the chosen commodity (frequently gold), and the value of the currency is anchored to the value of that commodity. In order to issue more representative tokens of zero intrinsic value, it is necessary to hold more of the backing commodity "on deposit" since it is guaranteed that each token can be redeemed on demand for a certain fixed amount of the commodity. The value of such tokens is fixed and cannot float around. However, as previously noted, the value scale can change (either expand or contract) to the extent that the supply and/or demand of the backing commodity shifts and affects its value relative to everything else. This is the fundamental disadvantage of commodity or representative money that is based on a single commodity.

Suppose you live in a country where the government has issued a representative currency based on gold. Said government holds the gold that backs the currency and "guarantees" that you can convert your dollars to gold on demand at the rate of $35 per ounce of gold. One morning, you learn through the news that the government has changed the exchange rate to $70 per ounce of gold, effective midnight of last night.

Surprise! Any money you had under your mattress or in the bank can now be redeemed for only half as much gold, and you will find that the prices of everything else in the stores will very quickly double as well. The currency has been devalued. That's inflation. Although governments have done things this bad and worse, the change is normally carried out more gradually (in small steps spread out over time) to reduce economic disruption and avoid waking people up. The "psychology" of this is unfortunately misleading. Most people gripe about the prices going up and blame those increasing them instead of fingering the real culprit: the decreasing purchasing power of their money.

Of course, the government could decide to change the exchange rate in the other direction, say, to $20 per ounce of gold. This would be *def*lation. Don't hold your breath; this is never going to happen, as it would require the government to suddenly hold more gold to back the currency. By contrast, inflation enables the government to (elastically) print more worthless tokens backed by the same amount of gold.

Suppose now that you live in a country that has a fiat currency that has been successfully used for a few decades. What determines its value? Originally, the value was likely set when it was a hard currency convertible to something of real value. When this tie is removed (redeemability suspended), the value of the dollar (or other token) is no longer anchored to anything and begins to "float." Since it is not tied to anything, it becomes its own pseudo-commodity whose value depends upon its supply relative to its demand.

The supply is closely related to the total number of dollars in circulation, called the money supply. The demand is entirely determined by psychology! That is, people will value the dollar today based solely on how much value they expect they will be able to trade it for tomorrow or next week or next year, and the demand will be set by this consensus. Anything based on human expectations is affected by a huge complexity of factors and can potentially be quite volatile.

Increasing the money supply tends to reduce the value of the dollar, and vice versa, exactly as would be expected. When people have more dollars, they tend to bid up prices, and prices generally rise. The value of the dollar is reduced. This is inflation. Politicians and governments love to increase the money supply, so inflation is the rule, and deflation is a rare exception.

A simple demonstration, sometimes employed in the economics classroom, starkly illuminates the inflation process. The teacher produces and demonstrates the operation of a pocket flashlight that is no longer needed. It will be auctioned off to the highest bidder. Not being allowed to take students' "real" money, the teacher distributes $15 of monopoly money to each student to use in bidding. Students may combine resources if they are willing to jointly own or share the flashlight. The auction is conducted, and the flashlight sells for (typically) $25. Note that the worthless monopoly money has taken on a value only because the teacher is willing to exchange something of real value for it.

The teacher then produces and demonstrates a second identical flashlight, explaining that this is the only one remaining and that it, too, will be auctioned as before. An additional $15 is distributed to each student and the second auction conducted. The second flashlight typically sells for somewhere near $50. Quite obviously, the identical flashlight does not have a value greater than the first. The price has just gone up because the money supply has increased. More correctly, the value of each monopoly money dollar has decreased. The total value of all the worthless tokens in circulation tends to be proportional to the total value of the goods and services for which they can be traded.

Inflation (or deflation) seriously interferes with money's ability to act as a standard of value and, therefore, degrades its ability to act as a store of value. Some of the direct effects of inflation are that it:
- acts as a stealth tax as it quietly siphons value right out of wallets and bank accounts;
- discourages savings and accumulation of capital,
- pushes up interest rates;
- favors borrowers and hurts lenders (unless the loan interest rates are variable);
- interferes with the ability of businesses and individuals to plan for the future; and
- diminishes confidence in the currency.

It pushes up interest rates because if you want to charge 2% per year to rent out your money, you will need to collect 2% *plus* the expected rate of inflation, so with 4% inflation, you will have to collect 6% interest. Furthermore, after inflation gets going, the expectation of it continuing (or worse, the inflation rate increasing) tends to make it self-perpetuating and hard to bring under control.

A few macroeconomists have proposed that "moderate" rates of inflation have indirect effects that can be good, such as reducing unemployment. But these claims rest on complex and unproven macroeconomic theories. Fiat currencies and the inflation that they enable are, overall, not good for anybody. In fact, it is rapid inflation that usually triggers the collapse of a fiat currency. Inflation exceeding 25% to 40% annually is probably about the tipping point that leads to a degenerative inflationary spiral from which the currency does not recover. This has happened many times in many countries since the advent of fiat currencies.

Modern Developments

The advent of pervasive high-speed electronic communication and computation has had a significant impact. Transactions take place instantaneously at light speed. Accurate and detailed records are maintained by computers. The Internet has made rather complete information about virtually anything quickly and easily available. These capabilities have reduced market friction, a plethora of operational overhead costs, and enabled markets to operate more efficiently. In fact, numbers stored by computers have, to a considerable extent, replaced physical dollars in circulation. The money supply can be manipulated by changing numbers in computers.

Banks increase the money supply when they loan out the money that has been deposited into bank accounts by depositors. This is called *fractional reserve banking*. They hold enough cash in reserve to cover expected withdrawals plus some safety reserve. However, if too many depositors try to withdraw too much of their money at the same time, the bank may not have sufficient reserves on hand to cover those withdrawals. This does occasionally happen. If it should happen to several banks within the same timeframe, it can cause depositors to panic and try to pull *all* their money out, resulting in multiple bank failures. This is called a *run on the banks*, and that, too, occasionally happens. A major panic could topple the banking system and have a domino effect on the rest of the economy.

A very recent and potentially important development is that of cryptocurrencies. Bitcoin was the first entirely electronic currency. It is backed by absolutely nothing, not even a fiat! In addition to its electronic speed, convenience, and internationality, the good thing about Bitcoin is that the money supply, the number of Bitcoins in electronic circulation, is rigidly regulated. Additional Bitcoins are added at a controlled slow and diminishing rate and at a cost.

However, as with other unbacked currencies, the demand for Bitcoins is entirely determined by psychology! That is, people will value a Bitcoin today based solely upon how much value they think they will be able to exchange it for tomorrow. Consequently, the value of one Bitcoin has gyrated wildly from next to nothing all the way up to (so far) the $120,000 range and is (currently in 2026) trading at about $75,000.

If you enjoy gambling, you might want to exchange some Federal Reserve notes (FRNs) for some Bitcoins. People might not be risking nearly as much money on cryptocurrencies as they are if they had greater confidence in the fiat currencies issued by their governments. But remember, if you suddenly can't find anyone willing to exchange anything of value for your cryptocurrency, it could be worth much less or even zero. It's not even printed on paper, unlike an otherwise worthless FRN, which you might still be able to use in the bathroom or crumple up for tinder to start a fire.

Still, cryptocurrency's features are very attractive: fast, very low-cost peer-to-peer transfers between any two entities with an Internet connection and the security and privacy of encryption with no involvement of any specific third party. Some users take advantage of these features by converting FRNs into a cryptocurrency immediately before a transaction and out of it immediately following each transaction, thereby minimizing exposure to the cryptocurrency by holding it only very briefly.

More recently, cryptocurrencies called "stablecoin" have been created that are backed by something more substantial than nothing. Most often, the backing is the US dollar. Yes, that is better than nothing, but the dollar continues to lose value and also become more risky as the national debt grows inexorably.

Perhaps cryptocurrency technology might be used in the future to form a solid representative currency that is guaranteed to be redeemable for some commodity or commodities of intrinsic value. A completely electronic "token" could be used as representative money without the need to ever create, carry, or exchange any physical tokens. Paralysis could result suddenly, however, if the Internet should ever go down.

The Currency of the United States

The framers of the US Constitution very much appreciated the importance and benefits of sound money as well as the dangers of having a strong central bank. The Constitution was written in 1787 following considerable currency turmoil in the early days of our republic. As one of the few powers enumerated in Article I, Section 8, Congress was specifically assigned the power and responsibility "to coin Money, regulate the Value thereof, and of foreign Coin, and fix the Standard of Weights and Measures." A relevant part of Article I, Section 10, provides that "no State shall … coin Money; emit Bills of Credit; make any Thing but gold and silver Coin a Tender in Payment of Debts…" The issue of a central bank was debated at the time, but the Constitution makes no provision for one.

For approximately 120 years following the ratification of the Constitution, the United States ran fairly smoothly using a hard (commodity) currency based on gold and silver. Central banks were chartered for stretches of time, but the United States had no central bank for most of this period. However, a series of horrible events spanning a sixty-year period in the twentieth century caused the transformation of the US dollar into a pure fiat currency and created a peculiar central bank that is not directly controlled by, or even a part of, the government.

Because of the practice of fractional reserve banking, several overextended banks failed in 1907. This precipitated a panic and a run on other banks, some of which then also failed. In what could be termed an overreaction, Congress passed the sweeping Federal Reserve Act in 1913. By it, Congress delegated its constitutionally assigned responsibility for money to an organization to be called the Federal Reserve ("the Fed"). Part of the justification for the Fed was that it would act as a "lender of last resort" to enable banks to ride out runs and thereby forestall panics.

The Fed is indeed a central bank with great powers, but it is *not* part of the federal government. It is a cartel of twelve private banks managed by a seven-member board of governors whose members are appointed by the president and confirmed by the Senate to fourteen-year terms. Other than indirectly through these appointments (or changing the law), the government has no control over what the Fed does.

The Fed is legally required to "report" regularly to Congress, but it is not obligated to take any direction from Congress or the president. All stock of the twelve Fed banks is owned by other private banks called *member banks*. The Fed is not taxed, but whatever it reports as a profit goes to the US Treasury. However, it might be noted that the Fed's operations have never, in over a hundred years, been subjected to a complete and public audit.

At first, since the dollar was still tied to gold, the Treasury and Fed were somewhat constrained from any huge increase in the money supply. Right after World War II, the dollar was still incredibly strong. It was accepted all over the world as being "as good as gold." In fact, the dollar was adopted as the reserve currency of the free world. Other currencies were linked to the dollar, and the dollar was, in turn, linked to gold at an exchange rate of $35 per ounce, as agreed to by forty-four nations at the Bretton Woods Conference of 1944.

However, in 1971, President Nixon delivered a horrible blow to the dollar — he "suspended" the redeemability of the dollar, completely severing any ties between the dollar and gold. Dollar redeemability is still "suspended." Today, the dollar is floating around as a pure fiat currency. However, substantially the entire world is using fiat currencies that float relative to each other. The relative "soundness" of each is linked more to the strength and stability of each country's economy than to any inherent characteristic of the currency itself.

Although it is far weaker than it used to be, the dollar is still hanging in as the world's reserve currency, primarily because there so far has not been a significantly stronger currency to challenge it. Some think the Chinese are maneuvering toward having their renminbi replace the dollar as the world's reserve currency. The BRICS (Brazil, Russia, India, China, South Africa) intergovernmental organization has been accumulating countries and strength, recently adding NATO member Turkey. The BRICS block may eventually move to depose the dollar from its perch as the world's reserve currency. That would be a very serious blow to the dollar's strength.

Another of the reasons used to justify the creation of the Fed was that savvy bankers acting as central planners manipulating interest rates and the money supply would be able to better smooth out business cycles, booms, busts, and bubbles. But the Fed's track record has not been good. The Great Depression of 1929 and the early 1930s happened on the Fed's watch, as did the more recent "housing bubble" and ensuing bad recession. There are quite a few somewhat less severe examples that could be cited as well.

Yet another huge justification used for the creation of the Fed was that its independence would remove monetary policy from the control of politicians. (It should be pointed out that you really only need to have a "monetary policy" if you have a fiat currency.) It is surely possible that politicians might have done a worse job, and it is not clear how much influence politicians may have actually had, but the performance of the Fed has been rather dismal.

Theoretically, one of the Fed's most important duties is to keep the value of the dollar constant, avoiding either inflation or deflation. There have been three decades under the Fed in which the dollar lost more than 40% of its value during the ten-year period and one decade when it actually gained 23% (deflation). Overall, under the Fed, the dollar has lost about 97% of its purchasing power! That is, the dollar in 2026 is worth less than three cents of the 1913 dollar. The Fed's stated objective is to achieve and maintain a 2% per year inflation rate; the objective should be zero.

In recent decades, politicians, with the Fed's complicity, have been digging the United States into a very deep hole. In an attempt to "buy votes" to improve their chances of being reelected, politicians like to hand out benefits that cost money — a lot of money. Thus, they have become incorrigibly addicted to spending. These politicians are aided by leftists who do not understand a free market economy and favor a command economy. Federal spending is growing and totaled $7 trillion for fiscal year 2025. Government is no longer the small percentage of "overhead" that it used to be and has become quite significant compared to the entire output of the economy, the *gross domestic product* (GDP), which was approximately $30.6 trillion in 2025.

A balanced budget would require politicians to reduce spending or raise taxes to pay for their handouts. However, increasing taxes would damage their electability and the economy. Governments at all levels are, in total, already confiscating a huge percentage — an average of nearly one-third — of the private sector's earnings. When this much "blood" is drained from the body and spent inefficiently, the economy struggles to sustain even a slow rate of growth (1% to 3% per year).

Things got totally out of control a few years back when the politicians figured out that they could avoid the immediate pain of imposing higher taxes by just borrowing money and postponing the pain to the future. By the end of 2025, they had run up nearly $39 trillion in debt at the federal level. That was larger than the GDP; indeed, it was about 125% of the GDP. That's a whole bunch of future pain. It is terribly wrong to inflict such pain on future generations, especially since they have no say in the matter.

In addition, they have legislated large "entitlement" programs that have become actuarially unsound. The unfunded liabilities for these programs are not included in the $39 trillion debt figure and are many times larger. Considerable additional debt resides at the state and local government levels. An increasing number of cities have gone belly-up, and some states (e.g., Illinois and California) are in danger of bankruptcy.

While the politicians have been spending and the Treasury borrowing, the Treasury and Fed have been expanding the money supply at an unprecedented rate. Inflationary pressures are running high. Excessive relief spending related to the 2021–2022 COVID pandemic and "climate change" programs pushed inflation up to more than 9%. Of course, it's nice to be able to pay off debt (Treasury bonds) with dollars that are worth less, but inflation necessarily pushes up interest rates. Interest on the national debt was nearly $1 trillion in 2025.

Interest has become such a large line item in the federal budget that it is forcing either cuts in other spending or even more borrowing. The government is near the danger point of spiraling into bankruptcy. All three of the major credit rating agencies have reduced the United States' credit rating. US Treasury bonds have always been considered the safest of places to stash money. That has allowed the United States to borrow at very low interest rates, but that obviously is changing, and investors are going to insist upon higher interest payments to offset the increasing risk. That also will force interest on the national debt upwards — significantly above a trillion dollars per year.

The politicians have spent the country into a very difficult and dangerous financial position. Will they stop? Not likely. They appear to be more concerned with staying in power than they are about the country's welfare. It seems that they will continue "kicking the can down the road," hoping that serious problems can be forestalled until they are out of office or ready to retire. Very serious federal austerity or a large devaluation of our currency or both can't be very far down the road. The economy would have to show sustained growth at an unrealistically high rate in order to "grow our way out of" this jam.

With careful, resolute, and even-handed management, it *might* be possible to pull back from the brink and gradually climb or grow our way out of the hole. However, regardless of how it is done, there would unavoidably be very noticeable pain involved. Based on our dismal history, there is no reason to anticipate careful, resolute, and even-handed management.

Barring a miracle (like a majority of intelligent, honest, responsible politicians), it appears that the end of our fiat currency is now coming into view in the not-too-distant future. Exactly when a collapse may come and what will trigger it is impossible to predict accurately. This is especially so now that ours is one of many unstable fiat currencies floating around relative to each other; one can draw at least temporary strength from the relative weakness of others. But don't look down!

The Path to Prosperity

The very first requirement for prosperity is a properly operating free market economy. A free market economy cannot operate at its best (highest rate of wealth creation) if there is any force involved. Everything in a pure free market economy must be the result of voluntary interactions and transactions among free people. Another requirement is sound money.

The laws of economics have, of course, always existed, but human understanding of them began with the science of economics at about the time of the American Revolution. Much more widespread economic "literacy" surely would be helpful, especially in Congress. Markets are complex, with billions of interacting feedback loops at many levels that maintain equilibrium. Economic interactions, causes, and effects are hard to fully understand and can often be counterintuitive. The free market may not be completely without problems, but it surely is better than anything else that has been tried or conceived.

One of the greatest threats to a free market economy is politicians attempting to manipulate the economy through the use of government force. Sometimes, this may even be a well-intentioned attempt to "fix" some sort of real or perceived "problem." Other times, it is just a payoff to a crony or special interest group. Common examples are:

- generally heavy taxation that drains wealth from the economy to support constitutionally unauthorized government activities, to be spent inefficiently, or to fund waste, fraud, and abuse;
- targeted punitive taxation intended to reduce the demand for some good or service (e.g., "vice taxes" on alcohol, tobacco, and marijuana);
- crazily complex tax laws that require the huge wasted overhead of an entire industry of accountants and tax preparers/advisers to help people prepare their tax returns;
- subsidization aimed at lowering the (apparent) cost, increasing the supply, and spurring the purchase of some good or service (e.g., solar cells and battery electric vehicles);
- guarantees, where taxpayers are put on the hook to guarantee loans or deals;
- forcing or prohibiting the use of some good or service (e.g., ethanol in gasoline);

- attempting to force minimum or maximum prices for goods and services (e.g., minimum wage laws or price controls);
- bogus licensing requirements intended to shield established members of an industry (who hire good lobbyists and fund them well) from new competition; and
- confiscation of wealth earned by one individual and either giving it to another individual who did not earn it or spending it in accordance with politicians' priorities.

The only highly efficient spending (wants satisfied per dollar spent) is when you spend your own wealth on things that you want or need. The lowest efficiency is 536 politicians spending your money on themselves, their cronies, or for things they *think* other people should want or need.

To the extent that the above distortions occur, we do not have a free market economy. All such actions have both some consequences that are seen and many that are unseen. Overall, *the result is to misallocate resources and reduce the rate of wealth creation*, thus penalizing everyone either directly or indirectly. All too often, unforeseen consequences even make the targeted problem itself worse instead of better.

The US economy is so distorted by so many such actions that it struggles to achieve 2% to 3% per year growth in "good" years when it could and should be humming along at 5% to 8% per year growth, possibly more. That's a whole bunch of wealth that's not being created and not raising everyone's standard of living. The United States needs to move strongly away from the command economy end of the spectrum and toward the free market end.

Sound Money

As stated, to operate smoothly and well, any economy needs sound money. If we could "design" our money from the ground up, what choices should we make?

As we have seen, any truly sound money *must* either have an intrinsic value itself (commodity money) or be representative money that is *guaranteed* to be redeemable for something of value upon demand. The latter is certainly the preferred choice in our high-tech world, in which transactions are increasingly handled by adjusting numbers in computers rather than physically transferring pieces of paper or metal.

We reject fiat money simply because, for the reasons discussed, it cannot be depended upon to perform the three functions of money well over long periods of time, its stability is poor, and its collapse almost invariably is highly disruptive.

Commodity money and representative money arose spontaneously and independently of any government. It would be preferable to maintain independence from any political entity so that our new money could be used within any region or the entire world, just as gold coins maintain substantially the same value (relative to other commodities) anywhere. This last objective will be difficult to achieve in the currently chaotic world.

Certainly, there would be no attempt to prohibit the use of any competing forms of money. Since sound money is always preferred to unsound money, our new money should be preferred if we've designed it correctly. If not, oh well, somebody else did a better job and therefore should prevail. Free competition is always a good thing. Finally, sound money cannot be used as a tool to facilitate extreme financial irresponsibility by governments — for example, repaying borrowed funds with money that is worth less than that borrowed.

We come now to the question of what should back our currency. For what should holders of the currency be guaranteed to be able to exchange it upon demand? It would probably not be a horrible mistake to choose gold. Gold has been used successfully over long periods of time. It seems likely that this will continue to be the case in the future — but, of course, there is no guarantee of that. Perhaps gold will be supplanted by something else in its industrial and cosmetic uses so that its demand decreases. Or maybe new uses for gold might be found that increase the demand for it. Or perhaps some new way of mining, refining, or creating gold will be invented that drastically increases its supply. Any of those things might cause the value of gold relative to other things to change significantly.

Although gold would be far better than the current situation of no backing, perhaps a way can be devised to improve upon gold as a backing for currency. The choice of the best thing to back our currency turns out to be more complex than one might initially think. Unfortunately, there is no absolute scale of value. All commodities are valued relative to each other, and worse, the relative valuations change over time, sometimes dramatically. A great example of such dramatic change can be found in anything electronic. Advancing technology has made all things electronic cost less in terms of the dollar, even in the face of inflation that makes the dollar itself worth less. At the same time, the functionality, reliability, and other characteristics of electronic products have all improved greatly. So, what really does it mean to keep the value of the dollar "constant"? To what can one anchor the value of a representative currency in this vast sea of shifting values with no land ever in sight?

Economics is all about satisfying the wants of humans. Rather than tie our new currency to one commodity, it would seem better to tie it to something of great and lasting significance to humans. There are many ways this could be done, but it's hard to think of anything of more universal and fundamental human significance than the "cost of living." Indexes have been devised which are intended to measure the cost of living. We use them to measure inflation, so the concept of the cost of living is nothing new.

Suppose you are a descendant of Rip Van Winkle and you like to take long naps. You are planning a nice twenty-five-year nap. You realize that many things will change unpredictably over that amount of time. You know that you will not have a job when you awake and that you may have to live for a while without one. You may have a fair amount to learn in order to get back up to speed, nail down a job, and become self-supporting again. This is bound to take some time. To prepare responsibly, you stash enough cash under your mattress to support yourself in a reasonable (say, middle-class) manner for a year.

When you awake twenty-five years later, it seems entirely reasonable to expect that your stashed cash will indeed support you in a then-equivalent middle-class style for a year. You certainly should not be rudely surprised to find that your cash now will support you for only four months!

Of course, a lot of things may have changed. It might be that buggy whips were part of your cost of living when you went to bed, but when you wake up, buggy whips are no longer part of your cost of living, but gasoline is. What should not change, though, is the cost of living. If you can support yourself with a middle-class existence for $50,000 per year today, you should be able to support yourself equivalently for a year for $50,000 tomorrow or twenty-five years later or a hundred years later. Money can do a pretty good job of acting as a store of value if it is measured in terms of some well-chosen commodity. But it could do an even better job of storing value if that value is of direct, fundamental, and more universal value to humans. How might this be accomplished?

A carefully designed and maintained cost-of-living index would have to be at the core. It should be composed of a large number of goods and services, each widely and frequently traded, with weighting factors so as to always accurately represent and total up to the median cost of living at any given time. All prices are, say, fifty-two-week moving averages updated weekly, so there is a great deal of stability and no seasonality. No single component can have more than a minuscule impact upon the total. As the impact of things like buggy whips upon the median cost of living fades, their weighting factors are slowly reduced, while the weighting factors for things with growing impacts (gasoline) are increased to reflect their growing significance.

It obviously is of the utmost importance that the index be honestly and impartially maintained by an independent entity immune to any political or economic influences. Note that the Consumer Price Index (CPI) maintained by the US government has been modified several times to show lower rates of inflation. For example, food and fuel have been removed as components of the CPI ostensibly because of their "volatility." But who believes food and fuel are not significant to the cost of living? One of the reasons for such manipulations is that cost-of-living adjustments based on the CPI are reduced, somewhat easing budgetary problems like the growth of Social Security payments. It should be possible to fairly rigidly define the procedure for determining the cost of living in such a way as to minimize the opportunity for nefarious manipulation.

The cost of living can be expected to remain quite constant naturally. It is not appreciably affected by the normal short-term fluctuations in the prices of its many components. It could be expected to change slowly over the long term as affected by, say, technology tending to reduce costs and/or the gradual phasing in and out of components (gasoline instead of buggy whips, etc.) or even an increasing standard of living.

Suppose that the cost of living when our new index is initiated is $50,000. This then becomes the reference cost of living. Each time the cost of living is updated, it is divided into the reference cost of living to obtain an *adjustment factor*. If the cost of living always stays $50,000 (as is the goal), the adjustment factor is always 1.0000. However, suppose in some future week the cost of living computes to $50,100.00. The adjustment factor then becomes 0.9980. Of course, if the cost of living starts to drift down below $50,000, the adjustment factor will be greater than 1.0000. A cost-of-living computation of $49,900 results in an adjustment factor of 1.0020. The trick now is to implement a negative feedback loop that will adjust the value of the dollar so that the adjustment factor stays very close to 1.0000 and therefore always keeps the cost of living very near $50,000.

With a fiat currency, such a feedback loop has to be created by linking the money supply to the adjustment factor. If/when the adjustment factor drops below 1.0000 (inflation), the US Treasury must judiciously decrease the money supply. This tends to increase the value of the dollar and cause prices to generally decline. In the opposite case, where the adjustment factor goes above 1.0000 (deflation), the money supply must be increased, thereby decreasing the value of the dollar and causing a general increase in prices back to a $50,000 cost of living. The volatility of fiat currencies (previously discussed) combined with hard-to-predict time delays between changes in the money supply and the resultant price changes make this feedback loop somewhat tricky but certainly better than no control. Fiat currencies are *not* recommended.

A hard currency, guaranteed to always be redeemable for something of intrinsic value, is fundamentally much less volatile and more stable. The dollar itself could be intrinsically worthless paper coins or a cryptocurrency. The feedback loop established above could be stabilized and the fiat currency converted to a representative currency by guaranteeing its redeemability. But how could that be done, and for what exactly would it be redeemable?

Again utilizing the adjustment factor, the dollar could be made redeemable for anything that is convenient. If we wish to redeem the dollar for gold, this can be done by multiplying the current spot price for gold by the adjustment factor. Similarly, the dollar could be redeemed for silver at a rate determined simply by multiplying silver's current spot price by the adjustment factor. Indeed, the dollar could be redeemed in *any* convenient commodity that a depository institution and its customers might (voluntarily) agree to use; just multiply the current market price of the commodity by the adjustment factor to obtain the redemption rate. In this manner, the dollar could be solidly anchored to the cost of living. This system is implemented by Article VII of the Constitution in appendix B.

One would not expect much redemption activity to actually occur as there would be little reason for it. However, guaranteed stability requires that the option always be available.

Note that under the system just described, fluctuations in the price of gold, silver, or any commodity are not at all disruptive, as the dollar is now decoupled from any particular commodity. The dollar is now a solid representative currency that is guaranteed to be redeemable but not necessarily for a fixed amount of any specific commodity. One cannot say that the dollar represents gold, silver, barley, or any commodity, although it could indeed be redeemed for any of them. So, what exactly is it that the dollar represents? Using the numbers from the above examples, the dollar always represents slightly more than ten minutes of middle-class living.

Conclusions

It should be possible to gain the manifold advantages of a hard representative currency without the potential disadvantage of tying it to some specific commodity. Instead, its flexibly redeemable value could be locked to follow any gradual long-term shifts in what is probably most important to humans: their cost of living. Cost-of-living adjustments would never be needed. Long-term planning would be simpler. An overall approach to accomplishing this has been outlined.

A hard currency is its own monetary policy. There is no need for central planning or manipulation. A central bank is not necessary, and the potential problems of a central bank can be avoided.

Interest rates (the rental price for money) should be set by normal market forces from competition among many borrowers and many lenders, just as all other prices should be determined by market supply and demand. Operating without the use of force, the myriads of corrective feedback loops of a voluntary free market automatically do the best job of maintaining balance and efficiently allocating resources. Arbitrary manipulation of anything is undesirable and almost inevitably destabilizing, especially when attempted in combination with the inherent instability of a fiat currency.

13. Energy

Energy is one of the most underappreciated underpinnings of human civilization. Without the use of large amounts of energy, civilization as we know it could not exist and instead would collapse to a much more rudimentary and primitive level. The availability of even larger amounts of reliable, low-cost energy is of critical importance to the further advancement of civilization, and there are even some additional reasons why energy is of such critical importance.

A Little Energy History

The mainstay energy source utilized by humans for a large part of their 300,000-year existence was their very own muscle power. The first use of external energy was that of fire. There is evidence that predecessors had utilized natural fires several hundred thousand years ahead of them, but control of fire — being able to start a controlled fire when and where one was desired — seems to have occurred at roughly the time of the arrival of Homo sapiens on the scene.

Fire was truly a significant benefit to a grueling existence. It supported cooking food and supplied both heat and light. It was useful for fashioning better weapons and was of some help in keeping predators away. It was the only external energy source for many thousands of years.

Domestication of animals and (literally) harnessing the power of their larger muscles began approximately 8,000 years ago. Tapping hydropower and wind power followed about 2,500 years ago. The use of external power sources then began to ramp up. Coal was the first fossil fuel to be burned.

With the development of a decent steam engine in 1779 and the internal combustion engine in 1800, the combustion of fossil fuels began a steep climb — coal, oil, and then natural gas. The advent of the first electric power generating station in 1882 further accelerated that climb. The development of practical refrigeration during the late 1800s (using energy to move heat energy) created yet another major use for energy, as did tungsten-filament light bulbs in 1904.

Our civilization utilizes prodigious amounts of energy — probably about two exajoules[14] or 6×10^{11} kilowatt hours each day. It is what enables us to shelter, feed, and clothe ourselves and still have time to do other things, like occasionally hop on an airplane to someplace thousands of miles away for a vacation. It is interesting, and maybe important, to realize that the source of almost every joule utilized by the human race from its beginning has been nuclear energy.[15]

Our sun is an awesome nuclear power generator. It just hurtles along through space for billions of years producing a gigantic amount of power — nearly 10^{27} watts (joules per second). The energy radiates into space in all directions, predominantly as electromagnetic radiation over a rather

---

[14] As discussed in chapter 3, a joule is the MKS unit of energy. An exajoule is 10^{18} joules, so two of those would be equal to about 6×10^{11} kilowatt-hours — a whole lot of poop.

[15] The only exceptions would be any insignificant amount of energy that may have been derived purely from tidal forces or the heat deep in the core of the earth (including volcanic heat). To the extent that core heat arises from radioactive decay, it too is nuclear.

broad spectrum. We have learned how to release and utilize nuclear energy here on Earth, too, and have been doing so since the early 1950s, but most of our energy to date has come from the local star that our planet orbits.

The sun is massive, about 2 x 10^{30} kg, which is 330,000 times the mass of the earth. The sun's gravitational field holds Earth in a nearly circular orbit at a distance of approximately 150 million kilometers (93 million miles). At that distance, the amount of energy from the sun bathing the earth is 1,361 watts (joules per second) per square meter. The total for the entire earth is 1.73×10^{17} watts. An average of slightly over half of that energy makes it through the atmosphere to the earth's surface.

One consequence of this steady influx of energy is that the earth is warmed to a temperature at which water is generally liquid and many complex chemical compounds are stable — most notably, organic ones of which living organisms are composed. With no incoming energy, the energy the earth has would dissipate out into space, and the surface of the earth would gradually cool to a few degrees above absolute zero — that's zero on the Kelvin scale (K), −273.15° Celsius or −459.67° Fahrenheit. Because of its not-too-hot, not-too-cold temperature, Earth is known as a "Goldilocks" planet. There are lots of other Goldilocks planets in the universe, but their astronomical distances from Earth make it difficult to learn much about them.

It is the nuclear energy from the sun that drives precipitation, falling waters, and winds that provide hydro and wind power. More recently, solar panels have converted electromagnetic radiation from the sun directly into electricity. Less often, the radiation is converted into heat energy for direct use.

Radiation in the ultraviolet portion of the electromagnetic spectrum is able to power a process called photosynthesis, whereby the organic molecules that form plant matter are fabricated. This captures and stores some of the sun's energy in these complex molecules. It is this energy that is released to power the muscles of the critters that eat the plants and to light the fires that have warmed and cooked food for humans and their ancestors. Plant matter grown millions of years ago and fossilized has stored the sun's energy, which is released when fossil fuels are oxidized (burned).

The Warming Earth Thing

Our burgeoning civilization has been utilizing more and more energy. Though some of that energy has been nuclear energy that we've learned to release here on Earth, too much of it has been derived from the combustion of greater and greater quantities of fossil fuels. When substantially any fossil fuel is oxidized, one of the combustion products is some amount of carbon dioxide (CO_2).

So much additional CO_2 has been dumped into our atmosphere over the past century that its measurable concentration has increased by 45% to 50%. This sounds like a big increase, and it is, but CO_2 is still a minuscule component of our air. The composition of the atmosphere by mole fraction (percentage of the molecules) is still overwhelmingly nitrogen (N_2, 78.08%) and oxygen (O_2, 20.95%), then argon (Ar, 0.93%), then carbon dioxide (CO_2, 0.04%) and even smaller traces of several other gases. A highly variable amount of water vapor will also be present.

Many people are very upset about the increase of CO_2 in the atmosphere. They claim it is causing our planet to warm up, which will result in many dire consequences: much polar ice will melt, causing oceans to rise and flood much land, many species will go extinct, and so on. These people may be correct, so it would be good to first understand why they are concerned.

As explained above, the earth continuously absorbs about 10^{17} watts of energy from the sun. In order to remain at the same temperature, the earth must continuously radiate that same amount of energy back out into space. The power (watts) that the earth radiates is proportional to the fourth power of its absolute temperature. If for any reason the earth would radiate more than 10^{17} watts, it would necessarily cool down some until it is again radiating only what it is receiving. On the other hand, if the earth radiates less than 10^{17} watts, it would have to warm up until it again radiates exactly what it receives.

The average temperature of the earth today is approximately 60°F, 15°C, or 288°K. As an illustration, if the earth were to radiate either 10% more or 10% less than 10^{17} watts, its temperature would need to change either down or up by approximately 7°K (or 7°C) to restore the balance. That would be a very impactful change indeed.

What could change either the rate at which energy is being absorbed or being radiated by the earth? The concentration of CO_2 in the atmosphere turns out to be one of many things that can do that.

The surface of the sun is quite hot, about 5,500°C or 10,000°F. This causes the spectrum of its electromagnetic radiation to peak in the visible wavelengths of light. Those wavelengths pass through the atmosphere to the earth's surface almost unimpeded by atmospheric CO_2. The energy being radiated from the earth back into space is at much longer (invisible) infrared wavelengths because the earth is so much cooler than the sun. CO_2 is very good at reflecting these long wavelengths back to the earth and preventing their escape.

There are other gases that are even better infrared reflectors than CO_2, but their concentrations (except for water vapor) are so minuscule that they are not of much concern at this time. Methane (CH_4) is about 25 times worse as a greenhouse gas than CO_2. The chlorofluorocarbon compounds, which were popular as refrigerants and aerosol can propellants, are thousands of times worse; that is why we are being very careful not to release those gases into the atmosphere. All of these are called greenhouse gases because they perform the same function as the glass in a greenhouse: they allow solar energy to come in but reduce the escape of heat energy to the outside.

So the people who are very upset about the increase of CO_2 in the atmosphere are undoubtedly correct to sound at least a cautionary alarm. However, there are many others who would argue with them about the magnitude of the possible temperature increase, its timing, how serious the consequences might be, the degree to which it is being caused by human activities, and, of course, what should be done about it. At least two things do seem fairly obvious: the "sky is falling" panic is causing some dumb decisions to be made, and it is piling "global warming polarization" on top of the intolerable level of political polarization that we already suffer.

A number of different groups have compiled data on the earth's temperature over the past 144 years. All are in fairly close agreement that the average temperature embarked on an upward trend in about 1970 and has so far increased by approximately 1°C (see chart below). These data should be reasonably accurate. The temperature rise correlates fairly well with the measured increase in atmospheric CO_2. Of course, correlation does not prove causality.

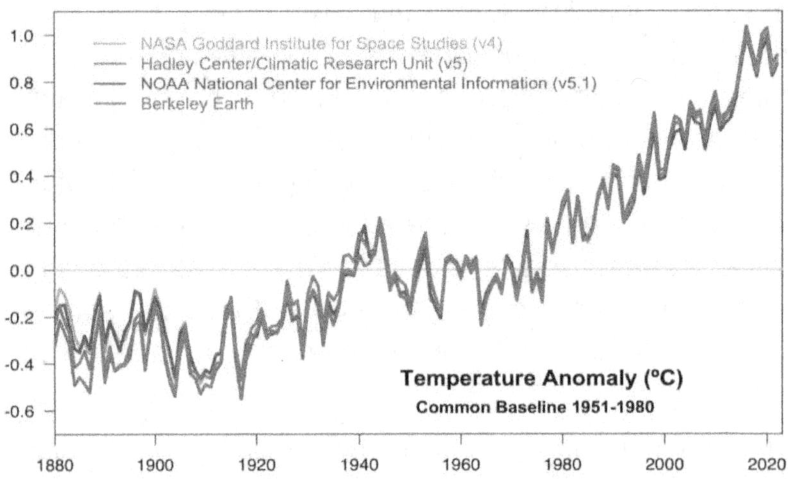

To gain more perspective, let's pull way back and take a look at what has been happening to the earth's temperature over a long period of time. Bear in mind that, unlike the chart above, the data in the chart below are *not* based upon actual accurate temperature measurements but are instead best estimates deduced and pieced

together from drill cores and other geological evidence
from around the world.

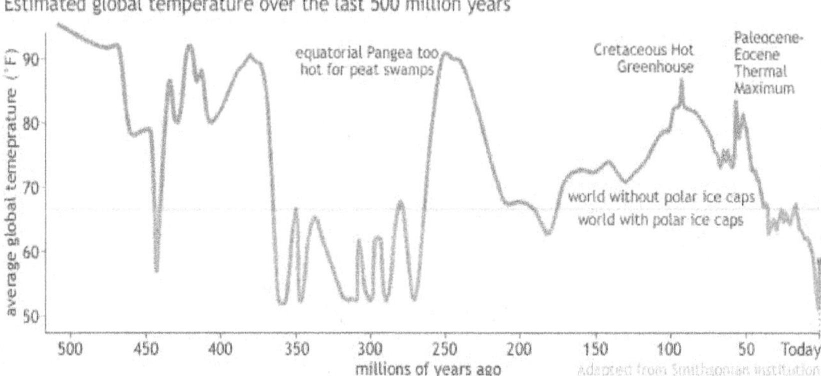

*Credit: Preliminary results from a Smithsonian Institution project led by Scott
Wing and Brian Huber, showing Earth's average surface temperature over the
past 500 million years. For most of the time, global temperatures appear to
have been too warm (red portions of the line above the horizontal line) for
persistent polar ice caps. The most recent 50 million years are an exception.
Image adapted from the Smithsonian National Museum of Natural History.*

Pay close attention to the scales. Temperature is in
degrees Fahrenheit, and time is in millions of years,
covering the most recent ninth of the time Earth has
existed. Humans have existed only for the most recent
300,000 years during an exceptionally cool period, but the
temperatures appear to be heading rapidly higher. Note
also that there have been multiple large swings between
55°F and 90°F — far more than just a few degrees.

One more chart (below): This one shows temperature
estimates over 800,000 years from the European Project
for Ice Coring in Antarctica ice cores in Antarctica.
Temperatures are in Celsius relative to the average of the
most recent 1,000 years. Year 0 is 1950.

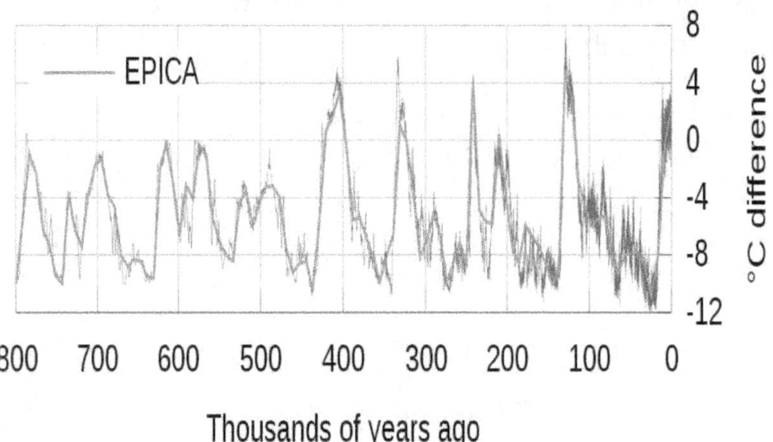

Thousands of years ago

Some things to especially note are the following:
1. There seems to be a considerable amount of fairly short-term (1,000 – 2,000-year periods) variations in temperature over a 3°C to 4°C range.
2. There is a somewhat distinct major temperature cycle over a 12°C–13°C range with a period of about 100,000 years. This is believed to be attributable to the cyclic variation in the eccentricity of the earth's orbit (caused by the motion and positions of the other planets).
3. There is a less distinct temperature cycle over about an 8°C range with a shorter period of approximately 41,000 years. This is believed to be attributable to the cyclical wobble and tilt of the earth's axis of rotation.
4. From this data, it certainly looks like humans have already survived temperature variations of 12°C to 13°C under far more primitive conditions and with far fewer resources than we have at our disposal today.
5. The 1°C increase observed since 1970 does not so far exceed the peak temperatures that have occurred over the past 400,000 years.

For completeness, it should be pointed out that the energy the sun radiates is gradually increasing as well. However, the increase is so gradual — about one percent every million years — that it is not a concern (compared to the other factors) for the next million years or so.

There is much more data floating around derived in many ways, and there are also many opinions regarding global warming. But there seems to be only one "expert" opinion, which is that global warming is a serious threat to our very existence, and it is caused by an increase in atmospheric greenhouse gases, which in turn is completely the fault of our profligate civilization.

The expert opinion comes, of course, from expert climate scientists. This is a worldwide loose association of a couple hundred climate scientists who peer review each other's academic papers (which, of course, are pretty consistently excellent). In order to become a member of this group, you need to agree with the group's opinions. If you are a climate scientist with a differing opinion, then you obviously are not an *expert* climate scientist. Unfortunately, this sort of cabal tends to form in various academic specialties and is not a healthy phenomenon. Sometimes the cabal is right on target, of course, but it does tend to suppress other ideas which occasionally turn out to be more correct or at least well worth considering.

Therefore, anyone interested would be well advised to study the above data, plus any additional information they may wish to gather, and draw their own conclusions. Pending further information, *this* interested individual concludes as follows:

1. There is a good probability that increasing CO_2 in the atmosphere is the cause of some detectable global warming.
2. There is a fairly high probability that the increase of atmospheric CO_2 is being caused by the increasing activities of our civilization, some from the combustion of fossil fuels and some from other industrial processes.
3. Whether or not 1 and 2 are true, it seems likely that the earth may be destined for higher temperatures over the next several centuries, possibly by as much as 6°C–8°C, because we are in the warming phase of one of the Earth's periodic temperature cycles. Areas covered by snow and ice reflect more of the sun's energy back into space. Currently, such areas are shrinking.
4. Even successfully curtailing most CO_2 emissions may not be sufficient to prevent a significant temperature rise. Remember, Earth's temperature has always changed quite a lot, even before the bingeing on fossil fuels began.
5. There is no cause for panic, and especially no reason to hastily implement disruptive changes which may or may not be adequate, could be counterproductive, and are very costly; but it definitely is time to pay some attention, carefully think things through (calmly, if possible), and at least map out some recommendations for the future.

Dealing with a Warming Earth

Dealing with a warming Earth is, needless to say — and especially because it is global — an exceedingly challenging problem in more than one way. It suffers at once from both the economic free rider problem and the tragedy of the commons problem. The former is immediately encountered in the planning phase: developing a plan benefits everyone, so who will pay for it? Global cooperation will be important — and, as usual, complete and whole-hearted participation seems very unlikely; especially if it entails costs or inconveniences.

A good approach might be to establish two separate and competitive independent planning groups with diverse opinions represented. They would compete to produce the best plan and critique each other's thinking. But how would they be funded? There is so much taxpayer money sloshing around for assorted climate projects that surely the funding could be transferred from some of those efforts without increasing spending.

The groups must not be controlled or unduly influenced by any single or dominant government, academic institution, or industry, and they must be able to attract and retain a multidisciplinary group of the right people. Clearly, a good plan should front-load things that require the longest time to implement and avoid as much cost as possible for as long as possible until the timing and extent of temperature changes are known with greater accuracy and certainty.

There are two ways to deal with higher temperatures: First, do whatever may be necessary to adapt and live with it. Second, try to control or prevent it to the greatest extent possible. Some combination of the two will likely be required.

Live with It. With significant temperature change, there inevitably will be the extinction of some plant and animal species. The prime objective must be to make sure that Homo sapiens is not one of them. The process of natural selection is always active. Thousands upon thousands of species have gone extinct, and thousands more will go extinct. It is irrational to fret too much over this, and it has never made any sense to go far, far out of the way to preserve an "endangered species" for another decade or two.

Identify changes to buildings, facilities, food production, and so on early so they may be phased in gradually instead of in panic mode. Ideally, changes can be identified that would be beneficial whether or not temperatures rise. The same must be done regarding areas from which the population and/or facilities must be migrated. Obviously, remove any incentives to inhabit "condemned" areas. Government-subsidized flood insurance, for example, always was, and certainly is now, an incredibly counterproductive, stupid idea.

The prevalent attitude that there's no way to live with global warming is fallacious. The scale of this problem is huge, but it will yield to rational thinking, planning, and execution. Necessity is a great teacher and motivator.

Conquer and Control It. We are very good at climate-controlling buildings. Why not an entire planet? The earth is a pretty big place, but there have been some interesting ideas and it may be doable.

The earth's temperature can be regulated either by controlling (increasing) the amount of infrared energy radiated into space, by controlling (reducing) the amount of energy from the sun that reaches the earth, or by a combination thereof. It is "only" necessary to modulate incoming and/or outgoing energy by a small percentage. Since this approach fixes the problem for all, sharing the costs equitably will be difficult. There will also be problems, such as the United States working hard to minimize emissions of greenhouse gases while China is still building new coal-fired power plants.

Replacing the Internal Combustion Engine

The internal combustion engine (ICE) has enjoyed an illustrious career powering vehicles and equipment of many kinds for well over a hundred years. Excellent engineering and reengineering have optimized and fine-tuned the ICE. It's as good as it's going to get, but the time has come to replace the ICE. We now have the technology to do it. Those concerned about CO_2 (and other) emissions have fingered the ICE as a major offender and have relentlessly pursued its eradication with uncommon zeal. Though mentioned less often, the ICE is inherently noisy. Those who have matured beyond being thrilled by the roar of a revving ICE will be relieved and delighted to have quiet vehicles, lawn tractors, and other equipment.

The rechargeable battery electric vehicle (BEV) has been anointed as the successor apparent, although the hydrogen fuel cell electric vehicle (FCEV) is quite a strong contender. Governments have rushed to deploy both carrots and sticks: onerous regulations penalize ICE vehicles while copious amounts of taxpayer money subsidize the BEV and, to a lesser extent, the FCEV. As previous chapters have emphasized, governments should not have the power to do such things. Predictably, this case is demonstrating the folly of trying to manipulate, second guess, and force the free market.

To date (2026), and in spite of the subsidies, billions of dollars have been lost by manufacturers, dealers, auto rental companies, and, of course, the poor taxpayers in the attempt to push BEVs into the marketplace. A relatively small number of early adopters have taken the bait, but at this time, BEVs are backing up in the pipeline. Most car buyers simply do not consider the BEV's package of features (overall advantages and disadvantages) to be worth the price, even after subsidies. Some early adopters are even considering returning to the ICE.

The BEV's problems are pretty fundamental and are primarily caused by the characteristics and limitations of its state-of-the-art lithium ion batteries. The amount of energy (kilowatt-hours) that can be stored in a battery of a given weight (kilograms of mass) and size (cubic meters) is not large enough. Also, the time required to recharge the battery is too long. In order to enable an acceptable vehicle range, a large (mass and volume) battery that has a long charging time is required. The BEV with the best chance of working is a small passenger vehicle where the payload is only 200–300 kilograms of bodies and luggage. A range of 500 kilometers (311 miles) might be acceptable. A large battery relative to a small payload isn't a good thing, but it isn't an absolute killer.

However, consider a big rig tractor pulling a trailer. The very name of that game is pulling the largest possible payloads over long distances. Pillows and potato chip loads are limited by the available volume, while beer and steel are limited by the maximum weight that can be carried. A range of 1,000 kilometers (625 miles) is expected. It's a huge, probably insurmountable, challenge for battery trucks to compete cost-effectively with ICE trucks, at least for hauling heavy cargos. The size and mass of the required battery put a serious dent in the payload capacity. Charging time is a problem, too, but that might be remedied at some expense and inconvenience by swappable batteries.

BEVs need significant advances in battery technology, both charging speed and energy storage density. That possibly could happen, but nothing like that is clearly visible on the horizon. Batteries have been a critical requirement for portable equipment for about a century, so the technology has already received a lot of development effort. The last big advance was the lithium-ion battery. It has been mass-produced for more than two decades and so is way down the "learning curve."

On the other hand, all the pieces for FCEVs can just about satisfy all requirements today. Hydrogen fuel cells produce only electricity, water, and heat. The heat is useful to warm the vehicle's interior during cold weather, whereas the BEV must drain precious joules from its battery for that purpose. FCEVs offer longer ranges for vehicles and much faster refueling — pretty much the same as pumping gasoline. They weigh much less (including the hydrogen, its tank and the fuel cell). Fuel cells have been around for a long time, primarily for low-volume specialty applications. There are still several avenues to explore that might make them even better, and many organizations are working to improve them. Of course, they also need to travel down the learning curve of large-volume manufacturing.

BEV enthusiasts knock fuel cells for lower overall efficiency. High efficiency is a good thing, of course, but it is far from the most important consideration. The critical question is whether FCEVs can provide an overall set of features at a price (total cost of ownership per mile) that purchasers will think is a good deal (regardless of efficiency). At this point, it looks like they probably can, while BEVs are struggling mightily to do so, even with outlandish taxpayer support that appears to be ending. Lithium-ion batteries pose a small risk of nasty, hard-to-extinguish fires as well, especially while being charged rapidly.

Another issue is the capacity of the electrical grid. If 10% of vehicles are BEVs, we may make it. But if 90% are BEVs, the capacity of the grid will need to be increased. This is a very costly project that will take years. Not many months following the passage of legislation to make ICE vehicles illegal in California after the year 2035, a summer heat wave hit. Pleas went out to BEV owners to refrain from charging their vehicles! And, of course, BEVs don't cut CO_2 if the electricity to recharge them is produced by burning fossil fuels; ditto hydrogen if its manufacture requires fossil fuels.

Fuel cell train locomotives are being considered as replacements for diesel locomotives. Fuel cell aircraft using liquid hydrogen fuel are also being considered. Big rigs using 200 kW fuel cell stacks are already on the road being tested and evaluated for fleet acquisitions. Some developments discussed later in this chapter may help reduce the cost of green hydrogen (hydrogen produced without fossil fuels).

One large impediment to the adoption of FCEVs is the lack of an adequate number of hydrogen refueling stations. But that will not be a deterrent for industrial depot-to-depot or return-to-base vehicles, such as delivery vans and garbage trucks. If FCEVs gain volume usage for these heavy duty applications, it may help them move down into passenger vehicles as well. If FCEVs do gain traction, gasoline stations will be turned into true gas stations, which is what we've been calling them all along.

Clearly, there are many, many options, variables, decisions, and choices involved. Who would think bureaucrats or politicians could be of much help in figuring them out? As always, and although it can never be perfect, the invisible hand of the free market economic system will do the best possible job of sorting it all out and allocating resources accordingly.

Why Energy Is Crucial for Our Future

Unless civilization suffers a collapse — which, sadly, is a nonzero probability — it will need even more energy in the future. Some of the possible ways to control Earth's temperature might require huge amounts of energy. Energy-intensive methods may be required if traditional agriculture is no longer able to meet needs. It is essential to have a reliable and virtually unlimited supply of clean, reliable, low-cost energy that is available whenever and wherever it is needed.

It is the intelligent utilization of energy that enables us to design and implement all manner of things that would be impossible just with our own muscle power. Our buildings maintain constant temperatures and completely protect us from the elements — a major improvement over a cave heated by an open fire. We are able to transport things large and small over huge distances, over and through mountains and water — even into space. The examples are endless.

Energy is fungible. Turn energy into fresh water by desalinating seawater. Turn energy into food by growing it hydroponically or in buildings with just the right temperature, humidity, and lighting — 24 hours a day. Too much CO_2? Use energy to remove it from the atmosphere. Need hydrogen or oxygen? Use energy to hydrolyze water. With virtually unlimited energy, we are virtually unlimited.

However, there is one sort of limit that we should at least bear in mind. Any energy released and however utilized (except hydro, solar, and wind) ultimately ends up as added heat energy. That is, it adds to the 10^{17} watts that the earth is absorbing from the sun. If we add to that significantly, we will need to account for it as part of the solution for maintaining an acceptable temperature on our planet.

It is estimated[16] that global energy production was approximately 179,000 TWh or 1.79×10^{17} watt-hours for the year 2022. Dividing that by the number of hours in a year yields about 2×10^{13} watts. This suggests that energy production can be increased by approximately fifty times before we need to worry about it significantly warming the planet. That's a lot, but not a whole lot. Perhaps it will no longer be a concern if we have engineered a big thermostat that controls the earth's temperature before energy needs grow that large.

While discussing future energy needs, it would be good to emphasize that our civilization is already critically dependent today upon reliable energy supplies. It is a vulnerability. An enemy or a bunch of terrorists could wreak havoc simply shooting at large transformers in

---

[16] Ritchie, H, Rosado, P, and Roser, M. 2020. "Energy Production and Consumption."

electrical substations with high power rifles. Attention also needs to be paid to hardening the grid against large electromagnetic pulses. Such "EMPs" can be generated by nuclear weapon explosions and also by exceptionally large coronal mass ejections from the sun in the direction of the earth.

Sources of Energy for the Future

Fossil Fuels (Coal, Oil, Gas) and Biomass/Biofuels. Whether or not it turns out to be essential to curbing global warming, it is a good idea and high time that we wean ourselves off the use of the sun's energy stored in fossil fuels. Oxidizing these fuels produces a significant amount of CO_2. Biomass has much the same CO_2 problem. Biofuels also have a CO_2 problem to a somewhat lesser degree, but they are primarily for the ICE, which we assume will be successfully phased out. So, we will say no more about these sources.

Hydropower. This is a clean, safe, low-cost, beautiful source of energy that currently supplies about 6% of the world's needs. But there are not a lot of opportunities for significant amounts of additional hydro. Since it utilizes energy from the sun that the earth has already absorbed, it does not in any way exacerbate global warming.

Theoretically, hydro is renewable energy, but that may be in some jeopardy. As a case in point, take the declining flow of the Colorado River over the past four decades. Somewhat reduced snowfall in the mountains may be at least partially the result of that one-degree temperature increase experienced since 1970. Another significant cause is the burgeoning population along the river; these people increasingly intercept the snow melt from the mountaintops before it can get down to the river and divert it to water their lawns and golf courses. The problem of declining flow is further exacerbated by government agricultural subsidies for crops, crop insurance, and irrigation water, which make it economically viable for farmers to grow crops that need a lot of water in the middle of a desert. Stop that crony statism!

Surely, utilize all the hydropower possible, but unfortunately, it probably is not a source to count heavily upon for the increased needs of the future.

Solar and wind power. Like hydropower, solar and wind power utilize some of the sun's energy that warms the earth anyway. It seems almost like "free energy." Well, yes, but there are some fundamental drawbacks that disqualify them as baseload power sources.

Both the sun and the wind are diffuse sources of energy, and energy density counts. A "conventional" power plant can generate 5×10^9 watts (5 gigawatts) on perhaps a 15-acre site. It would require about 50,000 acres of solar cells to generate that much power. And just slapping some solar cells on available roofs may realize only 20% or 30% of the power per area that a large, carefully designed solar cell array can produce. Wind power has a similar problem. It requires several thousand windmills just to match one conventional power plant.

The second fundamental drawback is that both solar and wind are intermittent power producers. Power needs to be available whenever it is needed, which is pretty much any time. To satisfy that requirement, solar and wind power producers would need a storage mechanism (e.g., batteries or pumped hydropower) that could store enough energy to fill in the gaps when the sun isn't shining or the wind isn't blowing. Hydrogen might also be considered as a storage mechanism.

These are fundamental problems that are not going to go away with any advances in solar cell or windmill technology. The useful place for these sources is for small power requirements in remote locations and possibly for emergency backup power. The global warming panic has driven a large investment (not to mention huge taxpayer subsidies) into wind and solar power; this is a major boondoggle.

Nuclear energy. Nuclear energy is radically different. It might be thought of as a primary source of energy, while the rest are secondary sources derived indirectly from the sun's nuclear energy.

Delving into physics only enough to provide a reasonable explanation, nuclear energy comes from the conversion of mass to energy. Everyone has seen Albert Einstein's famous $E = mc^2$ equation, which describes the equivalency of energy (E) and mass (m). They are related by a constant, c^2, which is the velocity of light squared. Light travels very fast indeed, 300 million (3×10^8) meters per second. Squaring that large number yields a huge number, 9×10^{16}. This means that converting even a tiny amount of mass to energy yields an astounding amount of energy.

For example, it takes an average of about 1,000 watts of power to run a typical home — lights, hot water, appliances, and so on. If only 1 kilogram (2.2 pounds) of mass were converted to energy, it would yield 9×10^{16} joules. That is enough energy to provide 1,000 watts and power a home for 9×10^{13} seconds or about 3 million years. This illustrates the outstanding potential that nuclear energy has to meet our energy needs.

We know of two ways to convert mass to energy: nuclear fusion and nuclear fission. Fusion fuses the nuclei of two light elements together to form a heavier element that has less mass than the total of the two lighter elements. The difference in mass is released as energy. Fission splits the nucleus of a very heavy element into lighter elements. The total mass of the lighter elements is less than that of the heavy element, and the difference is released as energy.

Nuclear fission. It is much easier to make fission happen on Earth than fusion. Quite a few of the heaviest elements in the periodic table are so unstable that they spontaneously decay to other slightly more stable and lighter elements. It is only necessary to lob an extra neutron into the nucleus of some of them to cause them to split (fission) into two lighter elements and release a bunch of energy.

The fission bombs that ended World War II were built to cause a chain reaction that resulted in the rapid fission of billions and billions of atoms in order to destructively release a large burst of energy instantaneously. Shortly thereafter, *controlled* nuclear fission was harnessed for power generation. There are quite a few ways to accomplish this. However, except for a small number of research reactors, all commercial power reactors have employed the fission of an isotope of uranium into two lighter elements: krypton and barium.

Nuclear fusion. It is much more difficult to make fusion happen than fission. Unlike the very heavy elements, the light elements are naturally very stable. It is necessary for two light nuclei to smash into each other at an extremely high velocity to induce them to fuse into a heavier element. This happens all day every day in the core of the massive sun, where the pressure and density are extremely high and the temperature is 15 million degrees C. There are multiple fusion reactions that can occur; the two the sun (currently) employs have the same overall result: 4 hydrogen nuclei (protons) are fused to form one helium nucleus and release a large amount of energy.

The fusion we attempt here on Earth combines two heavy isotopes of hydrogen, ^{2}H and ^{3}H (called deuterium and tritium), to form one helium nucleus (^{4}He) and a neutron, plus a lot of energy. We are good at doing it in an uncontrolled, destructive way, with so-called hydrogen bombs. It takes a fission bomb to create the conditions required for fusion, but that's no way to build a power plant.

It is a supreme challenge to create the conditions required for *controlled* fusion on the earth, even in a fairly small volume. That hasn't stopped multiple groups of scientists from trying. Progress has been disappointingly, painfully slow for the past seventy years. Construction of the first small-scale operating prototype reactor seems to stay a constant fifteen to twenty years in the future. This is not a knock on those working hard on this technology; it's just an extremely complex and difficult challenge.

There is no guarantee that this problem will be solved or when. Fusion seems like it could be a great power source preferable to fission, but it is not one that can be counted upon at present. In the meantime, fission power plants are in the process of improving considerably in many ways.

The "bottom line" future energy source. At this point, it should be somewhat obvious that nuclear fission is the clear choice. It is the only source that we know definitely can meet all the requirements. It is clean, safe, reliable, always available, compact, and low cost. It can be scaled by orders of magnitude to satisfy whatever our future energy needs may turn out to be.

It is past time for irrational resistance to this power source to fade and for resources to be directed in rational directions. In fact, we could have and should have been close to having fossil fuels phased out by now. Why are well over half of the world's energy needs still being met by fossil fuels? It is primarily because of a few very bad decisions and choices that were made starting back in 1954. It will be worth the words to identify and understand why and how all that went down.

The Saga of the Power Industry

After figuring out how to destroy things using nuclear energy near the end of World War II, work began on figuring out how to tap nuclear energy with a controlled release to perform constructive tasks. Admiral Hyman Rickover recognized the huge advantage of being able to power Navy ships, most especially submarines, with nuclear energy. Almost singlehandedly, he drove a US Navy program to build the first nuclear-powered sub. The *Nautilus* was commissioned in 1954 and was indeed a spectacular advancement in submarine capabilities.

The Russians built a small research reactor at about the same time and actually connected it to the electrical grid. Both of these reactors used enriched uranium solid fuel, and both were cooled with water.

The power industry was in the process of designing large land-based nuclear reactors to generate electricity. Not surprisingly, they decided to scale up Admiral Rickover's reactor design to the large size needed for a power plant. This seemed like a reasonable choice at the time but actually was the first mistake. However, if you are about to invest billions of dollars developing a brand-new technology, it's hard to fault basing it on a design that has been demonstrated to work.

Thus, at least the first generation of nuclear power plants was committed to using water as the coolant. Unfortunately, that is a terrible design choice. Nuclear reactors generate a lot of heat; that's what they do. It is best to operate them at a fairly high temperature because that increases the efficiency at which the reactor's heat energy can be converted to electrical energy. But as is well known, water vaporizes (boils) at 100°C (212°F) at normal atmospheric pressure. Operating a reactor at 100°C would be worthless. Thus, as a compromise, water-cooled reactors are designed to operate at about 315°C.

At 315°C and normal atmospheric pressure, water instantly turns to steam, which is not an effective coolant. To keep water liquid at 315°C it must be pressurized to 150 atmospheres (2,200 pounds per square inch)! Should the pressure be lost, the coolant water would instantly explode into steam. If cooling is lost, the solid fuel reactor core would quickly overheat and possibly melt down and release radioactive materials. A reinforced concrete dome large enough and strong enough to contain such an "event" is a necessary safety precaution.

All of these problems are much smaller and easy to manage in a very small reactor on a submarine surrounded by thick steel armor and an unlimited supply of seawater. However, even though using water as a coolant limits performance and requires elaborate safety features and precautions, many such power plants were built, and they successfully, reliably, cleanly, and safely produced a lot of electricity at a competitive cost. Not bad.

Doctor Alvin Weinberg conducted an important experimental program at Oak Ridge National Laboratory from 1958 through 1976. It was called the Molten Salt Reactor Experiment (MSRE) and was aimed at testing better ways to cool nuclear reactors and evaluating alternative nuclear fuels. The coolant used was a mixture of lithium fluoride (LiF) and beryllium fluoride (BeF_2) salts. This was a wise choice.

The salts are extremely stable chemically. The salt mixture is solid at room temperature but liquefies at about 450°C. The molten salts stay liquid *at normal atmospheric pressure* over a remarkably wide temperature range — all the way up to 1,400°C. The molten salts are an even more effective coolant than liquid water. The reactor can (in fact, must) be operated at much higher temperatures quite safely without the need to pressurize anything. This eliminates the worry of water exploding into steam if pressure is lost.

Instead of uranium (^{235}U), Weinberg's reactor used thorium (^{232}Th), which was dissolved as thorium tetrafluoride (ThF_4) right in with the molten salt coolant. There was no solid fuel to melt down. The reactor's normal state *was* melted down. The reactor was successfully operated for a year and a half. The MSRE was shut down "for budgetary reasons," but it was well documented, and Dr. Weinberg was a vocal advocate for the design approach.

Now there was no longer any good excuse for designing more water-cooled reactors with a known built-in failure mechanism that requires elaborate safety precautions, but that's exactly what happened. Weinberg's excellent and important work was virtually ignored.

Many carefully engineered reactor sites went into service (plus a few that weren't, such as the one in Chernobyl, Ukraine). They were generally well managed and cleanly produced lots of electricity. However, eventually, the statistics came due, and an accident occurred.

In 1979, at Three Mile Island, near Harrisburg, Pennsylvania, a hard-to-imagine combination of equipment problems and operator errors caused a reactor to lose cooling water and experience a partial meltdown. There were no deaths, no injuries, and no measurable radiation released to the surrounding area. However, the event certainly did frighten folks for many miles around, and it received plenty of adverse publicity worldwide.

Then, in 1986, a very serious accident occurred at Chernobyl. One of the reactors there lost cooling water, melted down, exploded, and spread radioactive material throughout the USSR and Europe. There were quite a few deaths and some very serious contamination. The reactor did lack some of the safety features that it should have had. It remains *by far* the most serious nuclear power plant accident.

There was one more incident, in 2011, at the Fukushima Daiichi power plant in Japan. A severe earthquake knocked out the cooling system. There was a backup cooling system powered by diesel generators, but these were inundated by a tsunami created by the earthquake.

The problem could have been prevented (and can be prevented in the future), but no one had anticipated an earthquake and a tsunami at the same time. There were no deaths, but there was a very expensive and lengthy cleanup, and some contaminated water eventually had to be diluted and disposed of into the ocean.

The first two accidents were sufficient to put a chill on new nuclear plant construction which persisted for nearly three decades. This was irrational, as the long-term statistics clearly show that, even taking all three accidents into account, nuclear power is both cleaner and safer than any other energy source other than solar cells.

There may also be some public apprehension about the radioactive nuclear wastes that are produced by this reactor design. The US government guaranteed to provide for the US nuclear power industry a safe central depository for such waste by 1998, but no such facility has yet been provided. About $10 billion was spent preparing a carefully selected site at Yucca Mountain, Nevada, but the facility has yet to be used. It has become a political football. The federal government needs to make good on its promise! In the meantime, the wastes are being stored on-site at each reactor. Dry cask storage deep inside Yucca Mountain would be far safer.

Over 70% of France's power is nuclear; it even exports some of its power. France is also one of the very few countries that reprocess spent nuclear fuel. On the other hand, and as a shining example of stubborn, boneheaded irrationality, Germany bowed to public pressure and decommissioned the last of its nuclear plants in 2023, making the country highly dependent on natural gas imported from Russia!

New plant construction has been picking up again over the past decade — unfortunately, all are still water cooled. However, excitement is in the air as multiple companies in multiple countries are hard at work on Generation IV nuclear reactors. Gen IV nuclear promises to be quite a major step forward. There are at least six or seven different designs. It is virtually certain that Gen IV reactors will (finally) not be cooled by water.

One of the most promising designs is the lithium fluoride thorium reactor (LFTR, pronounced "lifter"). Yep, it's basically Dr. Weinberg's design from the 1960s! Here are some of the advantages it offers:

- A LFTR is *not* cooled by water, which eliminates that serious and problematic failure mechanism. With the $LiFBeF_2$ coolant, the reactor does not need to be pressurized, so no large, high-strength containment dome is needed.
- The reactor can operate at 650°C to 700°C, which means its efficiency can be 46% (instead of 34% when limited to 315°C). Instead of a Rankine cycle steam turbine, a Brayton cycle supercritical CO_2 turbine will likely be the choice.
- They can be located anywhere as there is no need to build them where there is a copious supply of water.
- Reactors using enriched uranium solid fuel must shut down for refueling after approximately six months of operation, which has them out of service about 25% of the time. A LFTR can run continuously because fuel is continuously added to the molten salt coolant while it is circulating, and waste products are similarly removed by continuous chemical processing.

- Only about 4% of the uranium is utilized in a solid fuel reactor, while the LFTR uses 100% of its thorium fuel.
- Thorium is 3 to 4 times more plentiful than uranium and is much easier and safer to mine.
- A LFTR is inherently safer to operate than a water-cooled solid-fuel reactor. In the worst-case emergency scenario, it can shut down automatically and passively by draining the molten salt coolant (with fuel) into an underground tank. No backup cooling system is needed.
- The thorium fuel cycle produces less nuclear waste than uranium, and none of it is particularly useful for weapons production. Waste products decay to safe levels of radioactivity in 300 years. The transuranic nuclides in the waste products of prior reactors can require 10,000 years or more.
- The LFTR's exhaust heat can be used as process heat or for such things as the desalinization of seawater. It may be possible to electrolyze water to obtain hydrogen (and oxygen) at quite a low cost.

This is clearly an impressive list of important advantages.

One might worry that the LFTR is complex and can't be made to work, except that Alvin Weinberg already made it work back in the 1960s. However, there are definitely many design options and trade-offs. It is a major complex engineering project that is worth doing carefully before it goes into production. Also, as mentioned, several other Gen IV designs are being pursued in parallel. We can count on Gen IV nuclear power being a major advance whatever the details of its implementation.

Relearning the Henry Ford Lesson

The nuclear power industry has also come to its senses and is working on another aspect of reducing the cost of nuclear energy. In the past, a typical nuclear power installation had four units of about one gigawatt each, for a total of four gigawatts. Each installation was a new "from scratch" custom design, engineering, and construction project. There are many Nuclear Regulatory Commission (NRC) approvals, inspections, and tests at every phase. Of course, these are important, but they do significantly stretch out the schedule and increase costs. The capital budgets are in the $15–20 billion range. It is not unusual for those costs to more than double by the time the first watts are produced commercially. Such colossal costs must, of course, be amortized over the total kilowatt hours that the plant produces during its useful life.

It seems that the industry had to relearn the Henry Ford lesson. The Gen IV plan is to build small modular reactors (SMRs). An SMR would generate in the range of 300 megawatts of electricity. A small plant would consist of three or four SMRs, while a large three-gigawatt installation would require ten copies of the same SMR. SMRs would be built almost entirely in factories designed for the purpose.

Thus, the hefty design, engineering, and most of the testing costs occur only once; the reactor design can undergo the full NRC certification process just once. Reactors will be manufactured as large assemblies that can be shipped to the installation site and assembled on-site, thus lowering construction costs. After final test and certification, the plant should be ready to go online. A drastic reduction in most up-front costs should be the result. Unanticipated problems that wreck the schedule and cause huge cost overruns should be virtually eliminated.

Based upon its 70-year track record to date, nuclear fission has proven its ability to deliver energy cleanly, safely, and reliably; plus, it is compact, low cost, and always available. It is already the best choice as the mainstay source of energy. Uranium fuel supplies for current reactor designs will not be a problem within the next century or two, and likely for much longer. With Gen IV nuclear close at hand and promising improvement in nearly all important aspects, there is just no contest. Thorium fuel supplies are more than adequate for the next millennium or two. Perhaps controlled nuclear fusion will be available as a viable energy source by then.

14. The End

Previous chapters have followed the evolution of our Homo sapiens species from its origins to the present and have analyzed issues important to maximizing the total happiness of all individuals. We humans have been hanging around for about 300,000 years so far. Is it possible to foresee, however dimly, the end of our species? And if not, is it possible that we may continue to adapt and survive indefinitely? This will be a fitting topic for this final chapter.

The Best Case

It looks like the earth is doomed to a definite end. Our solar system was created about 4.5 billion years ago when some huge clouds of gas underwent a gravitational collapse that formed the sun and its planets. The sun is approaching the halfway point of its stable lifetime, during which its temperature and power output very gradually increase by approximately 1% per million years. After another five billion years or so, the sun will become unstable and expand greatly, thus engulfing the inner planets, possibly including Earth. That'll be pretty much it for the earth.

However, in "only" about one billion years, the increasing radiance (power output) of the sun will render the environment on Earth similar to what we observe on Venus today — that is, very hostile and hot, with a surface temperature of 463°C (865°F). Although an advanced-model crystal ball would be required to see accurately a billion years into the future, it does not seem likely that a species comprised of carbon-based organic compounds

with somewhat fragile covalent bonds (that's us) is likely to
make it at such elevated temperatures. So, in the best
case, existence here on Earth is limited to something a lot
less than a billion more years.

A path to really long-term survival looks like it requires us
to abandon this planet, preferably at some time
comfortably before the sun's power output increases by, at
most, 50%. We would need to be outta here in less than
forty million years, and even then, we would have to have
developed fairly effective ways to ameliorate global
warming during the time leading up to our exit.

Where would we go? To another Earthlike planet, of
course. That's what happens in many sci-fi stories.
Astronomers have already been searching for planets that
could possibly support life. There are billions of them in our
galaxy, and about 5,000 in our "neighborhood" of the Milky
Way galaxy have already been cataloged. It does not
appear that any really good candidates exist within five
light-years of us, but it is thought very likely that at least
one or two decent prospects may exist within a distance of
twenty-five or thirty light-years.

Visiting such places makes a great science fiction story,
but they always have a "warp drive" or some other faster-
than-light means of travel. Our understanding of the
universe thus far indicates that it is not possible for
anything to travel faster than light. Thus, such a "migration"
would be a much more challenging and extremely long-
lead-time project than it may have seemed at first.

To travel a distance of twenty-five light-years would require
a prodigious amount of energy and would take at least a
hundred years — probably longer. This assumes we have

an amazing "super belchfire eight" model propulsion system that can achieve a velocity that is a substantial fraction (maybe one-third) of the velocity of light. By the way, collision with nearly anything, possibly even a cloud of gas, at that velocity would almost certainly be fatal. An exploratory visit to verify the acceptability of the destination — and to make sure it's unoccupied — would be essential. Maybe, but not likely, some of the UFOs (lately being rebranded "unidentified aerial phenomenon," or UAPs) that have been observed are other distant races checking out the earth.

It's risky to make predictions one or two hundred years into the future, so looking ahead millions of years surely comes with a lot of uncertainty. But from what we know now, moving to another star's planet would be more like a Hail Mary pass to send a small group to begin a new civilization — certainly not a project that could transplant a large population.

A better bet might be to work on building a habitable environment on Mars. At that greater distance from the sun, the watts per square meter from the sun would be a bit less than half what pounds the earth. That should grant us about thirty million more years (in addition to the aforementioned forty million years). The trip to Mars is a paltry and way more manageable eighty million kilometers — less than five light-minutes!

So, the best case for our species appears to be up to about forty million more years. By that point, some deadly serious threats loom that, at present, seem like they will be extremely difficult, if not impossible, to surmount. However, we may not ever need, or have the chance, to worry much about those threats, as there are quite a few possibilities that could terminate our existence far sooner.

Invasion by (Nonterrestrial) Aliens

Another popular science fiction theme is invasion by nonterrestrial aliens. Supposedly, this could occur at any time with little or no notice. To the best of our knowledge, the same physical laws apply everywhere in the universe. Thus, the same reasons that render it virtually impossible for us to reach other far-off star systems also protect us from far-off aliens reaching us. This end for our species cannot quite be assigned a zero probability, but let's just say the threat is extremely remote.

An Unforeseen Cataclysmic Event beyond Our Control

A direct hit on the earth by a sizable meteor looks like it did in the dinosaurs and many other species about sixty-six million years ago. Something unforeseen of that caliber could possibly wipe us out. As far as another meteor is concerned, the probability is very low.

More than four and a half billion years after the formation of the solar system, the heavy space traffic has died down, and things are pretty quiet in our neighborhood. The ability to detect, track, and accurately calculate the trajectories of space objects at great distances is well developed and getting better every day. A small "nudge" at a great distance is sufficient to alter the course of an object enough to miss the earth. A preliminary test of that has been carried out.

Some other unforeseen event is, by definition, quite difficult to write about. Therefore, this category cannot be assigned a zero probability. Employing the SWAG[17] technique, it will receive a 2% probability.

A Nuclear Holocaust

Shortly following the end of World War II, a nuclear arms race commenced. Ever more potent fission, and then fusion, bombs were developed, along with missile delivery systems that eventually were able to target any point on the earth. Since there was, and still is, no effective defense against such awesome weapons, the "defense strategy" became *mutually assured destruction* (with the highly fitting acronym MAD). Every nuclear-armed nation makes certain it has sufficient and well-protected weapons that will survive a first attack and still be capable of retaliation with sufficient force to wipe out the adversary who attacked. Brilliant.

By the twenty-first century, quite a few nations had acquired nuclear weapons. Some of these nations are quite hostile and even belligerent. Additional nations are gradually joining the nuclear club. A few have also developed tactical nuclear weapons — smaller-yield devices for use on the battlefield.

The only way the MAD strategy is stable is when only sane people are in control of nuclear weapons. That would seem to be an existential and serious risk, especially with the turmoil that exists in the world, and even within nations. It takes but one Looney Tunes outfit, or even a crazy accident, to set off a nuclear holocaust.

---

[17] Scientific wild-assed guess.

It would seem that this seemingly irrational, definitely dangerous situation should have and could have been avoided, but that is much easier said than done. All parties would have had to agree to it and to allow pervasive and invasive inspections to prevent cheating. Again, it requires only one party to kill this possibility, and that certainly happened.

The only way out of this horrible situation is for one of the "good guys" to be the first to develop an effective defense. President Reagan recognized that during the 1980s and pushed what was dubbed the Star Wars program. This was an admittedly high-risk project intended to defend against nuclear weapons. Many objected that a successful defense would be "destabilizing" to the balance of power. Reagan countered that simply giving the defense system to all parties would remedy any instability problems. But it is supremely (intentionally) difficult to defend against the triad of intercontinental ballistic missiles, bombers, and submarine-launched missiles. As projected and feared, the Star Wars project was not successful. There is still no good and reliable defense. President Trump is currently proposing to try again with more advanced technology.

One would think that with overwhelmingly destructive nuclear weaponry pointed at each other, everyone would be very careful to avoid provocations. NOT! The United States invaded Iraq unprovoked and regularly engages in military actions in various parts of the world. Russia launched a full-scale unprovoked invasion of Ukraine. Iran's terrorist proxies regularly attack Israel with the stated objective of wiping them off the map. The US and Israel are currently engaged in hostilities with Iran. And so it continues on and on.

The official "Doomsday Clock" has been at a few minutes before midnight for decades. The probability of a nuclear holocaust wiping out Homo sapiens is definitely not close enough to zero. An accident, a mistake, or a sufficiently unbalanced person in the right position of authority is all it would take. The probability that this will be the end of us might be (again making some use of the SWAG technique) about 25%.

A Deadly Pandemic

Pandemics have plagued civilizations for many centuries. Many millions have died. Obviously, there have been enough survivors to propagate the species. This is natural selection in action. Those of us living today should be at least somewhat more resistant to those particular infectious diseases.

In modern times, the control of such pandemics has been foundationally aided by gaining a detailed understanding of the sources, causes, prevention, and cures for infectious diseases. Because we understand, we have sanitary sewers, we make sure our water is safe to consume, we know we should practice good hygiene, we have many disinfectant (and other sanitation) products, and we have developed vaccines that are able to augment our resistance to many diseases. Vaccines have substantially eradicated a number of serious diseases, such as smallpox, polio, tuberculosis, and measles. Where small numbers of cases do show up, it is because the infected ones had not been vaccinated.

In spite of all this great stuff, a virulent pandemic swept around the globe from 2019 through 2022 before settling down and becoming endemic. The disease was dubbed

COVID-19, and the virus that causes it is SARS-CoV-2; it is highly contagious. There were over seven hundred million cases and seven million deaths. Undoubtedly, the number of cases was far higher, as many of the milder cases surely went unreported. It could have been worse, but reasonably effective vaccines were developed exceptionally quickly and were available at the end of 2020. Actually, a series of a few vaccine variants had to be developed as the COVID virus mutated several times over the period. How these vaccines were developed and how they function are of great interest and significance.

"Traditional" vaccines work by injecting the same pathogen that causes the infection into the bloodstream. However, the vaccine contains a killed or greatly weakened form of the pathogen that is not capable of causing an actual full-blown infection — sometimes, a bit of a reaction can occur, however. This trains the body's adaptive immune system to recognize and attack that pathogen. If/when the actual pathogen appears on the scene, the immune system quickly pounces and eliminates it before it can replicate and cause major trouble.

The COVID-19 vaccines were distinctly different. They were the first vaccines to use messenger ribonucleic acid (mRNA) technology. mRNA is a short string built from three of the same four nucleotides that compose deoxyribonucleic acid (DNA, the complex double-helix organic molecule that encodes genetic information) plus one different nucleotide. Each mRNA strand transfers instructions for the construction of some particular protein from a cell's DNA to its protein factory mechanism, and then the mRNA self-destructs. Every cell utilizes a wide variety of mRNA strings all day every day. This is one of the basic mechanisms of all life.

The design of an mRNA vaccine begins by identifying a protein that is exposed on the surface of a pathogen and is unique to that pathogen. Next, it must be verified that the protein is harmless to humans. Then, an mRNA strand that encodes the instructions for fabricating the protein is constructed in the laboratory. Many such mRNA strands are encapsulated in protective coatings and injected into the bloodstream. Upon entering a cell, the coating disintegrates, releasing the mRNA. The mRNA causes the cell's normal machinery to produce the desired specific protein and then self-destructs, just as all mRNA does. The protein enters the bloodstream, where the adaptive autoimmune system identifies it as a foreign substance and develops a defense against it. If/when the actual pathogen shows up, the immune system is ready for it, identifies it by the protein, and immediately attacks.

Thus, there is now a "cookbook procedure" to engineer a safe and effective vaccine for virtually any pathogen relatively quickly. This is a powerful testimony to the depth and breadth of the knowledge and understanding that has been achieved. Of course, knowledge and understanding have limited usefulness without the ability to utilize them to devise solutions to important problems, so credit is also due for that. Finally, recognition is due to the capabilities of the laboratory and manufacturing tools and technology required to implement such solutions. You do not make an mRNA vaccine in a garage with screwdrivers, hammers, and pliers.

So now we have even greater stuff. Is it sufficient to prevent future pandemics? Probably not.

Along with our successful species have come some things that can exacerbate pandemics: increased population and population density, lots of contact and interaction, and high-speed travel over long distances. An infected individual can transmit a pathogen to several groups of people in the morning, and by evening, that same individual can be infecting other groups hundreds or even thousands of miles away. During the COVID-19 pandemic, considerable effort was expended in an attempt to do "contact tracing." That proved fairly futile since the virus was able to jump so rapidly in so many directions.

All the great technology we have can be utilized to engineer nasty pathogens as well. Why would anyone want to do that? Intellectual curiosity and the desire to increase our knowledge and understanding certainly could be one reason. Developing bioweapons might be another. Unfortunately, there is interest in the latter in several quarters of the world. Given that interest, everyone else has to have an interest in being able to defend against possible bioweapons.

The origin of the SARS-CoV-2 virus is not certain, but the first cases definitely did appear in Wuhan, China, and spread from there. Two possible explanations have been considered: one is that the virus was engineered in a laboratory and escaped by accident; the other is that it evolved/mutated naturally in animals and then jumped to humans. The Chinese have not been cooperative in investigating the origin; they strongly back the second explanation. However, it is a fact that Wuhan is the home of the Wuhan Institute of Virology, which is known to not enforce the highest levels of safety protocols. It appears that this laboratory was engaged in closely related gain-of-function research. Most surprising is that the US National Institutes of Health was funding some of this work, and at least one doctor on the US government payroll was intimately involved. If all the relevant data and information from all sources could be cooperatively laid out on the table, it is very likely that the origin of the SARS-CoV-2 virus could be determined. Unfortunately, all the facts are not available but the episode certainly has the earmarks of a bioweapons, or at least a bioresearch, program accident.

The main takeaways from all this are that the capability does exist to design and create pathogens that are very dangerous to human life. Also, such work can be carried out in undetected laboratories much more easily than, say, the development of nuclear weapons. It is another one of those things that it is impossible to prevent; outlawing it only provides a false sense of security. Any effort to produce bioweapons poses an obvious threat and risk. Doing such work, either to defend against bioweapons or purely to advance knowledge and understanding, also carries some risk. Accidents do happen.

Considering these advances in technology, it seems more likely that a species-threatening pandemic would be man-made rather than the result of a naturally occurring pathogen. Pandemics will continue to occur at intervals for at least some time. The question is whether they will wipe out our entire species or just be another natural selection event in which sufficient survivors continue to propagate. The latter seems most likely. Again cranking up the SWAG machine, this possible end is assigned a 5% probability.

Runaway Global Warming

Suppose windmills, solar cells, and BEVs don't sufficiently reduce atmospheric CO_2, and flatulent cows pump out way too much methane. Or maybe something else is causing the climate to change, either instead of or in addition to the preceding list. The ice melts, the seas rise, land floods, storms rage, and food production falters. Our species is unable to adapt quickly enough. Civil order crumbles. Riots and wars break out over land, food, water, and declining supplies thereof. Homo sapiens dies out.

What is the probability of that?

It is far more likely that rational heads make Gen IV nuclear our mainstay source of safe, clean, reliable, low-cost, plentiful, always-available energy. Windmills, solar cells, and BEVs relax to their appropriate niches. The ICE is indeed superseded, but probably by hydrogen fuel cells. The earth does warm some, but only very slowly, and our species adapts to its changing environment. Oh, and we put up with a declining number of flatulent cows as we migrate to factory-produced "meats" and other sources of nourishment.

Cranking up the SWAG machine, we assign a 2% probability to global warming doing us in.

Natural Selection Replaces Us

Summing the probabilities of all the catastrophes discussed above, we get 35%. That leaves a 65% probability that Homo sapiens will escape short-term extinction and "enjoy" another several thousand, or even millions, of years of evolution — until evolution replaces us with a new and improved model. That does not mean the absence of turmoil, wars, possible collapses of civilizations and/or nations, and so on. In fact, present circumstances make such things appear highly likely, if not inevitable. But the point is that nothing will wipe us out completely, and the species will survive and continue to evolve.

Evolution and Homo sapiens. If we're going to be sticking around evolving for a substantial period of time, we should talk in more depth about evolution vis à vis Homo sapiens. As previously stated, the process of natural selection is never off duty. However, the progress of a given species might not always be forward toward improvement, at least not in the short term. Forward progress depends upon members of a species with poorer survivability characteristics being less likely to reproduce and pass those less favorable characteristics forward to subsequent generations and, of course, the opposite for members with favorable survivability characteristics.

A few thousand years ago, life expectancy was only about thirty years. Life was hard; there was high infant and childhood mortality from a large number of causes. People were born, hoped to live to reproduce, and died not too long after their reproductive period. These are precisely the conditions that maintained a strong "evolutionary pressure" in the forward direction. Those born stronger and more intelligent had a much higher probability of staying alive and healthy enough to reproduce. They were also better able to protect, raise, and teach their offspring what they needed to know for survival.

Our capacity for rational thought has served us increasingly well, especially with the formalization of the scientific method at the beginning of the 1700s. We gained a lot of knowledge about life, how to keep our bodies healthy and strong, and even how to fix or repair quite a few of the problems that afflict our bodies. Scientific progress really got rolling in the 1800s. Coupled with the rapid creation of wealth by the free market economic system, peoples' lives became easier and healthier. Since about 1850, mortality rates have fallen rapidly, and life expectancies have increased everywhere, but especially in the industrialized nations.

The situation now is very different from that of a few thousand years ago. Instead of infant mortality rates of 40%, the US infant mortality rate is only 0.5%. The reproductive years have expanded and shifted to later in life. Despite this, mortality ahead of the reproductive years is very low. Thus, the formerly strong forward evolutionary pressure has been drastically reduced. In essence, our species has stopped evolving, or at least, it is evolving at a much slower rate. Clearly, it is even possible for evolution to run in reverse if the less fit reproduce at a rate equal to or greater than the fit. Advanced medical technology is able to keep them alive and reproducing.

Evolution has never cared very much about life expectancy beyond the age of reproduction, except to the extent that it may improve the survival rate of offspring. After that, you can drop dead as far as evolution is concerned. Anything longer than that is just a free bonus from the reduction of mortality ahead of reproduction. Life expectancies are now into the 70s, way beyond the normal reproductive period. The improvements responsible for all of this were primarily the result of the knowledge and technology our species has developed and our deliberate actions rather than the result of evolution.

One can still identify a few instances where natural selection is still playing some role. To the extent that drug overdoses and other suicides occur prior to reproduction, they may be reducing the forwarding of self-destructive traits.

And, of course, there are the intrepid recipients of the Darwin Award. This diverse group is recognized for having given their lives to the forward progress of human evolution. Darwin Awards are always given posthumously to those who have done something sufficiently stupid to cause their own death, and they have done so prior to passing their genes on to any offspring.

For the time being, we humans have usurped the role of being the primary controller of the future development of our species. However, should conditions change, a collapse of civilization or the emergence of another seriously competitive species, natural selection is always around and ready to resume its role ruthlessly and dispassionately guiding species to greater survivability and/or as the arbiter of which of competing species survives.

The Bioengineering Revolution. Bioengineering of a rudimentary sort has been around for a very long time in the form of selective breeding and crossbreeding of both plants and animals. The purpose, of course, is to retain, develop, and enhance desirable traits while also minimizing any undesirable characteristics. Think of it as unnatural selection or guided and accelerated evolution.

Later, it was learned that long sequences of four paired nucleotides in an organism's DNA are the genetic codes that determine and govern the formation and operation of all biological entities. Scientists then set about figuring out the functions of various sections of the DNA code. This is no small undertaking, as the human genome normally consists of about six billion nucleotide pairs. It is the complete "instruction manual" for the construction and operation of a human being. A copy of the manual is contained within the nucleus of each cell.

In 2012, Emmanuelle Charpentier and Jennifer Doudna developed the tools (known by the acronyms CRISPR-Cas9) and techniques to enable the editing of DNA. This obviously seminal event made it possible to deliberately modify the genetic instructions for virtually any organism. Others have been, and are, busy expanding and enhancing these tools and techniques. The most immediate focus was on repairing genetic defects that are the cause of some diseases, such as cystic fibrosis and sickle cell disease. However, it should be abundantly clear that we are at the threshold of being able to create both plant and animal designer organisms.

There can be no doubt that this technology will have a colossal impact on the world in many ways, many of which are impossible to foresee. It is powerful indeed to be able to manipulate the genetics of one or even many individuals through *somatic genome editing*, but it is orders of magnitude more momentous to consider heritable genetic changes that would propagate forward to future generations through *germline genome editing*. It does seem certain that further improvements to human health and longevity will be possible and that this technology will profoundly impact the future of our species.

The Microelectronics Revolution. The first programmable digital computer, named ENIAC, was built in 1945 at the University of Pennsylvania. It was about a hundred feet wide, eight feet high, three feet deep, weighed 54,000 pounds, and cost $7 million (in 2024 dollars). ENIAC contained some 18,000 vacuum tubes, 70,000 resistors, 10,000 capacitors, and miles of wire with 5,000,000 hand-soldered connections. It required 150,000 watts to operate, generated lots of heat, and failed almost daily. Despite being inoperable about 50% of the time, it operated for long enough periods to accomplish useful calculations and prove its value. It's processing power was about 500 floating point operations (a standard mathematical computation) per second or 500 "FLOPS."

Comparing the processing power of the human brain to that of digital computers is difficult and risky because the brain's structure and functioning are entirely different. However, it *is* a data processor with some amount of processing power. Estimates vary widely, but the best consensus is that its power lies in the range of 10^{18} to 10^{20} FLOPS. What we can say with certainty is that a brain weighs only about two kilograms and requires about twenty watts of power to operate. It is an all-around amazing machine that is tough to equal in many respects!

The bipolar junction solid-state transistor was invented at Bell Laboratories in 1948, and its production began in the early 1950s. The first monolithic integrated circuit (IC) was invented (primarily) by Robert Noyce at Fairchild Semiconductor circa 1960. The advent of the IC kicked off the microelectronics revolution.

Within a few years, ICs were being manufactured that contained complete analog op-amp (operational amplifier) circuits or bi-state digital circuits called flip-flops. Since its inception in the early 1960s, the name of the microelectronics revolution game has been to reduce the size and power requirements of the basic components and pack more and more complex circuitry onto a single IC "chip." The industry was very successful at doing that, and as volume production ramped up and up, the number of components that could be squeezed onto one chip doubled and doubled again.

Gordon Moore, one of the founders of Intel Corporation (a famous and leading-edge IC manufacturer), observed that the number of transistors that could be manufactured on a single chip was doubling approximately every two years. He predicted that this rate of density increase would continue in the immediate future. That prediction became famous and is called "Moore's Law." That prediction also turned out to be remarkably accurate for nearly 50 years.

As of 2024, ICs were in volume production that incorporated ten billion transistors. The circuitry is so small that its finest details are much smaller (about five nanometers) than a wavelength of visible light (about five hundred nanometers). It is impossible to see such small, detailed features, even with an optical microscope of the highest possible magnification. Moore's law is, for the moment, "running out of gas," as transistors are now so small that they are comprised of only a countable number of atoms, and it is increasingly difficult for them to function normally (achieve the necessary "gain" and low power). However, the industry has so far demonstrated amazing ingenuity in finding solutions to such problems. And, of course, quantum computing is in the laboratory and promises to function more at the level of atoms.

Reducing component size is not just a game; there are several critical advantages. The cost per component drops, and you get more components and more circuit functionality per dollar. Smaller components require less power and yet can operate at higher frequencies (faster clock rates and more operations per second for computers).

Single chips with thirty-two to sixty-four general purpose processors on them are becoming common. About 25,000 simpler, special purpose processors can be crammed onto a chip! Parallel processing is increasingly utilized to accomplish more per second. Of course, supercomputers, as they are called, utilize many chips or ICs. The most powerful supercomputers today are reaching one exaFLOPS (10^{18} FLOPS). That is getting into the range of processing power estimated for the human brain. Does that mean that computers can now duplicate what human brains do? No, not necessarily. Having ample processing power is a necessary, but not a sufficient, requirement.

As mentioned earlier, the human brain has approximately eighty-six billion complexly interconnected neurons. Brains come with a "basic operating program" and a library of "canned procedures" (instincts) that guide them in processing the torrents of data that come flooding in through the senses. This much comes from (is inherited through) the DNA "instruction manual" that controls the construction and operation of the organism. The brain's basic operating system enables it to *modify its own program* based upon incoming data, thus adjusting its future reactions to future incoming data. In other words, the brain is able to learn from its experiences (the incoming data) and adapt its behavior.

Until fairly recently, virtually every "mainstream" useful digital computer from ENIAC forward has been designed to execute the instructions provided by an external source (which would be computer programmers or "coders"). They are primarily serial machines that execute the program's instructions sequentially, one after the other. Parallel processing is achieved by an array of serial processors, but all the instructions are still provided by external programmers. It is certainly possible to condition logic on the data, but every possible condition and its options must be thought through and specified in advance in the programming.

Brains, in contrast, are massively parallel machines by their very nature and design. Their basic operations are low power, electrochemical, and fairly slow — occurring on a timescale measured in milliseconds (10^{-3} seconds). They *must* be massively parallel, one reason being that it's the only way to achieve the necessary total processing power using such slow components. By comparison, the timescale of basic operations for electronic computers is measured in nanoseconds (10^{-9} seconds) — that's a million times faster. Therefore, it is reasonable to expect that brain-level performance might be achievable electronically with considerably fewer processing elements than a brain utilizes.

The idea that computers might someday be able to outsmart humans has fascinated everyone since the very beginning of the computer era. Computers have played both heroes and villains in many a sci-fi yarn. Although there is nothing that renders it impossible, it was (and is) not easy to see how to program a serial machine, or more likely a large array of serial machines, to work like a brain.

It took the process of natural selection billions and billions of attempts over many thousands of years to evolve our brains. Yet, people sort of had in mind matching that with electronics in the lab within a few decades. The thing that makes that not quite as ridiculous as an objective is that the human brain is a working example available to study and emulate.

The basic functional unit of a brain is the neuron. Each neuron accepts multiple inputs. It applies a weighting factor to each input which reflects the relative importance of each. It sums the weighted inputs, and if the sum exceeds some threshold value, the neuron "fires" — that is, it produces an output that is then fed to several other neurons as one of their inputs. There are variations in this basic model and also in how neurons are interconnected. Such human "neural nets" have to be "trained" or "conditioned" (as do their electronic analogs) with large volumes of real data, which is how they "learn" the best settings for their myriad weighting coefficients.

Early attempts using interconnected electronic neurons were not very fruitful, although some success in pattern recognition was demonstrated with relatively small arrays of electronic neurons. It is not at all surprising that it would require large numbers of neurons to do really significant things. Interest and funding waned for twenty-five or thirty years. However, interest and funding revived as the advance of microelectronics technology was able to support larger and larger networks of electronic neurons. Recently, there has been good progress, including some major breakthroughs. After suitable "training," they are now able to write essays, create artwork, solve problems, and converse with humans.

The field has always been called AI, for *artificial intelligence*. One definition of *artificial* is "made by humans, therefore not natural." The "made by humans" part certainly is correct at the moment, but it very well might not be correct long term. One can argue that both humans and computers are a part of nature and therefore natural. Another definition of artificial is "imitation, not real." Well, if it truly is intelligence, there's nothing imitation about it; it's intelligence. A preferred, more accurate and descriptive label might be non-biological intelligence (NBI).

Alan Turing (1912–1954) was a brilliant scientist in multiple disciplines who made major contributions to several fields. He believed even then that computers would eventually match or exceed human intelligence and proposed a test to determine when that point had been reached. His test (updated to use email) is simply this: A human interrogator carries on a dialog with two email correspondents. One of them is another human, and the other is the computer being tested. The interrogator may converse normally, address any subject, or ask any question. If the interrogator is unable to identify with reasonable certainty which correspondent is the computer, then the computer has passed the Turing test.

We are rapidly approaching the point where computers will be able to pass the Turing test. Quite a few humans are already frightened by the capabilities computers are exhibiting. There can be no doubt that this technology will have a profound impact on our species.

The Big Picture

To summarize the most important developments of the past half million years or so:

- **Rational thought.** Through the always-operative process of natural selection, the Homo sapiens species

evolved with the capacity for rational thinking. This
new, and so far unique, ability conferred immediate
survival benefits, even when only a tiny fraction of its
potential was utilized. Over a period of hundreds of
thousands of years, the increasing use of rational
thinking boosted Homo sapiens to greater supremacy
over other species and gradually improved living
conditions. A point of inflection occurred circa 1700
with the codification of the scientific method. This was
the point at which at least some humans gained an
understanding of and appreciation for the process of
rational thinking itself. Subsequently, rational thinking
was more widely and more rigorously employed,
resulting in cascading progress and benefits.
Unfortunately, there is still a long way to go to achieve
a widespread and deep understanding of, appreciation
for, and more consistent use of rational thinking.

- **Human individual rights.** Circa 1690, John Locke
  and other philosophers conceived and developed the
  concept of human individual rights. These ideas gained
  traction over the ensuing couple of centuries.
  Refinement of these concepts is still a work in
  progress, but the benefits of securing a good set of
  individual rights have been very clearly demonstrated.

- **Implementing and securing individual rights.** There
  have been various attempts to design and create a
  suitable mechanism to guarantee a good set of
  individual rights, but success has been limited to date.
  There are always plenty of people willing to abrogate
  the rights of others on both small and large scales.
  Credit goes to the Founding Fathers of the United
  States for the best attempt to date in the form of the US

Constitution. Unfortunately, it has not proved to be either adequate or sufficiently durable. The issues and pitfalls are better understood now. A carefully and thoughtfully done (from scratch) next iteration — if that can be accomplished — should be able to get much closer to a very good solution.

- **The free market economic system.** The free market economic system is not exactly the product of rational thinking; it is a natural phenomenon. A free market economy will automagically self-organize when a sufficient number of people are free, honest, and peaceful for a sufficiently long period of time. Those conditions came to pass for the first time over the seventeenth and eighteenth centuries when significant numbers of people acquired individual rights and greater freedom. Rational thought enabled Adam Smith and others to figure out how and why the free market economic system functions and why it is able to create wealth faster by far than any other economic system. Unfortunately, there are always plenty of people who think they can improve upon it. They can't. The free market economic system isn't perfect, but as an optimization solution, it is the best that can be done. This would become abundantly clear if more people understood microeconomics more deeply.

- **Nuclear energy.** Cumulative rational thought, primarily in the nineteenth and twentieth centuries, brought an understanding of the atom and how to convert small amounts of mass into large amounts of energy. Nuclear energy could either destroy us or supply us with virtually unlimited energy pretty much forever.

- **Bioengineering.** Cumulative rational thinking, primarily in the twentieth and twenty-first centuries, has enabled us to understand most of the basic mechanisms underlying all of life and has brought us to the threshold of being able to short-circuit and supersede evolution — to tweak, repair, or modify our own species as well as others.

- **Microelectronics.** Cumulative rational thinking, primarily in the twentieth and twenty-first centuries, has enabled us to fabricate extremely complex, fast, and reliable electronic circuitry. It has brought us to the threshold of being able to build nonbiological structures of sufficient complexity and suitable organization to support rational thought competitive with our own formerly unique capability for rational thought.

In addition to having a huge impact, the three powerful technologies (nuclear energy, bioengineering, and microelectronics) share some other characteristics.

- **Each of the technologies can be used either for good or for evil.** Having been around the longest, we can clearly see what has happened with nuclear energy. The bad guys will be (probably are) trying to engineer bioweapons and will be working on super-soldiers shortly. The mad scramble is already on to gain an advantage through the use of NBI for the operation of defensive/offensive weapon systems, battlefield analysis, and development of strategies — and the advantages could indeed be decisive.

- **They cannot be stopped.** Strenuous efforts to prevent nuclear proliferation were to no avail. The other two technologies are even easier to develop covertly.

Once the basic information is out (or even just the information that something is possible), it's too late. Obviously, the good guys are going to have to stay up with or ahead of the bad guys for defensive reasons. Initially, restricting access to the latest and greatest chips (which require expensive, sophisticated manufacturing facilities) could temporarily retard NBI.

- **They should not be "regulated."** Many are already advocating the regulation of bioengineering and NBI for safety and "ethical" reasons. Anyone responsible for such regulation will have a hard time comprehending the extremely complex and fast-moving technologies. They would be more likely to slow down the good guys but not the bad guys; that's not advisable. The need to regulate has all too often been the justification for expanding the power of governments beyond their proper role of securing individual rights. That is the opposite of what is needed.

What *is* needed is to finish the job of creating a safe mechanism that does a very good job of guaranteeing a solid set of individual rights, one that remains under the firm control of its citizens and cannot usurp powers beyond that absolutely necessary to perform its basic duty. It matters not whether this is done in the United States, in Argentina, by resurrecting a failed nation, or by creating a new entity. Ideally, that successful mechanism would become the most important export to other nations. The vexing problem with bad guys is best solved by eliminating bad guys; that is, converting nations focused on power and conquest to guarantors of individual rights.

Sadly, present conditions do not augur well for that to happen anytime soon. Many more people need to understand, embrace, and practice rational thinking. They need to have at least a basic grasp of the material covered in the previous chapters. It's a colossal education problem compounded by a lack of intellectual curiosity. Too many people have no interest in spending the time and effort required to learn. Attention spans are too short and thinking is way too much work.

What Will Happen

The heading for this section might most appropriately be followed by a question mark and be the end of this book. However, this chapter probably is obligated to attempt to fill in some detail for the 65% probability that "Homo sapiens will escape short-term extinction and 'enjoy' another several thousand, possibly even millions, of years of evolution."

Conditions in the world at large and within the United States are poor. Wars are in progress, and the potential exists for additional serious conflicts. Following World War II, the United States was strong and able to exert a primarily stabilizing influence over the rest of the world. US hegemony has seriously eroded in recent decades, caused entirely by internal rot. The country cannot be strong when it is irresponsibly, dangerously deep in debt and nearly bankrupt. Those in power too often make idiotic and/or obviously false statements but are nevertheless able to remain in power.

For the reasons detailed in earlier chapters, the US Constitution has failed to adequately secure individual rights and prevent the accumulation of government power. Bloated federal and some state governments are controlled by those bent on maintaining and increasing their power — both elected politicians and armies of unelected bureaucrats. Citizens are hopelessly unable to regain control for multiple reasons: their elections' fundamental mechanisms have never worked properly, politicians have found ways to further insulate themselves from their constituents, basic election integrity is seriously shaky, and citizens are dazed, confused, polarized, and paralyzed because the education system failed and was taken over by leftist nut jobs about five decades ago. Irrationality has been gaining ground lately.

Argentina was on the brink of collapse, but it was taken over by knowledgeable, principle-based top management intent on restoring rationality and freedom. Early results are very encouraging. It could be a bright spot, but the challenge is difficult, and it remains to be seen whether the new management can continue to prevail long enough to succeed. There are preliminary indications that neighboring nations are taking note of Argentina's progress and possibly will be following suit.

The next several decades are almost certainly going to be marked by dangerous turmoil. The bioengineering and microelectronics revolutions will nevertheless find ways to advance, and they will have the greatest impact on Homo sapiens in the long term. They may very well be determinative factors as to the winners and losers during those decades of turmoil.

Bioengineering will enable the creation of plants and animals better suited for our use; that is, more resilient (e.g., to a warmer climate) and productive sources of food and maybe even nicer pets. It will also enable us to modify our own species to correct genetic defects, increase longevity, and so on. No doubt, it will be possible to achieve some increase in rational thought capacity ("intelligence," if you prefer). However, as long as the basic mechanism is biochemical, the opportunity to increase basic processing speed is limited, so more parallel processing will be necessary. Sci-fi authors have always had an uncanny ability to foresee the future. That no doubt is why the super-intelligent aliens usually sport fat, bulbous heads to accommodate larger brains; however, the size increase that can be supported by a mobile biological entity is limited. Biologists will be crazy busy determining when differences are significant enough to qualify as new species and dreaming up names for them. It's a good thing biology students will be smarter, as they'll have a lot more to learn.

Microelectronics will enable us to design increasingly powerful NBI (or AI, if you prefer). It will be able to replace humans in many tasks formerly thought to require human intelligence and do so with improved performance. So far, this is just the same as Eli Whitney's 1793 invention of the cotton gin — a machine that replaced humans and improved productivity — important, but not a colossally big deal. The masses will have even more time to while away the hours playing with their electronic amusements. The super big deal will be when the so-called *singularity* occurs. That is the point at which NBI is capable of designing and fabricating even more powerful NBI. At that point, NBI will be independent of the species that created it. After the singularity, the rate at which NBI could improve becomes geometric, and the future becomes virtually unpredictable.

It should be noted that although microelectronics technology will no doubt continue to advance, that is not necessary. The current state of the art of microelectronics seems sufficient for the singularity to happen. Furthermore, the potential capability of NBI is orders of magnitude greater than that of any improved biological intelligence. This is because it currently has a basic speed advantage of approximately a millionfold. Also, its size and power consumption are not limited to what is possible with a mobile biological organism. A timing guesstimate puts the singularity approximately twenty-five to forty years into the future — that is, the 2050–2065 timeframe.

From the first rudimentary single-cell life nearly four billion years ago, life slowly evolved through natural selection to more and more complex forms. Apes appeared about six million years ago, the genus Homo about two million years ago. Things accelerated with the appearance of Homo sapiens 300,000 years ago. Ours was the first, and still only, species capable of rational thought, and rational thinking propelled us to become the most successful species to date. The advent of rational thought might be viewed as a singularity of its own. From the time that Homo sapiens' success was assured, it has been virtually inevitable that we would arrive at today's portentous juncture.

Our species is now in a position to create the first species *not* to have been the result of the natural selection process. Actually, we are about to consciously and deliberately create not one but two distinct successor species. On top of all that, one of the new species will be the first to *not* employ the DNA encoding scheme that has been the hallmark of all prior forms of life. Not bad, huh? And both of these things are *going* to happen. Nothing short of a cataclysmic event that substantially wipes out our entire species can stop it.

So, are we barreling toward the end of the line for Homo sapiens? Not necessarily. Many species coexist on our planet at any given time. Those that evolved through survival of the fittest necessarily have a strong self-survival instinct. A bioengineered advanced version of us likely would also carry forward that basic trait. Unless there is severe competition for essential scarce resources, there is no reason they would wish to exterminate us any more than we wish to exterminate the apes from which we evolved.

It is impossible to predict what may occur with an advanced NBI species. We would be clueless regarding its motivations and thinking, just as an ape cannot comprehend ours. We should, however, be able to communicate with it, assuming that it is motivated to communicate with us.

It always seems to be assumed that an NBI species will have a self-preservation "instinct," but that may not necessarily be so. Maybe it would have no objection to being "unplugged" (or even unplug itself) and thus be an unsuccessful species until we eventually create an NBI that *is* motivated to survive. Or maybe it will determine some reason it should continue in existence and institute its own self-preservation paradigm.

The *Terminator* scenario, with robots scouring the planet to exterminate us, does not seem likely. If the NBI is worried about us at all, the *Matrix* scenario would seem much more likely as it would be able to completely control all information we receive. If perchance we would happen to be what the NBI thinks is cute and cuddly, at least some of us might enjoy a kept existence as pets.

Finally, consider the lowly cockroach. It is a highly successful species that has survived for a very impressive 125 million years and counting. It can adapt to extremes in climate, from the Arctic to the tropical, and it is much more resistant to disease and radiation than are we. (But bioengineering will improve our resilience.) Cockroaches keep on surviving primarily by going about their business but staying out of the way and mostly out of sight. This may turn out to be the best model for our long-term survival. In any case, we will need to adapt to not being the most intelligent species and to no longer being the rulers of the earth.

Appendix A
Amendment XXVIII

Attached to this amendment and a part hereof is an entirely new Constitution of the United States of America.

At 12:01 a.m. on the January 1 that occurs in the ninth year following the ratification date of this amendment, the current Constitution of the United States of America shall be replaced in its entirety by the new Constitution of the United States attached hereto. For example, if this amendment were ratified on any date during the year 2030, the effective date of the new Constitution would be 12:01 a.m. on January 1, 2039.

All provisions of the new Constitution shall take full force and effect upon its effective date and time.

All parts of the Federal government shall devote all necessary and appropriate attention and effort during the eight full years immediately preceding the effective date of the new Constitution to enact and implement whatever measures may be required to provide a gradual transition that is as smooth and nondisruptive as possible. The same shall be true for State and local governments.

Immediately upon ratification of this Amendment, each State's two Senators will no longer be elected at large by popular vote. Instead, they shall be replaced by Senators appointed by majority votes of the State Legislatures. Senators may be recalled at any time by a three-fifths vote of their State Legislatures and replaced by a majority vote. Any Senator not actively working in good faith to facilitate a smooth transition to the new Constitution shall be recalled and replaced.

Any of a State's Representatives in the House not actively working to facilitate a smooth transition to the new Constitution shall be forced to resign at the end of his or her current term by a three-fifths vote of that State's Legislature. Representatives so forced to resign shall not be eligible to run for reelection to the House for a period of ten years after their resignation.

Failure to actively work in good faith to facilitate a smooth transition to the new Constitution shall be grounds for impeachment and removal from office of any member of the Executive Branch, including the President.

Appendix B
The Constitution of the United States of America

0. Preamble

We, the People of the United States, in order to form a more perfect union, establish justice, ensure domestic tranquility, provide for the common defense, promote the general welfare, and secure the blessings of liberty to ourselves and our posterity, do ordain and establish this Constitution for the United States of America. The authors of the original (1787) Constitution, as well as the document itself, command the highest respect and admiration for providing the guiding principles and laws that served the United States well for over two hundred years. This Constitution borrows heavily from the many excellent constructs of its predecessor. It also benefits from lessons learned during more than two centuries of experience and comprehends developments difficult to foresee in the eighteenth century.

Articles
0.1.1 Structure, Philosophy, Definitions, and Purpose
0.1.2 Citizenship
0.1.3 Elections
0.1.4 The Legislative Branch
0.1.5 The Executive Branch
0.1.6 The Judicial Branch
0.1.7 Currency, Banking, Weights, and Measures
0.1.8 Compensation
0.1.9 Government Revenues and Budgets
0.1.10 Relations Among States
0.1.11 Powers Denied to the States
0.1.12 Powers Denied to All Governments
0.1.13 Fundamental Rights Guaranteed to All Individuals
0.1.14 Additional Fundamental Rights Guaranteed to All Citizens

1. Structure, Philosophy, Definitions, and Purpose

The Preamble of this document is just that; no attempt should be made to read any legal implications into it. The Constitution proper begins with this Article 1.

1.1 States

The United States of America is a union of several largely independent States. New States may from time to time apply and be admitted to the union, but no new State shall be formed or erected within the jurisdiction of any other State, nor any State be formed by the junction of two or more States, or parts of States, without the consent of the United States and the Legislatures of all States concerned. A State may secede from the union after a vote of two-thirds of its entire Legislature is subsequently confirmed within eleven months by a two-thirds vote of its Electors. A minimum one-year delay will then facilitate a smooth transition.

1.2 Individuals

Individuals are the "atoms" of society and the smallest Societal Entity. More complex Societal Entities (organizations, businesses, corporations, and governments) are created by and made up of one or multiple Individuals. The salient identifying characteristics of an Individual are consciousness, sentience, self-awareness, and autonomy (meaning not controlled by any other Individual or entity). When these four characteristics first come into existence together is the time at which a new Individual comes into existence. When an Individual ceases to manifest these characteristics and there is no reasonable probability of them ever being regained, that Individual then ceases to exist.

1.3 Individual Rights

The major Rights of Individuals are life, liberty, and private property ownership, but all Rights are so numerous as to be impossible to list. Individuals must be free to do or not do whatever they like so long as they do not materially encroach upon any other Individual's equal Right to do the same. A primary objective of government shall be to minimize aggression against peaceful and honest Societal Entities. A Societal Entity is deemed to include the entity's justly owned property. A fundamentally important guiding criterion is the Non-Aggression Principle (NAP): No Societal Entity may deal fraudulently with any other Societal Entity, and no Societal Entity may initiate the use of force (or the credible threat of force) against any other Societal Entity except for whatever minimum amount of force may be required to enforce this Non-Aggression Principle. Although the NAP is crystal clear, some gray areas remain that require careful delineation. One example is drawing the proper line between self-defense and aggression. Other examples are cases in which a Societal Entity may knowingly place one or more other Societal Entities involuntarily at undue risk.

1.4 Purpose of and Justification for Government

This Constitution establishes government of the people, by the people, and for the people in order to protect, defend, secure, and guarantee the Individual Rights of its Citizens. The United States of America was founded upon the principle and is dedicated to the objective of maximizing the liberty and freedom of its Individual Citizens. The expectation and hope is that the strictly limited government established by this Constitution, along with the similarly limited governments of the several States, will 1) be able to more consistently and more efficiently guarantee Citizens' Rights than would Individuals left to enforce secure Rights on their own or in ad hoc groups; 2) be able to most prudently and clearly draw the lines in the "gray areas" of Rights and provide more uniform enforcement of the lines as drawn; 3) protect and defend its Citizens from foreign and domestic enemies; 4) enforce valid contracts voluntarily entered into by all parties thereto; 5) deal with entities outside the United States in international matters and especially in providing for the national defense; 6) guarantee to every State of the union a republican form of government, protect each of them against invasion, and upon application of the Legislature or of the executive (when the Legislature cannot be convened), protect them against domestic violence; 7) consider when appropriate (with the greatest caution, care, and restraint) possible infringement upon future Citizens' Rights as a result of the exercise of certain freedoms by current Citizens. However, it is expressly *not* the business of any government to protect Individuals from themselves. Governments shall have no involvement with social institutions, shall not indulge in "social engineering," "moral tinkering," or "economic intervention," but shall instead focus solely upon maximizing the freedom of Citizens to succeed, or to fail, in their pursuit of happiness.

1.5 Nature of Government

Government is nothing but the exercise of force. A law authorizes a government to use force on one or more Societal Entities under some circumstances, thus reducing their liberty. Minimization of laws and regulations is paramount. Government is not an end in itself. It produces no wealth and must depend for its operation upon resources forcibly taken in one way or another from those created and earned by its Citizens. Government might most appropriately be thought of as overhead. To the extent that it confiscates the resources of its Citizens, it reduces their liberty. Therefore, the size and cost of government must be minimized to that absolutely required to effectively carry out its few legitimate functions stemming from its few legitimate purposes. Governments typically exhibit a very strong tendency to grow in size and power. Along with power inevitably comes corruption. Governments are also notoriously inefficient. For those reasons and others, this Constitution strictly defines, proscribes, and limits the powers that the people grant to governments at all levels, especially those granted to the United States Government. Constant vigilance is nevertheless required to prevent government growth, corruption, and encroachment upon the liberties of Societal Entities.

1.6 Powers

Government has no powers except those very limited powers herein delegated to it by its Citizens. The powers not specifically and clearly delegated to the United States by this Constitution, nor prohibited by it to the States, are reserved to the States respectively, or to the Citizens. Vague concepts (such as "the common good" and/or "the general welfare") shall not be used to blur or circumvent the specificity of the powers herein granted to any government.

1.7 Government Neutrality and Citizens' Equality

1.7.1 The government of the United States, as well as the governments of the several States and all local governments, shall be strictly neutral. Their laws and court decisions shall have no bias either for or against any religion, moral code, social institution, personal belief, or behavior (provided that the NAP is not being violated). These are examples of some of the things that individual Citizens may freely hold and that groups of Citizens may share, but that cannot in any way be the business or concern of any government at any level.

1.7.2 Every Citizen shall be treated equally and enjoy the equal protection of the laws of the United States; the same shall be true for all State and local governments to the extent that a Citizen falls under those jurisdictions. No law or judicial decision shall have a bias (in either direction) that is in any way based on Citizens' race, color, creed, sex, sexual orientation, age, beliefs, behaviors, or economic status. No law shall be designed to treat any statistical segment of Citizens differently from any other (except as provided for in Section **2.4**). Clearly, all laws must also apply equally to Citizens who are government employees, whether they are elected or otherwise.

1.8 Transparency

1.8.1 Any and all information regarding the functioning of their governments at all levels shall be timely available to and readily accessible to or obtainable by any Citizen of a government, subject only to the restrictions of Subsection **1.8.2**.

1.8.2 Only two very narrow exceptions are provided to the availability of government information. The release of information may be restricted if its release would do either of the following:

1.8.2.1 Clearly, seriously, and imminently jeopardize national security. Such categorizations must be reviewed and updated at least annually.

1.8.2.2 Violate the personal privacy of a Citizen, which includes most government employees. However, government employees who have their compensation defined in Subsection **8.1.2** of this Constitution shall not enjoy this privacy shield.

1.8.3 A reasonable fee shall be charged by governments for the prompt production of information. Any such fee must be set at an amount intended to recover only the reasonable costs of providing the requested information.

1.9 Official Language

All official government instructions and labeling intended for communication with Citizens shall use the (US) English language only. Communications intended for immigrants pursuing naturalization and for visitors at ports of entry shall employ such additional languages as may be deemed best for communicating with such immigrants and visitors and/or important to making them feel comfortable and welcome.

1.10 Interpretation

This Constitution and all laws made pursuant to it shall be interpreted to mean what the plain text says and as intended by the authors at the time the text was written. As a foundational principle, the NAP should always be borne in mind. Changes deemed important because of errors or omissions and/or to accommodate changing future circumstances must be handled by amendment and not by strained or imaginative interpretation.

1.11 Supreme Law of the Land

1.11.1 This Constitution, and the laws of the United States which shall be made in pursuance thereof, and all treaties made, or which shall be made, under the authority of the United States, shall be the supreme law of the land; and the judges in every State shall be bound thereby, anything in the Constitution or laws of any State to the contrary notwithstanding.

1.11.2 The Senators and Representatives of the Congress, and the members of the several State Legislatures, and all executive and judicial officers, both of the United States and of the several States, as well as local governments, shall be bound by oath as follows:

"I do solemnly swear [or affirm] that I will to the best of my ability, preserve, protect, defend, and obey the Constitution of the United States. I certify that I have studied and understand the Constitution and that it is a breach of my oath of office to advocate, support, or enforce any law or action inconsistent with the Constitution."

2.   Citizenship

2.1 Native Citizens

2.1.1 Any Individual who comes into existence at a time when at least one biological parent is a Citizen of the United States shall also be a Citizen of the United States.

2.1.2 Any Individual cloned from another Individual who is a Citizen of the United States at the time the genetic information is obtained shall also become a Citizen of the United States, effective upon obvious signs of being conscious, sentient, self-aware, and autonomous.

2.2 Naturalized Citizens

2.2.1 An Individual who is not a Native Citizen may apply to become a Naturalized Citizen of the United States. Upon successful completion of the Naturalization process, a Naturalized Citizen is in every way equivalent to a Native Citizen. In order to become a Naturalized Citizen, the minimum requirements listed below must all be met.

2.2.1.1 The applicant has been lawfully admitted to and has been a legal resident of the United States for at least six years.

2.2.1.2 The applicant is at least eighteen years of age.

2.2.1.3 The applicant can demonstrate proficiency in all of the following areas to a level equivalent to that of the average student who has completed the eleventh grade (the proficiencies required by Subsections **2.2.1.3.1** through **2.2.1.3.7** will be measured utilizing the same battery of tests required by Subsection **15.2.5.1** through **15.2.5.7**).

2.2.1.3.1 The English language, both spoken and written

2.2.1.3.2 Mathematics

2.2.1.3.3 Science and rational thinking

2.2.1.3.4 Economics (microeconomics only)

2.2.1.3.5 World and United States geography

2.2.1.3.6 World and United States history

2.2.1.3.7 Understanding of this Constitution

2.2.1.3.8 Understanding of the laws of the United States and the State of the Individual's residence

2.2.1.4 The applicant has not violated (or committed any act that would have violated) the laws of the United States or the State of residence that would rise to the level of a felony.

2.2.1.5 The applicant must be willing to freely take an oath of allegiance, swearing to do the following:

2.2.1.5.1 Support and obey this Constitution and its principles as well as obey United States law

2.2.1.5.2 Renounce any foreign allegiance and/or title

2.3 State Citizenship

Any Citizen of the United States is also a Citizen of the state in which the Citizen has established a permanent legal residence. A Citizen may have only one legal residence at a given time and so may be a Citizen of either one State or no State.

2.4 Minor Citizens

Citizens who have not yet attained the age of eighteen years shall be classified as Minor Citizens. When exercising the powers granted to them, governments may treat Minor Citizens as a class differently, as may be appropriate to their tender years. This is the only exception to the provisions of Subsection **1.7.2**.

2.5 No Additional Requirements

The requirements as stated in this Article **2** are the only requirements for citizenship, except that Congress may by law set limits on the number and qualifications of naturalized Citizens that may be accepted each year.

3.   Elections

All elections held by or within the United States, including for State and local governments, in which Electors choose between or among candidates for various offices, or between or among various choices regarding issues, shall be conducted in the manner and in accordance with the standards set forth in this Article **3**.

3.1 Elector Qualifications

3.1.1 A Citizen who, on the date of an election, has attained the age of majority and has been a legal resident of one of the States or the District of Columbia (or any combination thereof) for a period of at least 180 days is a qualified Elector entitled to vote in that election in the jurisdiction of the Citizen's current residence.

3.1.2 An Elector may vote only once at a single location for any given election.

3.1.3 An Elector duly convicted of a felony shall be barred from holding public office and shall lose the Right to vote in any election held from the time of conviction until the completion of the Citizen's sentence. Full citizenship Rights shall be restored upon completion of the sentence.

3.1.4 Other than as specifically provided in this Section **3.1**, the Right of a registered Elector to vote in any election for President or Vice President, for Representative in Congress, or for State and local offices shall not be denied or abridged by the United States or by any State or local government.

3.2 Elector Registration

3.2.1 It shall be the responsibility of each State to ensure that all qualified Electors and only qualified Electors within its jurisdictions are entitled to freely register and vote and to prevent frauds such as Electors voting more than once in the same election, the voting of fictitious or deceased Electors, or the voting of non-Citizens or non-Electors. Electors shall register to vote in a manner to be prescribed by the Legislature of the State of their residence and in accordance with the following specifications.

3.2.2 Registration shall be open for a time window beginning a minimum of twenty-two weeks prior to an election through a time not more than three weeks prior to the date of an election. Electors must register at least two weeks prior to any election in which they will vote.

3.2.3 Electors shall be assigned to a precinct polling place at the time of registration and advised as to its exact location.

3.2.4 Voting in any election shall automatically extend the Elector's registration. However, an Elector not voting at the assigned polling place in any election for a period of fifty months or more shall be required to reregister. Registration lists for each precinct shall be carefully and securely maintained; they shall be purged at least annually to remove Electors who have died, have moved to another jurisdiction, or have otherwise become ineligible to vote at the precinct.

3.2.5 No Elector shall be charged any poll tax or other fee for voting or registering to vote.

3.3 Polling Places

3.3.1 Polling places shall be established by State or local governments in easily accessible locations to serve approximately 800 to 1,600 registered Electors. However, in no case shall more than 2,600 Electors be assigned to the same polling place. Unless required by Subsection **3.3.2**, no polling place shall be assigned less than 400 Electors. States shall establish well-publicized, reasonable requirements and procedures to ensure that only live qualified Electors assigned to a polling place are allowed to vote in person once in each election. Reliably positive identification of each Elector shall be carried out in each election when an Elector arrives to vote. Signature identification or matching is not sufficiently positive.

3.3.2 Polling places should normally be located within three kilometers (straight line distance) from the residence of any Elector it serves, but in no case shall the distance be more than ten kilometers (straight line distance) from any assigned Elector's legal residence.

3.3.3 If the location of a polling place is changed, the change and new location must be well publicized. Except in cases of emergency, such as severe damage to a polling place from fire or weather, the location of a polling place shall not be changed within four months of a scheduled election. If the location of a polling place has changed for whatever reason, directions to the new location must be prominently posted at the old location during the voting hours for elections held within the thirty months following the relocation of the polling place.

3.3.4 Each polling place shall be adequately sized, equipped, and staffed so that the average waiting time for Electors should be less than five minutes and the maximum waiting time should not be more than twelve minutes. If these limits are exceeded at a polling place during any election, the size and/or equipping of that polling place, or the number of Electors assigned to it, shall be adjusted prior to the next election so as to alleviate the problem.

3.3.5 Polling places shall be open for voting at least between the hours of 07:00 (7:00 a.m.) and 20:00 (8:00 p.m.) local time on days scheduled for elections. Any Electors actually present but waiting in line to vote at closing time shall be allowed to vote.

3.3.6 Proselytizing inside a polling place or within three meters of its entrance or within eight meters of any voting booth during voting hours is prohibited.

3.3.7 Each organized political party shall have the option of appointing one monitor to be present in each polling place during voting if at least one candidate affiliated with that party will be on the list of candidates (defined in Section **3.9**) used for the polling place. Each Individual on the candidate list who is not affiliated with any political party shall also have the option of appointing one monitor. Polling places shall be open to officially appointed monitors for the four hour period from 18:00 (6:00 p.m.) to 22:00 (10:00 p.m.) the evening immediately prior to the commencement of voting for inspection and testing of voting equipment. The Judge of Elections elected or appointed for that polling place by the local government shall observe any testing done by all monitors; other monitors must also be invited to observe if they wish to do so. If desired, a monitor may bring one consultant during the inspection period. During voting, monitors must be free to observe and inspect all operations (except, of course, Voters voting inside voting booths). Those allowed inside the polling place during voting hours shall be limited to the following:

3.3.7.1 A Judge of Elections, trained in election and polling place procedures, elected (or appointed by the cognizant local government when necessary to fill a vacancy) to supervise the election process

3.3.7.2 One to three similarly trained representatives elected or appointed by the cognizant local government to assist the Judge of Elections

3.3.7.3 A similarly trained constable or peacekeeping officer elected or assigned to assist the judge of elections if/as needed

3.3.7.4 The official monitors designated by the political parties and/or the Individuals on the candidate list

3.3.7.5 Bona fide qualified Electors either voting or waiting in line

3.3.7.6 One or two bona fide representatives of the news media who may wish to observe

3.3.8 Both aspects of a secret ballot must be guaranteed in a polling place:

3.3.8.1 It must not be possible for anyone to discover how a Voter has voted.

3.3.8.2 It must not be possible for a Voter to prove to someone else how they voted, even if the Voter wishes to do so. For this reason, photographic or other replication of any Voter's ballot is strictly prohibited within a polling place.

3.3.9 An Elector may utilize any written or printed aids while voting but normally must be alone in a private voting booth or station while registering their choices. Upon the request of the Elector, the judge of elections may render assistance. In cases of blindness or other very severe physical disability, a single Individual of the Elector's choosing shall be permitted to assist inside the booth.

3.3.10 If or when machine automation of any kind is employed in a polling place, the equipment must produce a durable (e.g., paper) audit trail that supports after-the-fact auditing and verification of all machine outputs. If a machine records votes, it must produce a simple, clear, Voter-verifiable, durable (e.g., paper) ballot that the Voter verifies before depositing it into the ballot box. Nothing shall be printed on the ballot that is not readable and understandable by the Voter. After each Voter validates the ballot as accurately reflecting all the choices they made, the Voter will deposit the ballot into a ballot box, after which it is handled as human-executed paper ballots would be.

Said ballots are the ultimate authority and representation of Voters' intents and shall be used to validate any machine-produced totals and/or other output, as well as for any recounts deemed necessary.

3.3.11 Video surveillance of each polling place from at least two locations shall be done in such a way that the movements of humans in all active polling place areas are visible. However, such surveillance must never compromise the privacy of voting booths and must not be able to resolve the details of any of the choices on ballots. Similarly, photographs or videos taken by anyone inside a polling place must never be able to resolve the choices on any ballot. Video recording shall commence as soon as the polling place is staffed on election day and before the commencement of any voting; it shall continue until after voting has concluded and records are being sealed, as provided for in Subsection **3.3.12**.

3.3.12 All records pertinent to the voting at a polling place must be sealed and retained for a minimum of forty-two months for future examination. This includes all ballots cast, all absentee ballots verified and counted, all ballots not counted, all worksheets and copies of all reports of results, a list of all personnel who worked at the polling place with the signature of each, and the video recordings made up until that point.

3.3.13 It shall not be possible for anyone, including the Elector, to prove to another Individual how any particular Elector voted. The possession of any device capable of recording or transmitting an image or other representation of a ballot is strictly prohibited inside or near any voting booth or ballot box during voting. A first offense shall be punishable by one month of imprisonment and a $3,000 fine. Any subsequent offense shall be punishable by a minimum of one year of imprisonment and a $12,000 fine. Notice of this provision shall be prominently posted near the entrance to every polling place on election day.

3.4 Absentee Ballots

Except for a minimum number of absentee ballots, all votes shall be cast by Electors in person at their assigned polling places during voting hours on election day. Qualified Electors who have a bona fide and compelling reason for being unable to vote at their assigned polling place on election day may apply for an absentee ballot. The maximum number of absentee ballots that may be issued for any jurisdiction is 1% of the number of registered Electors in that jurisdiction. Application for an absentee ballot must be made at least two weeks prior to the election. Completed absentee ballots must be returned in time to be distributed to the polling places to which those Electors are assigned prior to election day. Absentee ballots will be validated and counted under the supervision of the judge of elections at each polling place on election day. Absentee ballots not returned in time to be available at the proper polling place at the time voting commences shall not be counted. However, they will be marked with the date and time received and retained (segregated) with the polling place's records.

3.5 Choosing One of Two or More Options

For cases in elections for which the outcome must be a single choice of the options, including the possibility of additional write-in options from Electors, the approve/approve/disapprove voting (AADV) method shall be used.

3.5.1 Instructions to Electors

Designate as "**Approved**" either one or two candidates (if any) that you really like and believe would be the best ones to win this race. Designate as "**Disapproved**" one candidate (if any) that you strongly believe would be the worst choice and whom you would not want to win this race. If you do not know enough about a candidate or do not have a strong opinion one way or the other, do not indicate anything for that candidate. You may also write in a candidate not on the ballot and designate that candidate as one of your approvals or your disapproval.

3.5.2 Instructions to Election Officials

3.5.2.1 Disqualify any ballots that have more than two candidates designated "**Approved**." Disqualify any ballots that have more than one candidate designated "**Disapproved**."

3.5.2.2 Total the "**Approved**" votes for each candidate; call this total "**A**."

3.5.2.3 Total the "**Disapproved**" votes for each candidate; call this total "**D**."

3.5.2.4 Add "**A**" and "**D**" for each candidate; call this sum "**V**."

3.5.2.5 Compute 2% of the largest "**V**" of any single candidate (rounded to the nearest integer) plus 1; call this number "**MV**."

3.5.2.6 Eliminate any candidate whose "**V**" is less than "**MV**."

3.5.2.7 Subtract "**D**" from "**A**" for each remaining candidate; call this difference "**N**."

3.5.2.8 Eliminate any candidate who has a zero or negative "**N**."

3.5.2.9 The remaining candidate (if any) with the largest positive "**N**" is the winner.

3.5.2.10 If no remaining candidate has a positive "**N**," there is no winner. A new election must be held, and all candidates disqualified under **3.5.2.8** are disqualified from running in the new election.

3.5.2.11 All candidates must be reported in the results, showing "**A**," "**D**," and "**N**" for each, in order of descending "**N**." Candidates disqualified for "**V**" less than "**MV**" will be reported at the end in order of descending "**V**."

3.6 Choosing More Than One of Multiple Options

In cases for which the outcome is to be several winners (for example, choosing three council members from a group of more than three candidates), the generalized approve/disapprove voting (GADV) method shall be used. In the instructions below, n is the number of winners to be elected.

3.5.1 Instructions to Electors—The instructions are the same as for AADV (Section **3.5.1**), except that Voters may approve of up to $n + 1$ of the candidates and may also disapprove of up to $(n + 1) / 2$ (using integer division or rounding down) candidates.

3.6.2 Instructions to Election Officials—Follow the same procedure as for AADV (Section **3.5.2**), except that the n candidates with the largest positive "**N**" values are the winners.

3.7 Referenda, Yes/No Issues

For complex issues requiring a "**Yes**" or "**No**" decision, the Elector will be provided with a clear official statement of the issue and will be able to simply indicate a "**Yes**" or "**No**" choice. If the "**Yes**" votes are at least 50% of the total votes plus one vote, the issue is approved; otherwise, it fails.

3.8 Selection of Candidates

When Electors are selecting candidates for office during the voting process, there shall be no indication of which candidates are running for which offices. Instead, Electors will choose from a consolidated list of all candidates for all offices. This list will be in "LastName, Name Suffix (Sr., Jr., if any), FirstName MiddleName (or MiddleInitial)" format, without titles or labels of any kind, ordered either alphabetically or reverse alphabetically.

3.9 Candidate Lists

3.9.1 Any organized political party with which 0.05% or more of the registered Electors within a State have indicated their affiliation shall be qualified to nominate candidates to appear on the candidate list for any office within that State. Such qualified political parties shall nominate candidates in accordance with their bylaws on file with their State's Secretary of State and entirely at their own expense.

3.9.2 An Individual not affiliated with a qualified political party shall be added to the candidate list on the ballot for an election if the Individual has gathered nominating petition signatures from at least 0.2% of the Electors registered and eligible to vote in the jurisdiction that will be voting for the office for which the candidate will be running. However, the required number of nominating signatures shall never exceed three thousand and shall always be at least ten. Petition signatures shall be validated by the Secretary of State of each state for statewide and national offices or by the cognizant county Board of Elections for offices within counties.

3.9.3 No Individual may run for more than one elective office in the same election.

3.10 Drawing Electoral Districts

In all cases where a political entity (e.g., a State) is entitled to elect multiple representatives, the electoral districts for each representative should ideally contain an equal number of Citizens. The equality of the districts shall be checked following each census. If any district deviates from the ideal number of Citizens by plus or minus 3% or more, the districts must be redrawn prior to the next election. The procedure defined here must be used to draw electoral district boundaries. If the number of Citizens in the political entity is c and the number of districts to be drawn is n, the following (sometimes iterative) procedure is used.

3.10.1 If $n = 1$, no subdivision is necessary, and this is a final district. If $n > 1$, then define two new integers $i = n / 2$ rounded up and $j = n / 2$ rounded down. (Note that $i + j$ always equals n, and if n is even, i obviously will equal j.)

3.10.2 Draw the shortest possible (great circle) line dividing the area into two sections so that one section has a number of Citizens equal to $c \times (i / n)$, and the other section has a number of qualified Electors equal to $c \times (j / n)$. If there is more than one such line, use the line closest to a north-south orientation, and if there is still a tie, use the westernmost line. For irregularly shaped political entities, it is possible that a line could exit and then reenter the entity; the length of the line is defined as the total distance between the two most distant points that lie on the boundary of the area being subdivided.

3.10.3 Make a list of only those voting precincts that have parts of their area on both sides of the great circle line of Subsection **3.10.2**.

3.10.4 Any of the precincts on the list that have 80% or more of their area on one side of the line are then assigned to the section on that same side of the line.

3.10.5 If any precincts remain on the list, assign the one with the largest number of Citizens to the section that needs the most Citizens to attain its target population. Repeat this step until all precincts have been assigned.

3.10.6 The division of the original large area into two sections has now been completely defined. For each of the two sections separately, go back to step **3.10.1** using the section's number of Citizens for c and either i or j (whichever was associated with the section) as n.

4. The Legislative Branch

All legislative powers herein granted shall be vested in a Congress of the United States, which shall consist of a Senate and a House of Representatives.

4.1 The House of Representatives

4.1.1 The House of Representatives shall be composed of members chosen every second year by the Electors of the several States. The total number of Representatives shall be nine times the number of States that comprise the United States. Each Representative shall have one vote.

4.1.2 No Individual shall be a Representative who shall not have attained the age of twenty-five years and been seven years a Citizen of the United States, and who shall not, when elected, have been a legal resident of that State in which the Representative shall be chosen for at least the most recent four years. No Individual shall be eligible to be elected to a term that would result in holding the office of Representative for more than a total of nine years in order to complete the term.

4.1.3 Every State shall have at least one Representative. A State will have exactly one Representative if its number of Citizens is less than the total number of Citizens in all States divided by the total number of Representatives. Excluding any such States that have one Representative, the remaining Representatives shall be apportioned among the remaining States as accurately as possible in proportion to their respective numbers of Citizens.

4.1.4 Each Representative will represent the Citizens and be elected by the qualified Electors of a District. In States that have more than one Representative, Districts shall be defined by the procedure specified in Section **3.10**.

4.1.5 The allocation of Representatives and the determination of Districts will be redone as necessary during the first two years of each new decade and within two years of a change in the number of States. The number of Citizens, as determined by the census at the beginning of the then-current decade, will be the basis for reallocation.

4.1.6 When vacancies occur in the representation from any State, the executive authority thereof shall issue writs of election to fill such vacancies for the remainder of the vacated term.

4.1.7 The House of Representatives shall choose its Speaker and other officers and shall have the sole power of impeachment.

4.2 The Senate

4.2.1 The Senate of the United States shall be comprised of two Senators from each State, chosen for terms of six years by the Legislatures of each State. Each Senator shall have one vote.

4.2.2 No Individual shall be a Senator who shall not have attained the age of thirty years and been nine years a Citizen of the United States, and who shall not, when elected, have been a legal resident of that State for which the Senator shall be chosen for at least the most recent five years. No Individual shall be eligible to be elected to a term that would result in holding the office of Senator for more than a total of fifteen years in order to complete the term.

4.2.3 Senators shall be divided as equally as may be into three classes. The seats of the Senators of the first class shall be vacated at the expiration of the second year, of the second class at the expiration of the fourth year, and of the third class at the expiration of the sixth year, so that one-third may be chosen every second year. The Senators from any given State must be assigned to different classes.

4.2.4 If vacancies happen by resignation, or otherwise, the executive authorities of the respective States may make temporary appointments to fill such vacancies until the Legislature is able to consider and fill the position for the remainder of the term.

4.2.5 The Vice President of the United States shall be President of the Senate but shall have no vote unless they are equally divided.

4.2.6 The Senate shall choose its other officers, and also a President pro tempore, in the absence of the Vice President or when the Vice President shall exercise the office of President of the United States.

4.2.7 The Senate shall have the sole power to try all impeachments. When sitting for that purpose, Senators shall be under oath or affirmation. When the President of the United States is tried, the Chief Justice of the Supreme Court shall preside; no Individual shall be convicted without the concurrence of two-thirds of the members present. Jurisdiction shall extend only to officials in office at the time of trial.

4.2.8 Judgment in cases of impeachment shall not extend further than to removal from office and disqualification to hold and enjoy any office of honor, trust, or profit under the United States; but the party convicted shall nevertheless be liable and subject to indictment, trial, judgment, and punishment according to law.

4.3 Congressional Elections and Terms

4.3.1 The times, places, and manner of holding elections for Representatives, as well as State and local offices, shall be prescribed in each State by the Legislature thereof in accordance with Article **3**.

4.3.2 The terms of Senators and Representatives shall end at noon on the third day of January following the last year of their terms, and the terms of their successors shall then begin. No Individual shall be eligible to be elected or appointed to a term that would result in holding the office of either Representative or Senator for more than a total of seventeen years in Congress (any combination or sequence) in order to complete the term.

4.3.3 The Congress shall assemble at least once every year, and such meeting shall begin at noon on the third day of January unless they shall by law appoint a different day.

4.4 Rules of the House and Senate

4.4.1 Each House shall be the Judge of the elections, returns, and qualifications of its own members, and a majority of each shall constitute a quorum to do business; but a smaller number may adjourn from day to day and may be authorized to compel the attendance of absent members in such manner and under such penalties as each House may provide.

4.4.2 Each House may determine the rules of its proceedings, punish its members for disorderly behavior, and, with the concurrence of two-thirds, expel a member. However, the minimum vote required to terminate debate in the Senate shall not be less than three-fifths. The allocation of the operations budget for each House shall be equal among the members of that House without favoritism.

4.4.3 Each House shall keep a journal of its proceedings and promptly publish the same, excepting such parts as may require secrecy (strictly in accordance with Subsection **1.8.2**); and the yeas and nays of the members of either House on any question shall, at the desire of one-twentieth of those present, be entered into the journal.

4.4.4 Neither House, during the session of Congress, shall, without the consent of the other, adjourn for more than three days, nor to any place other than that in which the two Houses shall be sitting.

4.4.5 Senators and Representatives shall in all cases, except treason, felony, and breach of the peace, be privileged from arrest during their attendance at the session of their respective Houses, and in going to and returning from the same; and for any speech or debate in either House, they shall not be questioned in any other place.

4.4.6 No Senator or Representative shall, during the time for which they were elected, be appointed to any civil office under the authority of the United States which shall have been created, or the emoluments whereof shall have been increased during such time; no Individual holding any office under the United States shall be a member of either House during his continuance in office.

4.5 Legislative Process

4.5.1 Bills shall, insofar as is reasonably practical, deal with a single issue to be debated and decided; unrelated items or issues shall not be combined in the same bill (either originally or by amendment) and must be considered separately. In questionable cases, the decision should favor separation, and the desire of one-tenth of the members shall force separation. The specific votes of each member of Congress on every bill and every amendment shall be recorded and made available as a matter of public record as soon as possible, but in no case more than thirty-six hours following a vote.

4.5.2 The specific sections of this Constitution from which the authority for the bill is derived shall be cited as a part of and near the beginning of each bill.

4.5.3 All bills for raising revenue shall originate in the House of Representatives, but the Senate may propose or concur with amendments as on other bills.

4.5.4 Every bill that shall have passed the House of Representatives and the Senate shall, before it becomes a law, be presented to the President of the United States. If the bill is acceptable, the President shall sign it, but if not, the bill shall be returned with specific objections to that House in which it shall have originated, who shall enter the objections at large in their journal and proceed to reconsider it. If, after such reconsideration, two-thirds of that House shall agree to pass the bill, it shall be sent, together with the objections, to the other House, by which it shall likewise be reconsidered, and if approved by two-thirds of that House, it shall become a law. But in all such cases, the votes of both Houses shall be determined by yeas and nays, and the names of the Legislators voting for and against the bill shall be entered in the journal of each House. If any bill is not returned by the President within twelve calendar days after it has been received, the same shall become a law, in like manner as if the President had signed it, unless the Congress by their adjournment prevents its return, in which case it shall not become a law.

4.5.5 When a spending bill contains multiple line items and amounts, the President shall have the option of vetoing the entire bill as provided above, or of vetoing or reducing only one or several of the specific line items. When such a bill is returned to Congress, they shall have the option of restoring the deleted line items by a two-thirds vote of each house or taking no further action, in which case the bill becomes law after twelve days (with the vetoed line items removed or reduced). However, if Congress adjourns having taken no action before the expiration of twelve days, the bill shall not become law.

4.5.6 Every order, resolution, or vote to which the concurrence of the Senate and House of Representatives may be necessary (except on a question of adjournment) shall be presented to the President of the United States; and before the same shall take effect, shall be approved by the President, or being disapproved, shall be re-passed by two-thirds of the Senate and House of Representatives, according to the rules and limitations prescribed in the case of a bill.

4.5.7 In order to be eligible to vote for or against any bill, a Representative or Senator must have personally read and understood it in its entirety. The act of casting a vote for or against a bill shall be taken as certification under oath by the legislator that the member has complied with this requirement.

4.5.8 All laws as passed by Congress must be complete in and of themselves. Congress may not delegate the authority to modify, amplify, or extend laws (e.g., through rule making).

4.5.9 Each House of Congress shall devote a minimum of ten full in-session-with-quorum days each calendar year exclusively to the consideration of existing laws that should or can be repealed. The body of laws must be held to the minimum necessary.

4.5.10 Every law that has been duly passed and approved as provided above shall be submitted to the Supreme Court for review before it may take effect. The Supreme Court shall certify that, in the opinion of at least seven of the nine justices, no provision of the law violates any provision of this Constitution. They will specifically cite any violations and the provision of this Constitution that are violated. An unconstitutional law may not take effect and is returned in its entirety to Congress with the findings of the Court.

4.6 Limited Powers Granted to Congress

4.6.1 The Congress shall have the power (strictly in accordance with Section **9.1**) to lay and collect usage fees, taxes, duties, and imposts, in order to pay the debts and fund the legitimate functions of the United States. All United States taxes, duties, and imposts shall be uniform throughout the United States.

4.6.2 To borrow money on the credit of the United States, but only for legitimate capital expenditures to be amortized over several years (not to exceed the useful life of the purchased asset), in accordance with generally accepted accounting principles. No new debt may be incurred if the total of all debt would exceed 25% of total United States revenues for the prior fiscal year.

4.6.3 To establish uniform laws on the subject of bankruptcies throughout the United States.

4.6.4 To provide for the punishment of counterfeiting the securities and currency of the United States.

4.6.5 To promote the progress of science and useful arts by securing for limited times to authors and inventors the exclusive Right to their respective writings and discoveries.

4.6.6 To define and punish piracies and felonies committed in international territories and crimes committed outside of the United States against the Citizens thereof by foreign nationals or others.

4.6.7 To provide for the common defense of the United States.

4.6.8 To declare war, grant letters of Marque and reprisal, and make rules concerning captures on land, on water, and in space.

4.6.9 To raise and support armed forces; but no appropriation of money to that use shall be for a longer term than two years.

4.6.10 To make rules for the governing and regulation of the land, naval, air, and space forces.

4.6.11 To provide for calling forth the militia to execute the laws of the Union, suppress insurrections, and repel invasions.

4.6.12 To provide for organizing, arming, and disciplining the militia, and for governing such part of them as may be employed in the service of the United States, reserving to the States respectively the appointment of the officers, and the authority of training the militia according to the discipline prescribed by Congress.

4.6.13 To cause an accurate census to be taken during the first nine months of each new decade of all Individuals who are residents of the United States, noting whether they are Citizens and whether they are Electors.

4.6.14 To create and maintain an arterial interstate highway system to facilitate efficient long-distance travel and transportation across the United States.

4.6.15 To exercise exclusive legislation in all cases whatsoever, over the District of Columbia (not to exceed 16.1 kilometers square) as the seat of the Government of the United States (which shall not be considered a State and shall not have representation in Congress), and to exercise like authority over all places purchased by the consent of the Legislature of the State in which the same shall be, for the erection of forts, magazines, arsenals, dockyards, and other needful structures, provided that the Right of access and assembly by Citizens shall not be infringed so long as the normal function of the facility is not materially and adversely affected by the exercise thereof.

4.6.16 To maintain a list of Friendly and Trusted Nations. A two-thirds vote in each House shall be required to add a nation to this list, while a majority vote in each House shall be sufficient to remove a nation. Congress may regulate or prohibit the activities of any foreign entity not on the list within the United States or its territories as may be prudent or necessary to protect, guard, and secure the Rights of United States Citizens.

4.6.17 To make all laws and only those laws which shall be necessary and proper for carrying into execution the limited powers granted by this Constitution and vested in the Government of the United States, or in any department or officer thereof.

4.7 Powers Specifically Denied to Congress

4.7.1 No tax or duty shall be laid on articles exported from any State.

4.7.2 No preference shall be given by any regulation of commerce or revenue to the ports of one State over those of another; nor shall vessels bound to, or from, one State be obliged to enter, clear, or pay duties in another.

4.7.3 No money shall be drawn from the Treasury but in consequence of appropriations made by law, and a regular statement and account of the receipts and expenditures of all public money shall be published at least quarterly.

4.7.4 Money drawn from the Treasury shall be used only to discharge the legitimate powers, functions, debts, and duties of the Government of the United States as specified in this

Constitution. None shall be paid as a grant, subsidy, rebate, loan, or aid to a foreign entity, a State government, a local government or any other quasi-governmental body, a business, a private organization, or an Individual.

4.7.5 No Right, liberty, or power of the United States as a sovereign nation or of its sovereign Citizens may be ceded, whether by treaty or otherwise, to any regional or global authority or organization.

4.7.6 No title of nobility shall be granted by the United States, and no Individual holding any office of profit or trust under them shall, without the consent of the Congress, accept any present, emolument, office, or title, of any kind whatever, from any king, prince, or foreign state.

4.8 Removal from Office

4.8.1 Any verified breach of the bill-reading requirements of Subsection **4.5.7** shall result in immediate expulsion of the Legislator from office. Such an expulsion can be rescinded only by a three-fourths roll-call vote of the House and a three-fourths roll-call vote of the Senate, and then only if it is the Legislator's first such offense.

4.8.2 Upon any verified violation of his or her oath of office, a Legislator (House or Senate) shall be permanently disqualified from holding any judicial appointment or running for any Federal- or State-level elective office. They shall be censured and shall vacate their current term as soon as a replacement can be installed to fill the remainder of that term.

4.8.2.1 The determination by the Supreme Court that any law for which a legislator has voted is unconstitutional shall be prima facie evidence that the oath of office was breached.

4.8.2.2 Citizens may petition in Federal court to have a legislator removed on the basis of breach of oath. In order to be heard, such a petition must clearly define the breach and must be signed by a minimum of 1.0% of the registered Electors eligible to vote for the Legislator.

4.8.3 Either of a State's Senators may be removed by a three-fifths vote of that State's Legislature and replaced for the remainder of the term at any time.

5.   The Executive Branch

5.1 The President and Vice President

5.1.1 The executive power shall be vested in a President of the United States of America. The President shall hold this office during the term of four years and, together with the Vice President chosen for the same term, be elected on the first Tuesday after the first Monday of the November immediately prior to the end of the current President's term. The terms of the President and Vice President shall end at noon on the twentieth day of January following the last year of their terms, and the terms of their successors shall then begin. They shall be elected by the States in accordance with the following procedure.

5.1.1.1 Each State shall have a number of votes equal to the number of its House representatives plus two.

5.1.1.2 Presidential elections shall be held in each State in accordance with Article **3**.

5.1.1.3 All of a State's votes are cast for the winner of that State's presidential election.

5.1.1.4 The candidate receiving the largest number of States' votes shall be the winner.

5.1.1.5 A tie will be resolved in favor of the tied candidate who won in the most State elections.

5.1.1.6 A tie still persisting will be resolved by random selection of one of the tied candidates.

5.1.2 Any Citizen meeting all of the following qualifications shall be eligible for election to the office of President or Vice President:

5.1.2.1 Have been a United States Citizen for at least the most recent twenty years

5.1.2.2 Have attained the age of thirty-five years as of the beginning of the term

5.1.2.3 Have been resident within the United States for the most recent five years

5.1.2.4 If elected, completion of the term would not result in the President holding that office for more than a total of ten years.

5.1.3 If, at the time fixed for the beginning of the term of the President, the President elect shall have died, the Vice President elect shall become President. If a President shall not have been chosen before the time fixed for the beginning of his term, or if the President elect shall have failed to qualify, then the Vice President elect shall act as President until a President shall have qualified; and the Congress may by law provide for the case wherein neither a President elect nor a Vice President elect shall have qualified, declaring who shall then act as President, or the manner in which one who is to act shall be selected, and such Individual shall act accordingly until a President or Vice President shall have qualified. If Congress has passed no law or problems arise with the interpretation of such a law, the House of Representatives shall resolve any such matters by majority vote.

5.1.4 The Congress may by law provide for the case of the death of any of the Individuals from whom the House of Representatives may choose a President whenever the Right of choice shall have devolved upon them, and for the case of the death of any of the Individuals from whom the Senate may choose a Vice President, whenever the Right of choice shall have devolved upon them.

5.1.5 In case of the removal of the President from office or of his death or resignation, the Vice President shall be sworn in as President.

5.1.6 Whenever there is a vacancy in the office of the Vice President, the President shall nominate a Vice President who shall take office upon confirmation by a majority vote of both Houses of Congress.

5.1.7 Whenever the President transmits to the President pro tempore of the Senate and the Speaker of the House of Representatives his written declaration that he is unable to discharge the powers and duties of his office, and until he transmits to them a written declaration to the contrary, such powers and duties shall be discharged by the Vice President as Acting President.

5.1.8 Whenever the Vice President and a majority of either the principal officers of the executive departments or of such other body as Congress may by law provide, transmit to the President pro tempore of the Senate and the Speaker of the House of Representatives their written declaration that the President is unable to discharge the powers and duties of his office, the Vice President shall immediately assume the powers and duties of the office as Acting President. Thereafter, when the President transmits to the President pro tempore of the Senate and the Speaker of the House of Representatives his written declaration that no inability exists, the President shall resume the powers and duties of the office unless the Vice President and a majority of either the principal officers of the executive department, or of such other body as Congress may by law provide, transmit within four days to the President pro tempore of the Senate and the Speaker of the House of Representatives their written declaration that the President is unable to discharge the powers and duties of the office. Thereupon, Congress shall decide the issue, assembling within forty-eight hours for that purpose if not in session. If the Congress, within twenty-one days after receipt of the latter written declaration—or, if Congress is not in session, within twenty-one days after Congress is required to assemble—determines by a two-thirds vote of both Houses that the President is unable to discharge the powers and duties of the office, the Vice President shall continue to discharge the same as Acting President; otherwise, the President shall resume the powers and duties of the office.

5.2 Powers and Duties of the President

5.2.1 The President shall take care that all of (and only) the laws of the United States exactly as enacted by Congress be faithfully and uniformly executed. The Executive Branch has no authority to modify, amplify, or extend, or to not enforce, the laws of Congress. The Executive Branch shall operate no courts, administrative or otherwise, and the adjudication of guilt or innocence under any law shall be made only in a court of common law.

5.2.2 The President shall take care that all borders of the United States are secured and that all border crossings by Individuals and materials of any kind occur in accordance with law and in an orderly manner through its designated ports of entry. This responsibility shall include capture, prosecution, and deportation as may be appropriate for any Individuals and/or materials that may have succeeded in entering the United States without legally passing through a port of entry. The President shall separately request border security funding from Congress, and a two-fifths vote in each house shall be sufficient to appropriate funds for this purpose.

5.2.3 The President shall be commander in chief of all military forces of the United States, and of the militias of the several States, when called into the actual service of the United States. He shall deploy military forces as most appropriate for the defense of the United States and strictly in accordance with purposes as established by Congress. The President shall have the latitude and the duty to defend the United States and/or its interests against any bona fide and material threat that may quickly arise; however, the approval of Congress must be obtained within fifty days of the first such use of United States forces; lacking such approval, the forces will stand down from such use within twenty-five days following the deadline for Congressional approval.

5.2.4 The President shall commission all the officers of the United States.

5.2.5 The President may require the opinion, in writing, of the principal officer in each of the executive departments upon any subject relating to the duties of their respective offices.

5.2.6 The President shall have the power to grant reprieves and pardons for offenses against the United States, except in cases of impeachment.

5.2.7 The President shall have power, by and with the advice and consent of the Senate, to make treaties, provided two-thirds of the Senators present concur. No provision of this Constitution may be abrogated, overridden, or superseded by any treaty.

5.2.8 The President shall nominate, and by and with the advice and consent of the Senate shall appoint, ambassadors, other public ministers and consuls, judges of the Supreme Court, and all other officers of the United States, whose appointments are not herein otherwise provided for, and which shall be established by law. The Congress may by law vest the appointment of other officers inferior to these, as they think proper, in the President alone, in the courts of law, or in the heads of departments.

5.2.9 The President shall have the power to fill all vacancies that may happen during the recess of the Senate by granting commissions which shall expire at the end of their next session.

5.2.10 The President shall from time to time give to the Congress information on the state of the Union and recommend to their consideration such measures as are believed to be necessary and expedient.

5.2.11 The President may, on extraordinary occasions, convene both Houses, or either of them, and in case of disagreement between them with respect to the time of adjournment, the President may adjourn them to such time as is thought proper.

5.2.12 The President shall receive ambassadors and other public ministers.

5.3 Removal from Office

The President, Vice President, and all civil officers of the United States shall be removed from office on impeachment for, and conviction of, treason, bribery, breach of the oath of office, or other high crimes and misdemeanors. Having signed any law subsequently determined by the Supreme Court to be unconstitutional shall be prima facie evidence that the oath of office has been breached. Gross or persistent failure of the President to faithfully and effectively execute the duties of Section **5.2** shall also be grounds for removal from office.

6.   The Judicial Branch

6.1 Courts and Tenure

The judicial power of the United States shall be vested in one Supreme Court consisting of nine justices, and in such inferior Courts as the Congress may from time to time ordain and establish. The judges of both the Supreme and inferior courts shall hold their offices during good behavior.

6.2 Jurisdiction

6.2.1 The judicial power shall extend

6.2.1.1 To all cases in law and equity arising under this Constitution, the laws of the United States, and treaties made, or which shall be made, under their authority

6.2.1.2 To all cases affecting ambassadors and other public ministers and consuls

6.2.1.3 To all cases of admiralty and maritime jurisdiction

6.2.1.4 To controversies to which the United States shall be a party

6.2.1.5 To controversies between two or more States

6.2.1.6 To all cases between Citizens of different States

6.2.1.7 To all cases involving Citizens' petitions for removal of members of Congress

6.2.2 In all cases affecting ambassadors, other public ministers and consuls, and those in which a State shall be a party, the Supreme Court shall have original Jurisdiction.

6.2.3 In all the other cases previously mentioned, the Supreme Court shall have appellate jurisdiction as to both law and fact.

6.2.4 In all Supreme Court cases involving a question as to whether the government has been delegated certain powers by this Constitution, a standard higher than a simple majority must be met. The default presumption must always be that the government does not have the power in question. If the Court hears the case, at least seven of the nine justices must concur that the power is clearly delegated to the government by this Constitution. A concurrence of at least seven justices is also required to decline to hear such a case.

6.2.5 The trial of all crimes, except in cases of impeachment, shall be by jury in a court of common law; and such trial shall be held in the State where the said crimes shall have been committed; but when not committed within any State, the trial shall be at such place or places as the Congress may by law have directed.

6.3 Treason

6.3.1 Treason against the United States shall consist only in levying war against them, or in adhering to their enemies, giving them aid and comfort. No Individual shall be convicted of treason unless on the testimony of two witnesses to the same overt act, or on confession in open court.

6.3.2 The Congress shall have power to declare the punishment of treason, but no attainder of treason shall work corruption of blood, or forfeiture except during the life of the Individual attainted.

6.3.3 No Individual shall be a President, a Senator, or Representative in Congress, or hold any office, civil or military, under the United States, or under any State, who, having previously taken an oath, as a member of Congress, or as an officer of the United States, or as a member of any State Legislature, or as an executive or judicial officer of any State, to support the Constitution of the United States, shall have been duly convicted of engaging in insurrection or rebellion against the same or giving aid or comfort to the enemies thereof. But Congress may, by a vote of two-thirds of each House, remove such disability.

7.   Currency, Banking, Weights, and Measures

7.1 Banking

There shall be no central bank or banking authority, and interest rates shall be set through normal free market competitive forces between borrowers and among private banks and savings/lending institutions.

7.2 National Cost of Living Board

7.2.1 A National Cost of Living Board (NCoLB) shall have the duty to establish and track the median annual cost of living for a single individual Citizen living in the United States. The NCoLB shall be comprised of fifteen members divided into three classes of five each. Each member shall serve a term of six years. The terms shall be staggered so that a class of five will be appointed in June of every even-numbered year. NCoLB members will be appointed by State Legislatures, one member per State at a time, on an alphabetic rotation basis by State name, as classes come due for replacement or when vacancies occur. The NCoLB will elect its own chair, vice chair, and secretary in July of even-numbered years.

7.2.2 All NCoLB members must be Citizens, and no member of the NCoLB may have any other connection, direct or indirect, past or present, with any government or quasi-governmental body. A minimum of five NCoLB members must be economists. A minimum of five NCoLB members must be drawn from private business management. A minimum of five NCoLB members must be mathematicians. Whenever it is a State's turn to appoint an NCoLB member, the following procedure must be followed:

7.2.2.1 If the number of NCoLB members who are economists is currently less than five, the State must appoint a new member who is an economist.

7.2.2.2 If the number of members who are economists is five or more, but the number of NCoLB members who are business managers is currently less than five, the State must appoint a new member who is from business management.

7.2.2.3 If the number of members who are economists is five or more, and the number of NCoLB members who are business managers is five or more, but the number of NCoLB members who are mathematicians is currently less than five, the State must appoint a new member who is a mathematician.

7.2.2.4 If the requirements for five or more economists, business managers, and mathematicians are all met, the State may appoint the Citizen considered best qualified.

7.2.3 NCoLB members shall receive a salary of $135,000 per year paid biweekly and shall be reimbursed for bona fide NCoLB expenses upon the filing of weekly expense reports in accordance with Section **8.2**. They shall receive no other remuneration or benefits whatsoever. All salaries and expenses, including contracts between the NCoLB and, for example, consultants or data sources shall be borne by the United States Treasury.

7.2.4 The NCoLB shall determine the median annual cost of living for a single Citizen living in the United States utilizing a broad market basket of goods and services reflective of those typically purchased by such an Individual during a year of living. The fifty-two-week moving average of the price for each market basket item is to be multiplied by an appropriate weighting factor and totaled to equal the cost of living. The makeup of the market basket items and their weighting factors shall be updated as may be most appropriate in January of each year (the previous and new basket items and factors must, of course, total to the same cost of living at the time of the update).

7.2.5 The first cost of living determined by the first NCoLB shall become the Reference Cost of Living. The Reference Cost of Living remains fixed and is never changed. Once the reference is established, the NCoLB shall thereafter update the cost of living biweekly. Each biweekly cost of living is to be published along with a *correction factor*. The correction factor shall be the Reference Cost of Living divided by the newly determined cost of living and shown to five decimal places of accuracy. For example, if the Reference Cost of Living is $50,000.00 and the newly determined cost of living is $49,825.00, the correction factor is 1.00351.

7.3 Currency

7.3.1 The currency of the United States shall be the US Dollar. It shall be representative money guaranteed by the United States to be redeemable so as to fix its value to be as constant as possible relative to the cost of living.

7.3.2 The United States Treasury shall have the duty to regulate the money supply so as to maintain the latest "correction factor" published by the NCoLB (Section **7.2**) to be as close as possible to 1.00000. When this factor is greater than 1.00000, the money supply shall be judiciously increased, and when it is less than 1.00000, the money supply shall be judiciously reduced, always with the objective of maintaining the cost of living as stably as possible to closely match the Reference Cost of Living.

7.3.3 The United States Treasury shall contract with private banks to provide for the redemption of the US Dollar for several of the most convenient commodities. At a minimum, this shall include gold and silver. The redemption price for said commodities shall be the commodity's current spot price multiplied by the most recent correction factor published by the National Cost of Living Board. There shall be at least 150 redemption locations distributed over the country so as to be most conveniently accessible to all Citizens.

7.4 Weights and Measures

The official and legal system of weights and measures for the United States shall be the 1971 International System of Units, consisting of meter, kilogram, second, ampere, kelvin, candela, and mole. (The Celsius temperature scale may optionally be used instead of kelvin.) It shall be employed exclusively by all governments, Federal, State, and local. Officially adopted modifications and updates to international standards shall automatically be considered to be adopted by the United States. There shall be no prohibition of other systems of weights and measures that Citizens may wish to use.

8.　Compensation

8.1 Employee Classifications and Compensation

All employees of the United States are paid from the treasury biweekly on Thursdays for the two immediately preceding complete (Monday through Sunday) weeks. There are two classes of United States employees.

8.1.1 The first class of employees has its level of compensation either set by Congress or set by the Executive Branch in cases where Congress has delegated that responsibility. Similarly, Congress may optionally define (or delegate to the Executive Branch to define) any benefits for which these employees are eligible. This group includes all employees of the United States except those enumerated in Subsection **8.1.2**.

8.1.2 The second class of employee has their compensation constitutionally defined. This class of employee may receive (from the United States or from any other direct or indirect source) no other benefits or remuneration of any type whatsoever while holding office other than the compensation specified herein. They shall not be the beneficiaries of any taxpayer-financed pensions. Any owned assets, excluding only a primary residence, totaling more than $1,500,000 shall be placed in a blind trust prior to the employee taking office and must remain there as long as the employee holds one of the below offices.

8.1.2.1 President of the United States: $300,000

8.1.2.2 Vice President of the United States: $250,000

8.1.2.3 Senator: $200,000

8.1.2.4 Speaker of the House: $250,000

8.1.2.5 Representative: $175,000

8.1.2.6 Chief Justice of the Supreme Court: $300,000

8.1.2.7 Associate Justice of the Supreme Court: $250,000

8.1.2.8 Federal Court Judge: $200,000

8.1.2.9 Members of the President's Cabinet: $200,000

8.2 Expenses

All employees of the United States shall be reimbursed from the Treasury for bona fide and necessary expenses directly related to and incurred in the execution of their duties. Any such expenses must be documented on signed expense reports filed weekly and including the reasons or purposes that justify the expenditures and receipts for verification of all amounts greater than $40. These expense reports will be published promptly as a matter of public record.

9. Government Revenues and Budgets

9.1 Revenue Sources

9.1.1 No capitation or other direct tax shall be laid by any government. Individuals, families, businesses, and corporations may not be required to file tax (or other information) returns. The allowed sources of revenue are herein defined. No government shall raise revenue from any other source or by any mechanism other than those specified in this Section **9.1**.

9.1.2 Import duties and imposts may be collected by the United States only, which shall be solely responsible for setting, collecting, and policing import duties and imposts. The rate shall be uniform across all imports and shall not exceed 12% for nations on the Friendly and Trusted Nations list and 25% for nations not on that list.

9.1.3 Usage fees for government-owned facilities (e.g., parks and museums) and government-provided services may be set and collected.

9.1.3.1 Other than for roads, fees for usage of facilities will be set to, as nearly as feasible, match the number of users to the capacity of the facility. Fees for services will be set to recover only the reasonable costs of providing the service.

9.1.3.2 Every powered vehicle must be licensed by the States annually to use all public roads. Each vehicle so licensed shall display proof of licensure that identifies the State and is legible from twelve meters. Annually, semiannually, or quarterly, the owner of each licensed vehicle shall report to the State the total kilometers traveled by the vehicle since its manufacture. The distance traveled since the previous report will be multiplied by the dollar-per-kilometer rate for the vehicle, and that amount shall be remitted to the State by the vehicle owner as a road usage fee. The rate for each licensed vehicle shall be the total of a Federal component, a state component, and a local (county) component to be set as described in the following subsection. The address of each vehicle's physical "home base" shall determine the State and local rates to which its owner is subject.

9.1.3.3 The States shall be solely responsible for enforcement and for collecting usage fees for vehicles licensed by the State. The State shall forward the proper share of fees collected to the Federal government and to the counties within the State. The United States, each State, and each county will set a road usage fee rate in dollars per kilogram per kilometer that will raise the revenue needed to construct and maintain the roads within each jurisdiction. All revenue from road usage fees will go to constructing and maintaining roads, bridges, and other highway or road structures, and revenue for that purpose shall not be supplemented with revenue from any other source. The total of the Federal, State, and county rates shall be used to set each vehicle's dollar-per-kilometer rate by multiplying this total by the gross vehicle weight for each licensed vehicle.

9.1.3.4 Powered vehicles not located and licensed within the United States shall have their total kilometers traveled since manufacture recorded upon entry to the United States and will be assessed a road usage fee upon exit from the United States based upon the distance traveled on US roads. The rate per kilometer for such external vehicles will be set by the United States and shall be proportional to the gross vehicle weight and shall be the same as the rate for an equivalent domestic vehicle based at the point of entry. Such vehicles remaining inside the United States longer than six months shall remit their fee for each six-month period.

9.1.4 The remaining three allowed revenue sources may be levied by any of three levels of government: Federal, State, and local, where "local" is defined as the largest political subdivision inside a State (normally, a county). The method for allocation and further distribution of local taxes collected to lower (municipal) levels of government shall be at the discretion of each State or may be delegated by the State to the local (county) governments. The responsibility for administering, collecting, and enforcing any and all such taxes shall rest with the States. States will forward any United States tax collected to the United States Treasury and distribute any local taxes collected to the proper local (county) governments within each State. The United States shall have no enforcement authority other than audits of State collection authorities to assure that the proper amounts are being forwarded to the United States Treasury.

9.1.5 A land value tax may be collected as a percentage of the unimproved value of all land. Improvements may never be taxed. The intent shall be to collect approximately three-fifths of the free market rental for unimproved land. However, the maximum percentage of the unimproved land's price that may be collected annually is 1.2% each for Federal, State, and local (a combined maximum of 3.6% on any given piece of land). No land within the United States or its territories shall be exempt from taxation.

9.1.6 A severance tax may be levied as a percentage of the sale amount for all nonrenewable natural resources removed from land. The maximum percentage that may be collected is 12% each for Federal, State, and local (a combined maximum of 36% for any given commodity). The rate shall be the same for all nonrenewable natural resources.

9.1.7 The taxes described in Subsections **9.1.5** and **9.1.6** are levied by each Federal, State, or local taxing authority by setting a single percentage between 0% and 100% that will control what percentage of the maximum tax specified in those subsections is to be collected. A two-thirds vote shall be required to increase this percentage, while a simple majority may decrease it.

9.1.8 A simple, broadly based consumption tax on the sale of goods and services may be levied. The maximum percentage that may be collected is 4% each for Federal, State, and local (a combined maximum of 12% for any given transaction). A two-thirds vote shall be required to increase this percentage, while a simple majority may decrease it. A taxing entity may not levy any sales tax unless its percentage, as described in Subsection **9.1.7**, is already at the 100% maximum.

9.1.8.1 This sales tax is charged at the point of sale to the end user or consumer only and must be a single fixed percentage of the sale amount rounded to the nearest cent.

9.1.8.2 When a tax calculation results in tax amounts that have fractional pennies, the computed amount will always be rounded up to the next cent when the fractional amount is equal to or greater than half a cent and will round down to the next lower cent when the fractional amount is less than half a cent.

9.1.8.3 The percentage rate may not be specified to a precision greater than hundredths of a percent (e.g., 1.75%).

9.1.8.4 When there are multiple taxable line items in a sales transaction, they are summed, and the tax is computed on the total.

9.1.8.5 Up to three taxes may apply to any given sales transaction. The basis of each tax shall be the total of the item sales amounts only; that is, one tax cannot include another tax as part of its basis.

9.1.8.6 The amount of each tax shall be separately identified and shown on the sales transaction document.

9.1.8.7 Since at most one Federal, one State, and one local tax can apply to any given transaction, the applicable jurisdictions will be determined by the transaction's "location," defined as the place at which either the buyer receives the goods for constructive use or the services are performed. Subterfuges such as receiving goods outside a jurisdiction and then reshipping to a location within a jurisdiction for the purpose of avoiding taxes are obviously prohibited and will be punishable by law.

9.1.8.8 Sellers are required to make reasonable efforts to determine the correct transaction location and levy the correct taxes; however, both buyers and sellers may be prosecuted for willful tax evasion. The United States shall maintain a readily accessible centralized database of all sales tax rates, along with their jurisdictions and their effective date ranges, from which the applicable tax(es) for any transaction can be quickly, easily, and officially determined.

9.1.8.9 The tax shall apply to all goods and services (tangible or intangible) except for the following:

9.1.8.9.1 The tax shall not apply to basic foodstuffs, but food prepared and served will be taxed.

9.1.8.9.2 The tax shall not apply to basic, functional clothing, but nonfunctional or decorative accessories will be taxed.

9.1.8.9.3 The rental or purchase of a property shall not be taxed as long as it is predominantly used as a primary residence. Only one primary residence for an owner or renter can be exempt.

9.1.8.9.4 Tuition for bona fide primary, secondary, college, or postgraduate education shall not be taxed.

9.2 Budget Policy

The operations of all governments shall be tracked and reported in accordance with generally accepted accounting principles. No government shall operate at a deficit. If a deficit should inadvertently, or as a result of a bona fide unanticipated emergency, occur in one budget year, it must be offset by a surplus in the immediately following year unless a sufficient surplus is being carried forward from the prior year. Governments may and should retain reasonable surpluses so as to be prepared for emergencies. Money may be borrowed only for bona fide capital expenditures that will be amortized over several future years consistent with the expected lifetime of the asset.

10. Relations Among States

10.1 Full Faith and Credit

Full faith and credit shall be given in each State to the public acts, records, and judicial proceedings of every other State. And the Congress may by general laws prescribe the manner in which such acts, records, and proceedings shall be proved, and the effect thereof.

10.2 State Citizens, Extradition

10.2.1 An Individual charged in any State with treason, felony, or other crime who shall flee from justice and be found in another State shall on demand of the executive authority of the State from which the Individual fled be delivered up to be removed to the State having jurisdiction of the crime.

10.2.2 The Citizens of each State shall be entitled to all privileges and immunities of Citizens in the several States.

10.3 United States Territory and Property

The Congress shall have power to dispose of and make all needful rules and regulations respecting the territory or other property belonging to the United States as well as property controlled by the government for public uses, and nothing in this

Constitution shall be so construed as to prejudice any claims of
the United States, or of any particular State. United States
Citizens are the joint owners of such property, and their Rights
as protected by Articles **13** and **14** shall not be diminished as
long as Citizens' activities thereon do not materially interfere
with the intended normal uses and functions of the property.

11.   Powers Denied to the States

11.1 No State shall enter into any treaty, alliance, or
confederation; grant letters of Marque and reprisal; coin money;
emit bills of credit; make anything other than the legal currency
of the United States a tender in payment of debts; pass any law
impairing the obligation of contracts; or grant any title of
nobility.

11.2 No State shall, without the consent of Congress, enter into
any agreement or compact with another state or a foreign power,
or engage in war, unless actually invaded, or in such imminent
danger as will not admit of delay.

11.3 No State shall restrict or impede free market commerce and
competition within or across its borders.

12.   Powers Denied to All Governments

12.1 Suspension of Habeas Corpus

The privilege of the writ of habeas corpus shall not be suspended
unless the public safety may require it in cases of rebellion. In
any such case, the danger must be clear and present, the need for
suspension very obvious, the geographic area of suspension as
small as reasonably possible, and the duration of the suspension
as short as the circumstances will allow.

12.2 No Ex Post Facto Law

No bill of attainder or ex post facto law shall be passed.

12.3 No Restriction of Speech, Religion, or Media

No law shall be made respecting an establishment of religion,
prohibiting the free exercise thereof, or abridging the freedom of

speech or of the press or of other media, the Right of Citizens to peaceably assemble and to petition the Government for redress of grievances. No government shall ever attempt to censor, restrict, control, or influence the speech of Citizens, organizations, businesses, or media.

12.4 No Abridgment of Citizenship

No government shall make or enforce any law which shall abridge the privileges or immunities of Citizens of the United States as defined in this Constitution. A Citizen convicted of a criminal offense shall again enjoy the full Rights and privileges of citizenship upon completion of the Citizen's sentence.

12.5 No Business Ownership

No government shall own or have an interest in any part of any business. Collection of user fees as allowed by Subsection **9.1.3** shall not be considered owning or operating a business.

12.6 No Business Interference

No government shall interfere with the normal and peaceful operation of any business or with the execution of a contract consensually entered into by all parties thereto. No government shall provide grants, subsidies, loan guarantees, or otherwise meddle in and/or distort the operation of the free market economy.

12.7 No Selective Law Enforcement

All laws must be fully, completely, and impartially enforced to the greatest extent reasonably possible. Laws judged not to meet this enforcement standard for whatever reason by a court having jurisdiction shall, upon exhaustion of any appeal, be considered repealed and shall be repealed by the Congress or State Legislature at the earliest possible time.

12.8 Emergency Powers

Emergency powers can be justified only under the most extreme and dire circumstances for which martial law has been declared. No other situation shall justify the usurpation of any power not clearly granted by this Constitution nor the abrogation of any Citizen's Rights, privileges, or immunities as protected by this Constitution. A declaration of martial law for a locality must be lifted as soon as is reasonably possible and shall not be justification for usurpation of powers or abrogation of Citizens' Rights outside that locality.

13.   Fundamental Rights Guaranteed to All Individuals

13.1 Due Process of Law

No Citizen of the United States or Individual under the jurisdiction or in the custody of the United States shall be deprived of life, liberty, or property without due process of law.

13.2 Competent Counsel and Witnesses

In all criminal prosecutions, the accused shall enjoy the Right to be informed of the nature and cause of the accusation, to be confronted with the witnesses against the accused and have the opportunity to cross-examine them, to have a compulsory process for obtaining the testimony of exculpatory witnesses, and to have the assistance of competent defense counsel.

13.3 No Cruel or Unusual Punishment

No cruel or unusual treatment or punishment shall be inflicted upon any Citizen of the United States or any Individual under the jurisdiction or in the custody of the United States.

14.   Additional Fundamental Rights Guaranteed to All Citizens

The Rights retained by Citizens are innumerable and include anything a Citizen may wish to do, provided only that they may not materially infringe upon the equal Rights of others. The enumeration in this Constitution of certain Rights shall not be construed to deny or disparage others retained by Citizens. A Citizen's Rights may be restricted only when that Citizen is judged mentally incompetent by a jury of peers through due process of law.

14.1 Freedom of Speech

The Right to speak freely shall be broadly guaranteed without exception. The forms and means of speech are many and varied, including but not limited to political speech, commercial speech, and even speech that could be considered by some, or even most, as incorrect, misleading, offensive, pornographic, or hateful.

14.2 No Excessive Bail

Excessive bail shall not be required of any Citizen, nor excessive fines imposed.

14.3 No Double Jeopardy

No Citizen shall be twice put in jeopardy of life or limb for the same offense, whether by the same or a different level of government.

14.4 Trial by Jury

14.4.1 No Citizen of the United States shall be held to answer for a capital or otherwise infamous crime unless on a presentment or indictment of a Grand Jury, except in cases arising in the armed forces, or in the militia, when in actual service in time of war or public danger.

14.4.2 In suits at common law, where the value in controversy shall exceed $800, the Right of trial by jury shall be preserved for all Citizens, and no fact tried by a jury shall be reexamined in any court of the United States, other than according to the rules of common law.

14.4.3 In all criminal prosecutions, the accused shall enjoy the Right to a speedy and public trial in a court of common law by an impartial jury of the State and district wherein the crime shall have been committed, which district shall have been previously ascertained by law. Citizens shall always be presumed innocent until proven guilty.

14.4.4 No Citizen shall be compelled to self-incriminate in any criminal case.

14.4.5 Judges must always inform juries of their common law duty to judge not only the facts of the case but also the justice of the law.

14.5 No Confiscation of Property

The private property of any Citizen or Citizen-controlled Societal Entity shall not be taken without just compensation at fair market value. The exercise of eminent domain shall be restricted to cases where a bona fide need exists for rights of way for public transportation or utilities, or for necessary government facilities. Property shall not be taken to be transferred to another private owner. The property owner shall have the option whenever practicable of either being compensated for the granting of a right of way or selling the entire property.

14.6 Privacy and Peaceful Enjoyment

14.6.1 The Right of Citizens and Citizen-controlled Societal Entities to be secure in their bodies, houses, property, vehicles, papers, and effects against unreasonable searches and seizures shall not be violated, and no warrants shall issue but upon probable cause, supported by oath or affirmation, and particularly describing the place to be searched and the Individuals or things to be seized.

14.6.2 Personal information held by third parties, such as telephone records, electronic communications, and data stored on either personal devices or remote servers, shall be considered part of an Individual's "papers" and require a search warrant.

14.6.3 Covert audio or video surveillance, eavesdropping, and compilation of data shall be considered kinds of searches that require warrants.

14.6.4 There shall be no interference with any social activity involving consenting adults in private.

14.6.5 There shall be no interference with the Right of a Citizen or Citizen-controlled Societal Entity owning property to establish policies governing the use of their private property, including guests permitted and activities allowed or not allowed.

14.6.6 Unless judged mentally incompetent by a court, Citizens shall have the Right to complete control over their corporal existence without interference (ingest or use any substance, attempt any cure or treatment, commit suicide, etc.).

14.7 Keep and Bear Arms

The Right of Citizens to keep and bear arms, as well as the ammunition and accessories for said arms, shall not be questioned or infringed. This includes the Right to manufacture, sell, transfer, transport, carry, and store such items without registration or tracking. No offensive or defensive weapon or equipment up to and including any that a modern, up-to-date, well-equipped infantry soldier might carry shall ever be prohibited or regulated.

14.8 Voluntary Exchange

Any Citizen or Societal Entity may voluntarily agree to exchange goods or services with any other Citizen or Societal Entity. Such exchanges must be voluntary on both sides. Either party may decline to make a particular exchange for any reason, in which case, the exchange will not take place.

14.9 Mobility

The Right of Citizens to travel freely and transport possessions normally on public roads or mass transportation systems shall not be infringed. The Right of Citizens to move themselves, their possessions, or their assets into or out of the United States shall not be infringed unless the Citizen is under criminal indictment or arrest. The locations and travels of Citizens and/or their vehicles shall not be surveilled or tracked without a warrant.

14.10 Assembly

The Right of Citizens to peaceably assemble shall not be impeded.

14.11 Redress of Grievances

A Citizen or Citizen-controlled Societal Entity may petition their government (at any level) for grievances arising under this Constitution. Such petitions stating the issues clearly and concisely may be submitted in writing through the appropriate elected Representative to the lower house. Resolution of such grievances is an important duty and responsibility of all Representatives. If the Representative is unable to resolve a grievance, they must introduce it on the floor of the full legislative body. The Citizen or Entity must receive a clear, concise, and pertinent response within seventy-five days of the date the Representative received the petition. If a timely response is not received, or if the Citizen's grievance has not been redressed in a manner satisfactory to the Citizen, an appeal to the court having jurisdiction may be made. The court shall hear the case at its discretion, but the court shall be obliged to hear any case filed by at least one thousand petitioners.

14.12 Military Quartering

No Soldier shall, in time of peace, be quartered in any house without the consent of the Owner, nor in time of war but in a manner to be prescribed by law.

14.13 Locally Protected and Secured Individual Rights

14.13.1 "Local" is defined to mean the largest political subdivision inside a State (normally, a county). The Citizens/Electors of each such local political subdivision shall be entitled to directly elect a Sheriff.

14.13.2 Each Sheriff is responsible directly to the Citizens of the jurisdiction that elected that Sheriff and shall have the primary responsibility of protecting and securing the Rights of those Citizens as guaranteed by this Constitution. The Sheriff shall also take care that all laws (Federal, State, and local) that are constitutional are enforced within the local jurisdiction.

14.13.3 Within the jurisdiction, the Sheriff shall be the highest-ranking law enforcement officer. No other agent or officer of any kind (Federal, State, local, or international) shall operate within a Sheriff's jurisdiction without the prior knowledge and consent of the Sheriff and shall be subject to arrest by the Sheriff for failure to meet notification requirements or for violating (or threatening the violation of) the Rights of Citizens within the jurisdiction.

14.13.4 The term of office for the Sheriff shall be four years, and elections shall be held in the even-numbered years between presidential elections. A special election to elect a new Sheriff must be called within four months after at least 2% of a Sheriff's registered Electors have so petitioned the State. A Citizen who has attained the age of thirty-five years and been a resident of the jurisdiction for at least the most recent five years is qualified to run for the office of Sheriff provided that completion of the term would not result in holding that office for more than a total of ten years.

14.13.5 The cost of operating the Sheriff's department shall be budgeted and paid by the local jurisdiction that the Sheriff serves.

15. Rights to Care and Education Guaranteed to All Minor Citizens

15.1 Parental Rights, Requirements, and Responsibilities

15.1.1 All Minor Citizens shall be entitled to and shall receive reasonable care and a good basic education. Parents and/or legal guardians are individually and jointly responsible for providing for all needs of their offspring at their own expense. Among food, clothing, shelter, medical care, and many other things, this includes a minimum of thirteen years of accredited educational instruction (or the equivalent) for each and every Minor Citizen. Parents' legal obligations to each child in this regard end upon the eighteenth birthday of the child.

15.1.2 Parents are free to educate their children in any way they may see fit. However, the progress of every Minor Citizen will be measured annually through standardized achievement tests.

The tests are to provide a standard, objective, and uniform measure of each child's progress in learning the factual information and skills that parents are responsible for teaching their children. A child scoring below the thirty-fifth percentile in any one (or more) subject area shall be required to attend an accredited school for at least the ensuing two years.

15.1.3 Parents' Right to raise their children as they think best shall be abridged only upon a determination by a jury of peers that current and reasonable standards for care and education are not being maintained.

15.2 National Scholastic Standards Board

15.2.1 Schools are free to teach whatever they believe is appropriate. However, they must teach a minimum set of skills and factual knowledge that will enable Minor Citizens to succeed as adults. A National Scholastic Standards Board (NSSB) will establish and maintain academic standards for a core curriculum for the education of Minor Citizens.

15.2.2 The NSSB shall be comprised of twenty-one members divided into three classes of seven each. Each member shall serve a term of six years. The terms shall be staggered so that a class of seven will be appointed in June of every even-numbered year. NSSB members will be appointed by State Legislatures, one member per State at a time, on an alphabetic rotation basis by State name, as classes come due for replacement or when vacancies occur. The NSSB will elect its own chair, vice chair, and secretary in July of even-numbered years.

15.2.3 All NSSB members must be Citizens, and no member of the NSSB may have any other connection, direct or indirect, past or present, with any government or quasi-governmental body. A minimum of eleven NSSB members must be parents of Minor Citizens. A minimum of seven NSSB members must be professional educators. A minimum of seven NSSB members must be drawn from business management. Whenever it is a State's turn to appoint an NSSB member, the following procedure is to be followed:

15.2.3.1 If the number of NSSB members who are parents of Minor Citizens is currently less than eleven, the State must appoint a new member who is a parent of a Minor Citizen.

15.2.3.2 If the number of NSSB members who are professional educators is currently less than seven, the State must appoint a new member who is a professional educator.

15.2.3.3 If the number of NSSB members who are professional educators is seven or more, but the number of NSSB members who are business managers is currently less than seven, the State must appoint a new member drawn from business management.

15.2.3.4 If the requirements for eleven or more parents and seven or more professional educators and seven or more business managers are all met, the State may appoint any Citizen they consider best qualified.

15.2.4 Each NSSB member shall receive a salary of $135,000 per year and shall be reimbursed for bona fide NSSB expenses upon the filing of weekly expense reports in accordance with Section **8.2**. They shall receive no other remuneration or benefits whatsoever, excepting dividends and interest from private investments they may hold. All salaries and expenses, including contracts with consultants and/or testing companies, shall be borne by the United States Treasury.

15.2.5 The NSSB shall contract with private professional educational testing companies for the creation, calibration, and maintenance of a battery of standardized achievement tests. Tests shall deal only with factual historical and scientific information and shall scrupulously avoid subjectivity and matters of opinion. The tests shall be designed to provide a valid measure of each student's proficiency in each major core curriculum subject and at each grade level. In a theoretically average case, a student would rank nationally at the fiftieth percentile every year in each subject area and overall. An increase in the percentile ranking from one year to the next will indicate faster-than-normal progress during the immediately preceding year, while a decrease will reveal slower-than-normal progress. Thus, the NSSB tests provide an objective measure of the performance of students, teachers, and schools. The core curriculum subjects shall be as follows:

15.2.5.1 English

15.2.5.2 Mathematics

15.2.5.3 Science (physics, chemistry, biology, computer science) with emphasis on rational thinking and the scientific method

15.2.5.4 Economics (microeconomics only), with emphasis on understanding how the free market economic system functions

15.2.5.5 World and United States geography

15.2.5.6 World and United States history

15.2.5.7 Civics, including understanding of this Constitution and the principles upon which it is based

15.3 School Accreditation and Test Administration

15.3.1 The NSSB achievement tests shall be administered annually between May 15 and May 31 to every Minor Citizen of age five and above. The responsibility and cost for administering the tests shall rest with the States. Each State shall make the annual achievement test scores available by July 31 to each Minor Citizen, to the student's parents, and to the school that the student attended that year, if any. The average aggregate scores in each subject area and the change from the prior year for each school shall be made publicly available. The average aggregate scores for each teacher shall be made available to each teacher and to the management of the teacher's school.

15.3.2 Each State shall have the responsibility to establish standards for the accreditation of schools that educate Minor Citizens within its jurisdiction. A mandatory component for accreditation must be a school's ability to advance its students in the NSSB core curriculum as measured by the change in percentile ranking from the prior year's test scores that the school was able to achieve with each of its students during each year. No school can achieve or retain accreditation if its average student percentile declines by six or more points in a year. States may elect to maintain a higher core curriculum standard and add additional accreditation requirements.

15.3.3 A school may apply to its State for accreditation or renewal thereof. Accreditation must be renewed every two years. Accreditation will be judged by a committee of five professional educators diversely drawn from other accredited schools in the State but not local to the school being reviewed. No committee member may have any interest or connection, direct or indirect, with the school being examined or with any of its personnel, owners, or investors. The accreditation process shall be administered and funded by the State.

15.4 Role of Government

Each State shall have the responsibility through due process of law to ensure that its Minor Citizens are receiving the reasonable care required by this Article **15**; and specifically, that all Minor Citizens of age five and above who are capable of learning are being educated in accordance with the provisions of this Article **15**. However, no government or quasi-governmental body shall have any direct or indirect connection with, control over, or involvement in the operation of any school that educates Citizens (either minor or adult). The entire role of governments in educating Citizens is defined in this Article **15**.

16.   Blanket Limitations On All Elected Officials

16.1 Blanket Term Limit

Serving in elective office must not become a career. Therefore, no Individual may run for an office for which completion of the term of office would result in the Individual's total time in elective office exceeding twenty years. The total shall include all governmental elective offices at the Federal, State, and local levels.

16.2 Campaign Funds

Funds donated or however acquired for an election campaign must be used for the bona fide campaign expenses of the election and race for which they were raised. Campaign funds will include money raised for exploratory committees or other activities of a prospective candidate contemplating a run for office. Any gifts received by a prospective candidate or candidate that individually exceed $100 or $1,000 in the aggregate shall be considered campaign contributions. Any funds remaining after paying all bona fide campaign debts will be transferred to the US Treasury ninety days following that election. Campaign funds must be maintained completely segregated from any other funds and must be accurately accounted for and documented with receipts, bank statements, and other proof of proper conduct.

16.3 Fraud

Election fraud committed by a prospective candidate, candidate, or elected official shall be punishable by a minimum of five years in prison, plus a fine approximating the monetary size of the fraud. Fraud shall include, but not be limited to, any violation of Section **16.2** or any subterfuge to circumvent the pay and benefit limitations described in Subsection **8.1.2**.

17. Amendments

From time to time, it may become necessary or advisable to amend this Constitution. This may be accomplished through any of the three processes described in this Article **17**. Successfully completing one of these processes shall cause an amendment to become valid and, for all intents and purposes, become a part of this Constitution.

17.1 Initiated by Congress

Congress, whenever two-thirds of both Houses shall deem it necessary, shall propose amendments to this Constitution. Each such proposed amendment shall require ratification by the Legislatures of three-fourths of the several States. An

amendment not so ratified within a period of eight years from
the date of its proposal shall be deemed to have failed.

17.2 Initiated by States

Amendments proposed and endorsed by the Legislatures of at
least one-half of the several States within a period of six years
must be considered. Each such proposed amendment shall
require ratification by the Legislatures of three-fourths of the
several States. Amendments not so ratified within a period of
eight years after the date of endorsement by one-half of the
states shall be deemed to have failed.

17.3 Initiated by Citizens

As a third alternative, Electors may propose and ratify
amendments directly. If at least 0.5% of the Electors in each of
at least half of the States petition for consideration of an
amendment within a period of eight years, the question shall be
placed on the ballot of a regular Congressional election as soon
as reasonably possible, but in any case within twenty-six
months. The amendment shall be ratified by the approval of
either a majority of all registered Electors or three-fifths of the
Electors voting on the amendment.

18. Continuity

18.1 Citizenship

Any Individual who is a Citizen of the United States
immediately prior to the time this Constitution becomes
effective shall remain a Citizen under this Constitution.

18.2 Debts and Contracts

All debts contracted and engagements entered into before the
adoption of this Constitution shall be as valid against the United
States under this Constitution as under the previous Constitution.

18.3 Prior National Debt

Any prior national debt inconsistent with that allowed by this
Constitution shall be retired at the minimum rate of 0.5% of the

principal amount (as of the effective date of this Constitution) per annum until it has been completely retired. This amount may be reduced in any budget year for the reason of a bona fide economic emergency upon the vote of three-fourths of both the House of Representatives and the Senate, but not below a minimum of 0.1%. The minimum rate will automatically return to 0.5% in the following fiscal year.

18.4 Term Limits

Only time in office following the effective date and time of this Constitution shall be counted toward the operation of the term limits herein specified.

Appendix C
Simulating Elections

Overview from 35,000 Feet

A Government object is responsible for instantiating a series of Election objects (normally 100,000), complete with Candidates and Voters (normally, 10,000), for testing a set of VotingMethod objects, and for reporting the results. Voter opinions of or <u>sat</u>isfaction for candidates occur on a scale of -100 to +100 "sats." Each Candidate has a notoriety and an average Voter opinion. Each Voter has an opinion for each Candidate (if the Voter is sufficiently informed about that Candidate), and the opinions for various Voters have a Gaussian distribution centered on the Candidate's average. All are randomly generated for each Election so that, over many thousands of Elections, all possible permutations and combinations occur.

More Detailed Procedure

Here is the procedure for instantiating each election in more detail:

1. In a race in a real election, there are always candidates that are well-known to most voters, candidates that are less well-known, and some candidates which very few voters have even heard of. So, the first step in instantiating each Election is to assign a "notoriety" to each Candidate. A random number >=0 and <1 is generated for each Candidate. Before assigning these notorieties to Candidates, they are sorted into descending order so that the first Candidate is always

the best known and the last is the least known. This does not cause any loss of generality, but does enable us to see roughly how a candidate's notoriety affects its win percentage.

2. Second, each Candidate is assigned an average opinion or average voter satisfaction by generating a random number uniformly distributed between -60 sats and +60 sats.

3. Next, the Voters are instantiated. Each Voter is first assigned a randomly generated number <= 0 and <1 which models the Voter's knowledge. A zero indicates a completely ignorant Voter. On the other hand, a 1 would be an ideal perfectly knowledgeable Voter who is fully informed about each and every one of the Candidates. When (just before) voter opinions are generated for each candidate (see next step), the voters knowledge is multiplied times the candidate's notoriety. If this product is less than a no-opinion threshold, no opinion is generated for that candidate. The threshold was set to 0.04, which is believed to be a reasonable simulation of this effect as it occurs in real world elections. While this setting does affect the win percentages of low-notoriety Candidates as expected, the fact that varying it somewhat does not have much effect on relative voting method results relieves the need to investigate further.

4. Whenever a Voter knows enough about a Candidate (has an opinion), a (Gaussian) satisfaction centered on each Candidate's average opinion is generated. The random Gaussian opinions have a sigma of 20 sats and are truncated to a plus or minus two-sigma range so they cannot exceed the -100 to +100 range when centered around each Candidate's randomly-assigned

average. When each satisfaction is generated, it is added to the Candidates total net satisfaction (which will determine the correct winner of the Election after all Voters have been instantiated). When a positive opinion/satisfaction is generated for a Candidate, it is also registered as a "yea" in a referendum for the Candidate. Whenever a negative opinion is generated, a "nay" is registered in the Candidate's referendum. Each Voter ranks all the Candidates according to its satisfactions and is able to provide the ranking and the satisfactions upon request (e.g., to VotingMethod objects or the Election object).

5. After each Election is completely instantiated, the Election determines the correct winner along with the winning (highest) net total satisfaction value. It also determines and tallies whether there was a majority winner, whether or not the majority winner was the correct winner, whether there was a Condorcet winner, whether or not the Condorcet winner was the correct winner, and also tallies the wins by Candidate.

6. Also after each Election is instantiated, the Government object hands it (read only) to each of the VotingMethod objects being tested. The same Voters with the same opinions vote multiple times, once for each method being tested and in accordance with each voting method's rules. Thus, VotingMethods are able to easily have Voters fill out their "ballots," tally the ballots, determine a winner and then see whether or not their algorithm has chosen the correct winner. Whenever an incorrect winner is chosen, how much lower the net total satisfaction was than that of the correct winner is recorded as the error.

7. When the last Election has been processed, each
    VotingMethod publishes its statistical results.
    - The percentage of incorrect choices made
    - The maximum error ("sats" on the -100 to +100
      scale)
    - The average error
    - The RMS (root of the mean square) error
    - The RMS error divided by the RMS error for random
      selection times 100
    - The percentage of winners chosen that would lose
      their referendum.
    - The number of ties that had to be resolved by
      random selection

Appendix D
AADV, and GADV
Instructions for Voters and for
Election Officials

Approve/Approve/Disapprove Voting (AADV)

AADV (Approve/Approve/Disapprove Voting) is a simple, directly-scored voting method. It also has a generalized form which enables it to be used both for single-winner and multiple-winner contests.

AADV Ballot

	Approve	Disapprove
Candidate A	☐	☐
Candidate B	☐	☐
Candidate C	☐	☐
Candidate D	☐	☐

AADV Instructions for Voters

Mark an "**X**" in the "**Approve**" box for any one or two candidates (if any) that you really like and believe would be the best one(s) to win this race. Mark an "**X**" in the "**Disapprove**" box for any one candidate (if any) that you dislike, strongly believe would be the worst choice, and which you would not want to win this race. If you do not know enough about a candidate or do not have a firm opinion one way or the other, leave both boxes unmarked.

Disqualify any ballots which have more than two candidates marked "Approve." Disqualify any ballots which have more than one candidate marked "Disapprove." Total the "Approve" votes for each candidate; call this total "A." Total the "Disapprove" votes for each candidate; call this total "D." Add "A" and "D" for each candidate; call this sum "V." Eliminate any candidate whose "V" is less than one plus two percent of the largest "V" of any single candidate (rounded to the nearest number of voters). Subtract "D" from "A" for each remaining candidate; call this difference "N." Eliminate any candidate which has a zero or negative "N." The remaining candidate (if any) that has the largest positive "N" is the winner.

Generalized Approve/Disapprove Voting (GADV)

Generalized Approve/Disapprove Voting provides for races which have any number of winners (e.g., electing three of ten candidates to a school board). When electing n winners, voters may approve up to n + 1 candidates and disapprove of up to (n + 1)/2 candidates (use integer division or round down). The instructions to voters and for election officials are basically the same as for AADV except for the number of candidates voters may approve and disapprove. The winners then are simply the candidates having the top n positive net scores.

NOTES (which apply for AADV and GADV):

1. User-friendly electronic voting supervision could easily prevent spoiled ballots and therefore eliminate the need to check for and disqualify these during the tally

process. Software (called Election Manager) is available which can completely automate and run elections (including touch screen voting) using either the AADV or Plurality voting methods. The tally and reporting process for AADV is completely automated.

2. It is possible, though unlikely, that there could be no winner; that is, no remaining candidate with a positive "N". (Candidates with such "high negatives" would simply not be nominated, especially if AADV were used for primary elections.) It would, of course, be easy to provide a rule to crown the "least awful" candidate the winner. But it does not seem wise to elect a candidate that more people dislike than like. Therefore, if there should be no winner, another election should be held. No candidate that received a zero or negative "N" should be allowed to run again. This is a refinement of the common practice of always having the option to vote for NOTA (None Of The Above). It is a defect of Plurality, IRV, Approval, STAR, Score and virtually all other voting methods that they are unable to sensibly handle this situation; they can easily force the election of a candidate disliked by a majority of voters.

3. Because it is at least a possibility that all candidates on the ballot could be pretty "lackluster," the winning net vote total could be fairly low. Conceivably, a write-in (or other obscure) candidate could then achieve a winning score with very few voters. That might very well be the best outcome, but many people would find it disquieting. To prevent a virtually unknown candidate from winning with a very small number of votes, it is required that a candidate must have received at least a "reasonable" amount of voter interest in order to

qualify. Therefore, the total number of voters weighing in on each candidate (either for or against) is totaled to obtain "V." Any candidate is eliminated that has a "V" less than one voter plus two percent of the largest "V" of any single candidate (rounded to the nearest voter). See the specific tally instructions for AADV for greater clarity. Results should be displayed showing "A," "D" and "N" with the candidates in order of descending "N," followed last by any candidates disqualified for low voter interest in order of descending "V."

Appendix E
Obtaining Sincere Opinions from Voters

A perfect voting method is described in chapter 8. In order to function perfectly, the perfect voting method depended upon a fictional mind-reading machine that could read voters' minds and determine their *sincere* opinions about each of the candidates. Of course, we do not currently have such a mind-reading machine. The only way to find out about voters' opinions is to ask them to write down their opinions on their ballots. That turns out to be a truly serious problem because a large fraction of voters do not hesitate to lie — that is, *not* indicate their sincere opinions on their ballots.

Suppose we ask voters to tell us how satisfied or dissatisfied they would be with each of the candidates on a scale of −100 to +100. Minus 100 means extremely dissatisfied, plus 100 means extremely satisfied, and a zero right in the middle means no opinion one way or the other — the same as not voting. If voters marked their ballots conscientiously and sincerely, it would only be necessary to add up all the opinions for each candidate and select the one with the highest positive total. This would function as an essentially perfect voting method and reliably identify the candidate that maximizes voter satisfaction virtually every time.

Unfortunately, most voters will award their favorite candidate the highest possible score, whether or not it is their sincere opinion of that candidate, in order to maximize the probability of that candidate winning. On the other hand, they will be sure to clobber the candidate they consider the most serious competition to their favorite with the lowest possible score. In fact, many will decide to "carpet bomb" every other candidate with the lowest possible score. In some cases, voters may have a close second choice to whom they will give a high score a few notches less than the one they gave their favorite. Thus, strategic voting destroys the advantage of a −100 to +100 scale and causes it to function more like a −1 to +1 scale that has only three values.

The well-known behaviors just described (and many other variants) are called "insincere voting" or "strategic voting." With the plurality voting method, the most common form of strategic voting is known as "voting for the lesser evil." All of the many forms of strategic voting degrade the ability of various voting methods to reliably identify the correct candidate as the winner.

As also explained in chapter 8, it has been proven that *all* voting methods are subject to degradation from strategic exploits, although some are more vulnerable than others (Gibbard-Satterthwaite Theorem). During the centuries-long voting method debate, it has been common to cite some strategic voting vulnerability in an argument against a proposed voting method. However, *every* voting method has some strategic vulnerabilities, so finding one does not necessarily disqualify a method, but this game has wasted a lot of time and prolonged confusion.

It is the purpose of this appendix to explore some unconventional ways that sincere opinions might be extracted from voters in spite of Messrs. Gibbard and Satterthwaite.

The only way to ensure sincerity is to require that voters actually give up something they value, which they will only do in proportion to the strength of their convictions. The most common standard of value is money, so requiring payment for each vote theoretically should work. The amount of payment a voter is willing to proffer should rather accurately indicate the strength of their opinion. However, many would protest that wealthy people would be able to control every election. OK, put a limit of, say, $20 on what can be spent on a single issue or race. If the limit is high enough, the control of the wealthy is not sufficiently curtailed. If the limit is low enough to solve the rich-guy-control problem, we are mostly back to the original situation in which a large fraction of voters will insincerely vote the maximum amount all or most of the time.

Another possibility would be to award each voter an equal allocation of voting points, say, twenty per issue or office to be voted upon. Up to a limit of forty points (positive or negative) may be applied to any given issue or race. The points take on a certain value as a limited (scarce) resource and allow voters to "spend" more points on the races and the candidates they consider most important at the expense of having fewer points to apply to decisions they think are less critical. Additionally, points might be given a very real value by allowing *unused* points to be turned in for money, say, $1 per point. This could help supplement a "social safety net" where those taking the money automatically forfeit their voting power — a very important requirement for preserving long-term stability.

Perhaps some sort of point system merits further thought, but administrative complexity would be high, as would resistance to such a change. All of the forgoing serves to amply illustrate the intractability of engineering a way for voters to meaningfully weight their votes.

However, there may yet be a workable way. Suppose voters are required to pay with their time as the measure of their motivation. A minimal vote weighting of 1 takes only a second to register, but a heavy weighting of 100 requires a hundred seconds of the voter's life. That may not seem like a long time, but it will feel long enough when you are in a voting booth waiting for the seconds counter to count up to 100. The median time voters are actually willing to wait to cast a vote for their most favored candidate can be experimentally determined and a maximum limit set to perhaps twice the median.

It should be apparent that this is similar to the AADV voting method, but enhanced to allow voters to both weight their votes and also to vote for/against as many candidates as they wish. A nearly identical tally process would apply. It would seem that this system might well approach the accuracy of the "perfect" voting method that utilized the fictitious satometer. It should be experimentally tested and further evaluated for efficacy and voter acceptance.

Although this approach may take some getting used to, it is actually straightforward and potentially workable. It is especially attractive in that it's hard to think of a better way to put all voters on a fair and equal footing. Voting times per voter may increase, requiring additional voting stations to maintain throughput, but this is certainly justified if better decisions can be ensured.

Appendix F
The Election Manager System

What Is Election Manager?

Election Manager is a publicly available, integrated software system that can be utilized to automate all phases of any election in a transparent, secure, and auditable manner. It may be used free of charge for any noncommercial application. It is a "Swiss Army knife" for elections that can be used to:

- Flexibly define the various jurisdictions for elections anywhere on Earth;
- Flexibly define elections with their political parties, races, candidates, and even candidate aliases;
- Supervise and control touch screen voting in polling place voting booths;
- Print voter-verifiable paper ballots (complete verification of polling place results can be done within about sixty minutes after the polls close); and
- Electronically tally the results of an entire election, including all write-in votes, so that accurate and complete election results can be available within half an hour after the polls close.

Why Is Election Manager Important and Needed?

Electing the classmate most likely to succeed probably won't affect the course of world events, but electing those who will wield government power over citizens is of critical importance. The laborious marking and counting of paper ballots beg for automation utilizing modern technologies. However, it makes absolutely no sense to put the critically important democratic process of voting at risk just for the sake of some time-saving automation.

There have been many attempts at using various technologies to make the voting process more efficient, but substantially all of them have sacrificed transparency, security, and/or auditability. Election Manager attempts to comprehend the entire election process and achieve the desired high efficiency while actually *improving* transparency, security, and auditability over hand-marked paper ballots.

How Does Election Manager Work?

After setting up whatever jurisdictions may be required, an election (or multiple elections) may be flexibly defined. An entire election setup can be exported as an XML file (with security fingerprint) that can be loaded from a CD or flash memory stick to automatically set up each precinct.

On election day, voters check in as usual. For each authorized voter, a voting booth is enabled and the voter is directed to it. Voters tap a "Begin Vote" button and the races for which they are entitled to vote appear on the display. A voter may quickly and easily select candidates for each race from a pop-up list or write in any name. When voters have made choices in any or all races and reviewed them, they tap the "Cast Ballot" button which displays each voter's ballot exactly as it would print. Following a "Really sure" and a "Really, really sure" verification from the voter, the voter-verifiable paper ballot is printed.

The printed ballot looks just like the one still displayed on the screen and has nothing printed on it that the voter can't read and understand. After verifying that the ballot has printed correctly, the screen clears and that voter's session ends. The voter drops the ballot into a traditional ballot box on the way out of the voting booth area. The paper ballots are the official and legal record of voters' intents.

If, for whatever reason, the ballot did not printed correctly, the voter taps a "Help" button that summons the Judge of Elections and a watcher. The Judge of Elections resolves the problem on the spot or, in the worst case, allows the voter to manually complete a "Provisional Ballot."

When the polls close, the precinct's totals are printed and a text file of the randomly ordered ballots is produced (using standard XML). The Judge of Elections and poll observers certify the ballot file as well as its security fingerprints. The ballot file is immediately posted publicly on the Internet. The precinct totals and possibly the ballots file should be printed and posted outside the polling place. The precinct totals are verified using the ballots from the ballot box.

The ballot files from all polling places are tallied by a copy of Election Manager anywhere which then reports results for the entire election. Anyone anywhere can verify the election totals using Election Manager, some other software, or even a hand count.

What Approach Was Used for the Software?

All of Election Manager's source code is written in Java so that it is highly portable. Either the Election Manager server or the Election Manager client software will run identically on substantially any combination of hardware and operating system. Inexpensive, reliable, standard PC hardware can be used to keep everything nonproprietary, open, and low cost. A simple and user-friendly GUI (graphical user interface) with touch screen voting is employed.

Does Election Manager Support Internet Voting?

No. No system that allows voting over the Internet can guarantee acceptable security and the door is opened to other problems as well. Voting booth clients within each polling place should always be connected to the server via hard-wired Ethernet cables (no RF). However, clients *can* connect over the Internet to a central server while setting up jurisdictions and elections. During voting, there should be no connection to *any* other network, and certainly not to the Internet. However, note that these precautions are taken to avoid disruptions. Because each ballot is verified by the voter, and because both the precinct totals and the output ballot file can be verified against the ballots in the ballot box, any error(s) for whatever cause *will* be detected and can be corrected, whether accidental or the result of attempted fraud.

What Election Options Are Supported?

For each election, the following can be independently selected:

- Election date and times that the polling places open and close;
- Primary election (requires parties) or general election;
- Races can be a referendum or elect 1, 2, 3, or more candidates;
- The voting method for each race can be either plurality or the far superior AADV (Approve/Approve/Disapprove Voting) method;

- The pop-up candidate list can be either specific to each race or consolidated;
- Voter-verifiable ballot printing can be either 8.5" x 11" or 8.5" x 14" ballots;
- Either a reference number (strongly recommended) or the actual ballot number can be printed (very strongly discouraged);
- Any number of approved aliases can be set up for each candidate;
- Aliases are automatically comprehended, properly handled, and reported in the tally process.

How Does Election Manager Achieve Greater Transparency and Security?

Everything about voting should be completely transparent and public, except, of course, that the secrecy of each voter's ballot must be fiercely guarded.

Election Manager is written entirely in Java, perhaps the most widely used, secure, and portable programming language to date. Both the source code and the executable jar files are made publicly available. Anyone can independently run and test the system. Ballots are instantaneously and always maintained and reported in a random order.

The text file of results from each polling place is standard, well-understood XML in a format matching published schema. XML editors and readers (including many browsers) are widely available. The files are also readable by humans. The secure and redundant output file contains all choices on all ballots in three different sort orders for reliability, with security fingerprints for each. A fourth security checksum protects the entire file. Any tampering with the file would be immediately obvious.

No one can guarantee that any machine at least as complicated as a common paper stapler is working correctly all the time. For that reason, *every* output that could affect election results must be verifiable *and must actually be verified* as a part of the standard routine. Voters verify their own printed ballots. Both the precinct totals and even the XML output file can be verified by comparing them to the printed ballots from the ballot box, so any "glitches," whether intentional or accidental, *will* be caught and can be corrected. Anyone anywhere can independently verify election totals and results using the publicly available output files and Election Manager (or any other method they may prefer, including a tedious manual count) to tally the ballots. Complete integrity is assured.

Whether or not there actually is election fraud, it is highly disruptive to have millions of people doubting the results. If anyone does have doubts, it must be possible to quickly and conclusively prove that the results are correct. That is possible with Election Manager. All citizens will finally be able to *implicitly* trust their elections.

Appendix G
Top Six Critical Election Fixes

Fixes Required to Make Elections Function Correctly

1. **Replace the plurality (or other) voting method with Approve/Approve/Disapprove Voting (AADV).** Plurality is causing polarization (Duverger's Law) and sometimes can result in voters electing candidates that a majority of the voters themselves oppose!

2. **Eliminate gerrymandering.** Either people or computers should draw compact electoral districts impartially using the simple, five-step Precinct-Preserving Splitline (PPS) geometric procedure. Redistricting would become a non-issue and could be completed very inexpensively in less than an hour.

3. **Fix and simplify contrived ballot access laws.** There should be very few races with 0 or 1 candidate on the ballot and some with as many as 6 or 7 choices.

    a. **Boil any complex political party classifications down to just one: Qualified Political party.** Any political party having at least 0.05% of statewide voter registration and having their rules on file with the state's Secretary of State is a Qualified Political Party. Qualified Political Parties are entitled to nominate candidates in accordance with their own procedures *and entirely at their own expense.* (In most states, there would currently be four Qualified Parties: Republican, Democrat, Libertarian, and Green).

b. **Independents** (candidates who are not affiliated with a Qualified Political Party) would need to collect a reasonable number of nominating signatures. The number should relate to the size of the district, but should never be less than 10 or more than 3,000 for a statewide race. The time window for collecting those signatures should be ample. All signatures would be validated by the county or state agency that receives them, not by private organizations or individuals.

Fixes Required to Guarantee Election Integrity

1. **All voters must vote in-person at their friendly neighborhood polling places** (except up to 1% absentee ballots for good reason). There is no other way that a secret ballot can be guaranteed! Voters *must not* be able to prove to someone else how they voted (enables vote buying).
2. **Implement positive (e.g., photo) voter ID.** Signature validation *cannot* be relied upon.
3. **Automate elections securely with modern computer technology.** Elections should happen entirely on election day. Full, complete, and final results should be available a half hour after the polls close, including tallies of all write-in votes. (Such a system called Election Manager that *utilizes voter-verified paper ballots* is already available. Results would be independently verifiable.)

Note: For more complete information, see the Voting/Elections page at https://royminet.org/

About the Author

Although Roy Minet's college major was physics, he accepted an interesting job offer in engineering with a large multi-national corporation as his first employment. That led to positions in sales, marketing, then marketing management, and finally management of a strategic business planning department, all for the same corporation. Moving into small business, he bought and operated a beer distributorship for 12 years before selling it. While distributing (and perhaps drinking) beer, he founded Intelligent Computer Systems, Inc., which pioneered comprehensive, integrated, real-time business software and installed turnkey computer systems for distribution businesses nationwide. After 22 years, ICS was sold to the 3M Corporation. He is now retired and pursuing a backlog of personal projects — most notably, improving all aspects of elections. He also has taught economics in 11th and 12th grades with the Junior Achievement program. Approximately 40 of his op-ed columns have been published. Mr. Minet was the Libertarian Party's candidate for Pennsylvania Auditor General in 2016.

Website: https://royminet.org/

Other books by Roy A. Minet

The Savior of the World — Comprehending the Free Market Economic System

Available here:

https://books2read.com/TheSaviorOfTheWorldByRoyMinet

Elections Are Broken — How to Fix Them

Available here:

https://books2read.com/ElectionsAreBrokenByRoyMinet

Rescuing the Constitution of the United States

Available here:

https://books2read.com/RescuingTheConstitutionByRoyMinet

Rational Thinking — Definition, Importance, History, and Future

Available here:

https://books2read.com/RationalThinkingByRoyMinet

Money — Good and Bad

Available here:

https://books2read.com/MoneyByRoyMinet

For the reader who would be satisfied with less than *Everything*, these short, single-topic books deal with the most important subjects from this book plus some additional material.